Children of Victory

Children of Victory

*Young Specialists and the
Evolution of Soviet Society*

DAVID L. RUFFLEY

**Westport, Connecticut
London**

Library of Congress Cataloguing-in-Publication Data

Ruffley, David L., 1961–

    Children of victory : young specialists and the evolution of Soviet society / David L. Ruffley.
      p. cm.
    Includes bibliographical references and index.
    ISBN 0–275–97674–2 (alk. paper)
    1. Young adults—Soviet Union.   2. Specialists—Soviet Union.   3. Soviet
Union—Intellectual life.   I. Title.
    HQ799.8.S55R84   2003
    305.235'0947—dc21   2002019631

British Library Cataloguing in Publication Data is available.

Library of Congress Catalog Card Number: 2002019631
ISBN: 0–275–97674–2

First published in 2003

Praeger Publishers, 88 Post Road West, Westport, CT 06881
An imprint of Greenwood Publishing Group, Inc.
www.praeger.com

Printed in the United States of America

The paper used in this book complies with the
Permanent Paper Standard issued by the National
Information Standards Organization (Z39.48–1984).

10 9 8 7 6 5 4 3 2 1

Contents

Acknowledgments

First and foremost, I wish to thank my family for their endurance during the six years of work on this project, especially during the frequent trips abroad that kept us apart. They sacrificed a great deal to make it possible.

Thanks to several members of the history department at Ohio State University, for their support of this project from its earliest stages. Special thanks to the late Allan Wildman, who encouraged me to take on a topic that he considered important and worth pursuing, despite its unconventional nature. I thank as well David Hoffmann, for his advice and guidance upon Allan Wildman's death, and for pushing me to the highest possible standards, despite the geographical separation that made coordination that much more difficult. Ken Andrien helped me explore the applicability of the domination-resistance paradigm to Soviet society. Eve Levin was always ready to read yet another edition of the manuscript and to provide critical feedback.

Thanks to my colleagues at the Air Force Academy Department of History, especially Debbie Schmitt, for covering my classes and other duties so that I could work uninterrupted, while providing the friendship and support that kept me on track. I would never have finished this project without her. And to Bill Astore, who provided constant coffee, advice and friendship through the travails of manuscript preparation. Thanks also to Carl Reddel, who convinced me to undertake this project in the first place, and provided the time away from his Department for full-time study and research.

I also wish to thank Leonid Romanovich Weintraub, Elena Iurevna Zubkova, and Arch Getty for their help in locating and selecting archival materials during my 1999 research trip to Moscow. Special thanks to Georgie Anne Geyer, who gave me several hundred pages of notes from interviews with young Soviets in the early 1970s.

Introduction

In her groundbreaking social history of the immediate aftermath of World War II in Russia, Elena Zubkova noted, "While the political and economic structures of the USSR remained practically unchanged, a complex of hopes and expectations prompted by the sacrifices of the great victory led to major changes in Soviet society."[1] Her translator, Hugh Ragsdale, noted that Zubkova's key accomplishment was that she was "able to demonstrate . . . a considerable interaction of government policy and public mood. It may surprise the reader how sensitive the Soviet government was to public opinion—in fact, how responsive it was."[2]

While Zubkova was focused primarily upon the immediate postwar years, her observation applies with equal, perhaps greater force to the Brezhnev era as well. Between 1965 and 1982, Soviet society became increasingly dynamic; it included elements that were both capable of, and willing to develop, solutions to the USSR's problems. Huge numbers of specialists with higher education entered the Soviet workforce and came face-to-face with the country's problems. Naturally, they sought to alleviate those problems, putting their education and optimism to work. In many cases, the petitions, suggestions, and criticisms that they submitted to Party organs or the press represented potential solutions to problems. As it had in the immediate postwar period, the regime responded to public opinion in general and to these suggestions specifically as well. As always, some aspects of the response were negative, and some were positive, and in all cases the regime attempted to closely control the process. In many cases, the Soviet state censored citizens' petitions and stifled social initiatives in order to enhance society's short-term stability. This censorship led to the escalation of pressures and frustrations generated by the increasingly well educated society. Within this context, young Soviet specialists developed an ethos that stressed a commitment to moral principle and action to achieve practical results in solving problems.

Neither this social initiative nor its partial censorship represented new phenomena in Russian or Soviet history. In his work describing the interaction between the state and society of Imperial Russia, historian Gregory Freeze noted, "Supplication and petition was an endemic feature of Russian political culture, providing a partial substitute for popular representation and a vital bond between Tsar and people from medieval times."[3] What was new about the Brezhnev era was the dramatically increased level of education in Russian society, which gave rise to another new "complex of hopes and expectations" among the Soviet population. Well-educated Russian specialists grew increasingly aware of the fact that the political and economic structures of the Soviet state were not solving the problems facing the country. That awareness, the specialists' efforts either to live with it or to confront it, and the state's responses are the critical elements of this study. Specifically, this study targets the more than 12 million Soviet citizens who graduated from institutions of higher learning between 1965 and 1982, thereby earning the appellation "young specialists."

David Remnick, a Western journalist who viewed these specialists and their generation from the perspective of the post-Gorbachev years, concluded that, unlike the children of the Khrushchev-era thaw, who had been raised as true believers, then had to awaken after Stalin's death, "the young had never believed for a minute. They did not believe in Communism, the Party, or the system. They did not believe in the future." Never having known the ever-present sense of fear that their parents had faced, "a generation began to distance itself from the system and look at it with disdain; it saw all the strangeness and horror in all that had gone on before."[4]

Another Western journalist, Georgie Anne Geyer, said of the young Russians of Moscow: "In place of the children of the revolution, in place of the 'children of strife' has arisen a new generation that has known neither war, nor revolution nor Stalinism . . . the 'Children of Victory' the Russians sometimes call them—for they are what the revolution was fought for and what 50 years of agony were endured for."[5] Geyer concluded her evaluation of this generation with the insightful observation that change in Russia's youth would occur most quickly at the psychological and sociological level. Over the long term, she predicted that these changes "will lead to political change, but from within and probably non-violently."[6]

How did these "Children of Victory," principal benefactors of the Soviet military, industrial, and economic triumphs of the first 50 years of Soviet history, come to reject the basic premises of the system that had made them the most highly educated and materially affluent generation in all of Russian history? Did they, as a group, actually do so, perhaps as the result of Geyer's changes at the "psychological and sociological level"? Was Remnick's portrayal colored by the trauma of the Soviet collapse? Or did the truth of what happened actually lie somewhere in between?

Journalists, such as Geyer and Remnick, have made contemporary studies of the young Russians of the Brezhnev era. Both Western and Soviet sociologists have developed quantitative descriptions of the "Children of

Victory." But historians have to date not focused upon these people and their place in Soviet and post-Soviet Russian society. Even in the relatively open research atmosphere of the post-Soviet era, documentary sources of information on this generation's role in Soviet/Russian history remain scarce. But given the demographic realities of their numbers, their education, and the positions that they came to occupy in both Soviet and post-Soviet society, an understanding of the perspective and life experiences of young Russians who completed their university education in the Brezhnev years is absolutely essential to a fuller understanding of Soviet society, the collapse of the USSR, and the emergence of Russia today. This study turns to the Children of Victory themselves for such understanding.

The fact that young Soviet citizens left behind few written records of their beliefs and experiences is widely known and is discussed in more detail later. What is critical here is the understanding that this study does not focus primarily upon quantitative analysis or attempt any modeling of development for this generation. Likewise, this study does not pretend to offer a comprehensive portrait of the young specialists of the Brezhnev era. It offers an interpretive analysis of writings that the young specialists did leave behind, primarily in the form of letters to Soviet newspapers, Party committees, and government organs, as well as in the questions that they posed to the regime's representatives at political meetings in their workplaces. These texts are evaluated in terms of both their content and the language that they use and are compared to the texts of similar articles or pronouncements by government and Party officials, as well as to texts authored by specialists of other generations. Personal interviews with the young specialists, conducted by Geyer in the early 1970s and retrospective interviews conducted by the author in 1995-1999 provide insight into the historical context of these social "discussions" between the young professionals and Soviet authorities.

In some cases, young specialists apparently spelled out exactly how they felt in their letters and articles. For example, Alexander Rusov, a young doctor of chemistry working as a part-time writer for *Literaturnaia gazeta* in 1977, turned an article about a young Soviet researcher who abandoned his scientific post to become a cabdriver into a self-portrait of his generation. After denying that his writing represented his own disillusionment with scientific work and describing his encounter with this highly educated cabbie (who turned out to be a former student of his), Rusov admitted:

I could be combining in this image all the young, unsatisfied *vuz* [7] graduates who were assigned to Scientific Research Institutes and who left . . . . Those who complained about the insufficient knowledge of *vuz* graduates . . . and the "swamp life" at the institute [doing administrative paper work, manual labor and working in vegetable depots]. About those who cite the presence of wives and children, who complain about insufficient time for work on the side . . . who can't earn enough extra income through translations and synopses.[8]

This article generated a wide response from both sympathetic readers and concerned Party and government officials, most of whom were just as straightforward. Many of the readers used it to focus on flaws in the education and employment systems in the USSR, while academics and officials representing the "official" view focused on the shortcomings of individual *vuz* graduates as the center of the problem. These contrasting perspectives led to a sustained "discussion" of the topic in future issues of *Literaturnaia gazeta*, as will be discussed later.

Unfortunately, even apparently clear-cut examples such as this one merit analysis in light of the nature of censorship in the USSR. The censorship evolved over time, so that issues that were taboo at one point appeared in the public press at others. Such analysis becomes even more complicated when the source is less clear-cut, as the following example shows.

In 1982, a 28 year-old engineer was fired from his work as a factory supervisor. Officially, he was fired for repeated unexcused absences. In a complaint to *Literaturnaia gazeta*, his mother wrote that he really was fired for his refusal to bow to the factory administrator's pressure tactics, intended to force him to bestow bonuses "for assistance with new inventions" to workers selected by the administration (for reasons having nothing to do with invention). The young man and his friends insist that he acted in accordance with his principles (*po prinsipii*) and "for his conscience" (*za sovest'*). They are "shocked at the factory management's injustice." On the other hand, the young man's mother is outraged with the "Moral Choice" (*nravstvennyi vybor*) section of *Literaturnaia gazeta* for teaching people "to ask for trouble without protecting their own life." Clearly, the young specialist and his friends view life from a very different perspective from that of his mother. The notions of living "for conscience" and defiant action in this case serve as "generational markers," specific to the young. Such markers highlight differences in perspective among generations. Other such markers often appear in discussions in the Soviet press.

Analysis of such discussions is combined with the aforementioned interviews with members of the targeted generation. The public documents are compared to archival documents of a similar nature to discern how the young Russian specialists viewed themselves and their society and how they affected that society and the Soviet state. In so doing, this study demonstrates that Soviet society of the Brezhnev era, just like the immediate postwar society studied by Elena Zubkova, had an interactive relationship with, and a definite impact upon, the state.

Society's role in this interaction and impact may be considered as analogous to a fluid stream. As society developed impetus toward solving a problem, that impetus grew along channels where it met less resistance. In those social spaces where such growth was blocked, the movement stopped, but the pressure that it exerted continued to build and seek new outlets. The state, and more specifically, the censorship process, acted as a hydraulic engineer relative to this stream. At times, the regime might acquiesce to public opinion or social initiative—to open a spillway, if it so chose. But it also sought to channel, redirect, or sometimes block society's initiative via censorship.[9] The state did not merely prevent publication of certain petitions but also selected specific petitions or issues for publication in order to shape society's impetus and public opinion, in the same way that our hydraulic engineer might build a canal or irrigation network. This proactive aspect of Russian censorship was likewise not unique to the Soviet era. Gregory Freeze noted that he sometimes chose published documents over archival sources in his analysis of Russian society at the turn of the twentieth century: "I have deliberately preferred documents—especially from 1861-1906—that obtained broader publicity through the press; although archival materials are also readily available, the documents that appeared in the contemporary press hold greater historical importance, for they not only expressed but also molded group consciousness and public opinion."[10]

The young specialists at the heart of this study were born after 1940 and completed higher education during the Brezhnev era. They focused their attention primarily upon professional advancement and the acquisition of a high standard of living. They generally did not openly express political opinions or actively participate in the activities of the Soviet government or the Communist Party. Likewise, they did not openly break with the regime, as did their "dissident" contemporaries. In this way, these citizens upheld their end of an implicit social contract, the trade-off of political quiescence in exchange for stability and a basic modicum of material prosperity—often referred to by Western scholars as the "Little Deal."[11] Over the long term, however, young Soviet specialists became frustrated with their inability to fulfill their personal and professional potential within the confines of the Little Deal. Because of their isolation from the country's political power centers, aspiring young specialists also became disillusioned with their ability to improve the functioning of their social, professional, and economic systems, particularly when they compared that system's functioning to that of other "developed" nations. The arbitrariness and inefficiency of the Soviet economic and political systems inspired the specialists to seek to build a system that worked and that treated individual citizens with human dignity and respect. Limited discussions of such opinions in the Soviet press highlighted important differences in both personal and professional perspectives between the young specialists and their parents' generation (the anchor of the "stable cadres" of the Brezhnev years). In many ways, the young specialists held views and attitudes more similar to those of their grandparents, those who had earned the victories of the Revolution and World War II. Held in political check by the stagnation of the Brezhnev era, the young specialists nevertheless retained and developed keen interests in social, professional, and philosophical issues. Shared aspirations, attitudes, and opinions of these young specialists inspired them to attempt to establish some horizontal social and professional connections. The combination of these interests and connections generated social energies that were released by glasnost and directly contributed to the rapidity of the Soviet collapse and the evolution of post-Soviet society.

In order to demonstrate the unique contributions of this study to the understanding of Brezhnev-era Soviet society and the place of young specialists within that society, it is now necessary to more specifically define the identity of these young specialists and examine in more detail the importance of this generation. That definition is based upon the specialists' portrayal in demographic and sociological terms by both Western and Soviet social scientists.

THE TARGET COHORT, RESEARCH QUESTIONS, AND SOURCES

The most basic criteria defining the Soviet citizens targeted in this study are their age and education level. Citizens born between 1940 and 1958 would have been of age to complete the normal course of higher education in the USSR between 1964 and 1982 and at least start their work career during the Brezhnev era. As used here, "higher education" means the completion of a postsecondary course of study at a university or an institute leading to recognition as a "specialist." The "normal" course of study is defined as entry into university or institute study immediately following the completion of secondary education and completion of a four-to-six year curriculum, depending on area of specialty and educational institution.[12] While a significant number of people completed higher education programs via night school or other such alternative programs, the vast majority of those completing higher education did so through the "normal" course.

PORTRAIT FROM SOVIET SOCIOLOGY

As a percentage of the entire Soviet population, specialists with higher education were a rapidly growing segment of Soviet society in the Brezhnev years. Soviet sociologists, citing official Soviet statistics, place the absolute number of such specialists employed in the USSR at 8.4 million in 1973, 11.6 million in 1979, and 18.5 million in 1984.[13] Using official figures for the entire Soviet population, these specialists thereby represented 3%, 4% and 7% percent respectively, of the total population of the country in those years.[14]

More significantly for this study was the fact that, by 1980, one of eight of people aged 17 to 25 in the USSR was a student in higher education.[15] As shown in the Appendix, over 12 million people (4% of the total Soviet population in 1982) graduated from *vuzy* between 1965 and 1982, thus becoming potential members of the cohort to be studied here.

During the Brezhnev era, competition among graduates of secondary schools for admission to *vuzy* became increasingly competitive, so that the graduate of secondary school who applied for admission to a *vuz* had about a 20% chance of admission, as compared to a 65% chance for applicants at the end of the Stalin era.[16] In a sense, therefore, the target cohort of this study represents a very select group of Soviet citizens.[17] One had to pass a critical test to gain entry into this group. As the dropout rate among Soviet students at *vuzy* was relatively small, the vast majority of those gaining admission earned their degrees.[18]

An increasingly large portion of those who succeeded in gaining admission to higher education at the start of the 1970s were children of well-educated parents, who by example and active encouragement inspired their children to pursue higher education.[19] One Soviet sociologist who studied this phenomenon concluded, "It seems evident that the intelligentsia exercise a significantly greater influence on the transmission of occupational values to their children" than other groups in Soviet society.[20]   What exactly he meant by "intelligentsia" is addressed later, but the prominence of this issue in Soviet society is perhaps best demonstrated by its position at the center of a debate among "schools" of Soviet sociologists that swirled in the pages of the national press and sociological research publications from the mid-1960s until at least the mid-1970s.

M.N. Rutkevich and a group of Soviet sociologists centered on the Ural city of Sverdlovsk (now Ekaterinburg) noted a steady increase in the percentage of students who were the children of "employees" (*sluzhashchie*: those who performed mental labor of some sort), from 40.4% in 1964, to 50.7% by 1969. This increase was parallel to a corresponding decrease in the children of workers and peasants enrolled (from 53.0% to 45.3% for workers and from 6.6% to 4.0% for peasants). They rejected the Khrushchev-era concept of giving preferential treatment to children of workers and peasants in admission to *vuzy* but did call for "preparatory divisions" at *vuzy* to assist such children in preparing for the competitive entrance exams.[21] They were opposed by a group of sociologists grouped around V.N. Shubkin and centered in Novosibirsk, who called for "social planning" to offset the disadvantages faced by children of workers and peasants in seeking higher education.[22] That this debate occurred openly, with all of its implications for the existence of inequality in the "developed socialist society" of the Brezhnev years, demonstrates just how critical access to higher education was to both official and popular segments of Soviet society.

In large measure, the popularity of higher education was a by-product of the legacy of peace and prosperity enjoyed by the Children of Victory. A sociological review of surveys conducted throughout the 1970s concluded that "the optimistic character . . . of social expectations is related to attainment of a high level of living by the Soviet people." The study further noted that such optimism "places a serious obligation upon the Party organizations," with the clear implication that the "obligation" of the Party was to satisfy those expectations. Significantly, Alekseev et al. included tables measuring the satisfaction level of Soviet citizens with respect to their expectations. Those tables showed that while the expectations were both positive and modest, they were not satisfied in areas of living conditions, medical care, and the service industry. Yet the fundamental optimistic outlook remained, with "thirty-five percent firmly convinced that their housing conditions would improve."[23] Georgie Anne Geyer observed this optimism firsthand and speculated that "they have created a far more educated, far more cultured, far more aware young person. But they are now at the point that they have succeeded so well on that minimal level that they are reaching the level where the person—and the person's desires—are affecting the state in a syndrome of rising expectations."[24] Higher education and access to it therefore remained prominent public issues through the end of the Brezhnev era.[25]

A quantitative description of the target generation's political activity is difficult to achieve. In part this is due to the many different measures of what acts actually constitute genuine "political activity."   But some numerical indicators are available, particularly for those most prominent and official indicators of political activity, Komsomol and Communist Party Membership.

Between 1966 and 1981, 8.7 million people were admitted to "candidate" membership in the Communist Part of the Soviet Union (CPSU). In the same period, 8.4 million gained full membership.   Of the 8.7 million candidate members, 5.4 million (about 62%) were Komsomol members at the time of their acceptance as candidates.[26]   Since normal membership in the Komsomol ends at age 27, this figure represents a significant infusion of young people into the CPSU during the Brezhnev era.

The new candidate members were not only young but largely well educated as well. Of the 8.7 million new candidate members, approximately 2.6 million (30%) held positions as "engineering and technical workers, agronomists, zoo technicians, scientific workers, teachers, doctors and other specialists."[27]   In fact, the number of Party members with complete higher education nearly doubled from 15.7% of the Party in 1966 to 28.0% in 1981.[28] Unfortunately, available statistics do not directly break down Party members by age and education, but these numbers clearly indicate increased participation by young, well-educated citizens in Party affairs during the Brezhnev era.

How, though, do such statistics on Party membership relate to the target population of this study? After all, those upon whom this project is focused generally did not openly express political opinions or actively participate in the activities of the Soviet government or the Communist Party. Likewise, they did not openly break with the regime, as did their "dissident" contemporaries. Here it is necessary to define more closely the relationship between the subjects of this study and the Party and Komsomol.

Simply being a member of an "official" organization such as the Party or Komsomol did not prevent one from attempting to satisfy his or her interests "outside" that organization.   The Russians interviewed in 1995-1999 emphasized that they were "automatically" enrolled in the Komsomol as *vuz* students. Secondary sources indicate that many young, successful members of Soviet society belonged to Party and Komsomol organizations because such membership was a "normal requirement" for advancement and integration into Soviet society.[29] This study will therefore not exclude persons who joined these organizations. It will, however, exclude those who made full-time Party or Komsomol work their primary occupation.

Soviet-era sociologists normally defined the social status of citizens in terms of their "sociooccupational groups."[30] Those citizens at the heart of this study formed a subset of the general category of "employees" (*sluzhashchie*). The Soviets generally applied this appellation to all who performed "mental labor" of various sorts.[31] This amorphous group was further broken down according to the level of complexity of that mental labor and the education or training required to perform it. Thus, in 1983, L.A. Gordon and A.K. Nazimova declared, "Working people in highly skilled mental occupations still differ substantially, both in the nature of their labor activity and in many other features of their social position from all other working people," most notably in the absence of repetitive routines in their work, the presence of creative elements within that work, and their level of personal culture and lifestyle traits.[32] Gordon and Nazimova, therefore, made a critical distinction between various types of "nonphysical workers" in accordance with the complexity of their work. Highly skilled workers requiring specialized education (engineers, doctors, teachers, and scientific workers) were thus set apart from employees engaged in simpler nonphysical work (e.g., drafting, bookkeeping).[33]   This study is concerned with members of both sub-groups, because the primary qualifier for membership in the target group is the education level achieved, not the specific duties of the work position.

In terms of their occupations, the citizens targeted for study here represent what Vera Dunham once referred to as "middle-class." She said of them: "They are solid citizens in positions and style of life below the top official and cultural elite, yet above the world of plain clerks and factory workers, of farm laborers and salesgirls."[34] Rather than "middle-class," this study labels them as "professional specialists," a description more directly related to their education and outlook that still sets them apart from those immediately above and below.   The more traditional Russian appellation of "intelligentsia" is consciously avoided, and the reasons for that avoidance demand elaboration here.

Of all the descriptions of the target generation in the available literature, the one that most closely coincides with the purpose of this study is Vladimir Shlapentokh's appellation the "mass intelligentsia." Shlapentokh used this term to describe those well-educated citizens who were not members of the political elite, the Party apparatus, or the "intellectuals." The difference between his "mass intelligentsia" and these "intellectuals" was that the intellectuals were distinguished by their critical thinking and their roles as "ardent advocates of the democratization of society" and the "spokespersons for the masses." Thus, as defined by Shlapentokh, the "intellectuals" represented the successors of Russia's traditional eighteenth- and nineteenth-century "intelligentsia." The "mass intelligentsia," on the other hand, represented the unprecedented number of well-educated citizens who did not perceive themselves as spokespersons for the masses or successors of the traditional intelligentsia (they are the teachers, engineers, physicians, etc.). This distinction is critically important.   The "dissidents" of the 1960s fit Shlapentokh's definition of "intellectuals." The young citizens who constitute the target group of this study do not. Yet his term "mass intelligentsia" seems imprecise and potentially misleading, given the relatively small numerical size of the group, as well as the strong historical overtones for Russians of the "intelligentsia" label.[35]   Therefore, in order to more accurately emphasize their uniquely specific educational and occupational characteristics, the term "professional specialist" is preferred here.

No quantitative portrayal of the young professional intelligentsia of the Brezhnev years would be complete without some discussion of the large majority that women formed within this group.[36]   L.F. Liss made special mention of the concern extant at the highest political circles about the "complete feminization" of certain branches of the Soviet economy.[37]   While he did not specify these branches, he did study the preferences of male and female students with regard to area of specialization upon entering Novosibirsk State University. So distinct were these preferences that he labeled certain specialties as "primarily male" and "primarily female." Women dominated the enrollment of the faculties of chemistry, history, cybernetics, biology, and linguistics. Men, in turn, formed the majority in physics, geology, and mathematics divisions.[38] One Western source from the mid-1970s placed the female component of the total population with higher education at 58%, including 72% of all doctors, 70% of all teachers, 40% of engineers, and 30% of all Soviet lawyers.[39] Women's issues had a major influence upon the ethos of the young professionals studied here.

Male or female, free time was universally important to the young specialists. Equally important was their ability to choose for themselves how to spend that free time. In a 1977 study of young engineers in Leningrad, V. Iadov called "electivity" (izbiratel'nost) the "most common quality" valued by the engineers.[40] Yet this desire to control their own fate during leisure time did not necessarily indicate a desire to escape from the workplace. In a 1970 study of young specialists working in the elite academic/scientific environment of Akademgorodok, M.V. Timashevskaia found that the young specialists "socialized based upon common interests, not on geographic concerns [neighbors, etc.]." In addition, she noted that this was more true of those with higher education than of workers and other "employees."[41] O.I. Shkaratan had reached similar conclusions in his 1965 studies of specialists in Leningrad. "Personnel in highly skilled scientific and technical work named engineers and others with higher education as their closest friends 50.3% of the time, and named technicians and others with only specialized secondary education 21.5% of the time."[42]

PROFILE SUMMARY

In summary, the target cohort as depicted in the quantitative sources described previously was composed of men and women who had successfully overcome a major competitive obstacle in gaining access to, and completing, their higher education. In all probability, they were assisted in this process through both the active measures and passive influence of their parents, who were likely well-off in terms of their material living standard and well-disposed to the concepts of higher education.[43] Those among them who joined the CPSU or the Komsomol did so not out of ideological fervor but rather as a normal part of life, in order to facilitate their opportunities and advancement.[44] Upon completion of their studies, these young people entered the Soviet workforce as specialists in the performance of complex mental labor. In such positions, the young professionals of the Brezhnev era began to exert influence upon, and to be influenced by, Soviet society in a unique manner, a manner that set them apart from their historical predecessors as well as from their contemporaries in other socio-occupational groups. They developed a sense of themselves as a group, in that they specifically chose to spend their precious free time with others of similar education levels and interests.

IMPORTANCE OF THE TARGET COHORT

The lifestyles and formative experiences of members of the young professionals of the 1970s were rooted in the experience of the well-documented "Thaw Generation," that is, their parents' generation. That generation, born in the 1920s and 1930s, came of age during the last years of Stalin and was influenced most importantly first by Khrushchev's efforts at de-Stalinization, then by the conservative reaction that led to Khrushchev's ouster and culminated in the 1968 invasion of Czechoslovakia.[45] Many of these people, known as the "Children of the Twentieth Party Congress" were well-educated professionals who viewed Stalin and Stalinism as an aberration. They therefore placed themselves into varying degrees of opposition to the regime (whose cadres, the *vydvizhentsy*, had benefited from Stalin's patronage and purges). The most active among them sought to revitalize the Soviet Union through philosophical approaches that stressed either neo-Slavophile tendencies (epitomized by Solzhenitsyn), "purified" Marxism-Leninism (Roy and Zhores Medvedev), or the "convergence" of the socialist and capitalist worlds (Sakharov). Their courage to openly "dissent" earned them fame in the West, but only ruthless suppression at home.

Less openly defiant "Children of the Twentieth Party Congress" in many cases occupied posts in Party and government and had quietly developed their reformist notions in small groups with powerful "patrons" (e.g., Iakovlev at the CPSU Central Committee and Aganbegian in Novosibirsk).[46] On the whole, however, any reformist aspirations of this generation were held firmly in check by the straitjacket of the Brezhnev regime's conservatism.

Of course, it must be noted that no solid boundary exists between generations. Those referred to here as the "Children of Victory" or "people of the seventies" in actuality include those who finished their higher education between 1965 and 1982. Likewise, within the targeted "generation," great divergences among members may occur. Those oldest members of the target cohort may often hold dramatically different views from the youngest, as discussed later. The critical point is not that all members of the target group held the same views, but that they formed similar types of horizontal, unofficial connections that changed Soviet society.

The target generation of this study had its collective hopes for a promising future alternatively raised and dashed by the social and political conditions of the Soviet 1970s. Education and potential gave them a fundamentally optimistic outlook on life, yet their optimism was tempered by the discrepancy between the regime's ideology and the reality of their everyday lives. After the ruthless prosecution of the dissidents and the invasion of Afghanistan, many of them viewed themselves as a "half-lost generation."[47] Such a pessimistic outlook clearly separates this group from the official Soviet portrayals of them as the Children of Victory, that is, as the direct beneficiaries of the titanic struggle waged by the Soviet Union in World War II. Outside observers have termed them an "apolitical" generation that withdrew from public political life into the security of intimate circles of family and friends.[48] This study shows that the target group was indeed reluctant to participate in overt political activity yet retained a keen awareness of social and philosophical issues of the day. This political withdrawal also set them apart from their successors, the radical young reformers unleashed in the Gorbachev era. That group of young people (born in the 1960s) has been described as neither fearing nor respecting the Soviet system but willing to change or challenge anything in order to develop "a system that works."[49]

The "withdrawal" from political life helped conceal their social and philosophical activity from outside observation. The nature of their widespread participation in the precipitous events in Russia since 1985 suggests that, although hidden, this activity was nevertheless vital. The speed of the Soviet collapse and the widespread public participation in that collapse indicate that the basis of that participation was established via the expansion of unofficial horizontal linkages in Soviet society during the years of the alleged "withdrawal." Linkages such as common educational and professional experiences, common frustrations, and common concerns for issues such as the environment, family upbringing, and the future of Soviet society generated the evolution of public opinion that helped lay the foundation for the tempestuous changes that burst forth when the USSR collapsed. The fact that members of the target cohort have emerged as leaders all along the political and economic spectra in post-Soviet society attests to the diversity of these horizontal connections.[50]

The education and occupations of the young professionals guaranteed that they would have strong influence on Russian politics, society, and culture. Simply put, supervisors in all economic and cultural branches and in the "sphere of management" were, as a rule, recruited from the ranks of these specialists. As the "vydvizhensty" who epitomized Brezhnev's "stability of cadres" finally began to retire (or, as was often the case, simply died in office or became incapable of performing their duties), young, highly educated professionals replaced them with increasing frequency.[51] In addition to the formal influence that the young professionals gained through their positions, they gained an enhanced status in a Soviet society that was rapidly improving its overall education level. Gordon and Nazimova noted the growing sophistication of Soviet society as representing a direct consequence of the increased education level, asserting that when well-educated people become a majority, "their occupational orientation becomes a social norm."[52]

The well-educated citizen had long been a key goal and desired component of Soviet society. But the Brezhnev era marked the first time in Soviet history that such citizens constituted a large enough portion of the general population as to become this type of "social norm," prominent enough to influence the development of the state, the society, and the interaction between the two. The "stagnation" of the Brezhnev-era elite and the "alienation" of Soviet society formed the poles of a basic tension underlying that state-society interaction.   This tension manifested itself in the society's awareness and implicit acknowledgment of the "gap" between the regime's words and deeds. Such a gap and the tension from which it sprung were long-term features of the Soviet period.[53]   But the huge numbers of well-educated young specialists, as the most visible manifestations of Soviet success, altered the interaction between state and society.   Their efforts to resolve the fundamental tension of their time drove the evolution of late Soviet society forward in a uniquely Russian manner. To understand those efforts, it is critical to explore what these young citizens believed in and how those beliefs shaped their actions.

BASIC RESEARCH QUESTIONS

In order to examine the beliefs, characteristics, and values that form the "ethos" of the young Soviet specialists and to analyze the relationship of that collective ethos in terms of the evolution of civil society, this study pursues the following questions.   What avenues of social mobility were open to these citizens?   What kind of relationship did they have with the CPSU?   How did they regard the official Soviet ideology?   Did they hold common aspirations, frustrations, and fears?   Did they find satisfaction in their work?   How did they spend their free time and discretionary income?   What were their attitudes toward family life and friendship?   How did common educational experiences or certain career patterns influence their development?   Did they establish unofficial or horizontal social connections that facilitated the bona-fide evolution of "civil society"?   These questions will shed light on the mentalities, values, and ways of thinking of this pivotal group in Russian society.   In addition, these questions will lead to a view of Russian society from a perspective other than that of traditional, elite-centered studies.   Viewing late Soviet society from this perspective will contribute to a deeper understanding of the Russian society of the Brezhnev era and into the evolution of post-Soviet Russian society as well.

The ultimate goal of these questions is to shed light on how the young specialists of the Brezhnev era saw *themselves* and to explore the means by which they expressed themselves.   The nature of Soviet society forced that expression to occur in unique ways. Recent development of historical approaches to interactions between elite and nonelite elements of societies emphasizes that critical insights may be found at points where those elements interact.[54]   This study seeks out and explores points of interaction between the representatives of the political elite and the young, well-educated, often frustrated, alienated, or otherwise subordinated citizens at the heart of this study.

SOURCES

The most significant interactions for which written records are so far available are the discussions of social issues in letters to the Soviet press, Party organs, and the conversations between the specialists and those representatives of the regime who conducted ideological instruction in the workplace. A small number of KGB documents also are available and provide some interesting insight, if not outright interaction.

The most prominent and accessible "points of interaction" between the people of the 1970s and the elite of the Brezhnev era are to be found in the discussions of social issues in organs of the Soviet press. Letters written to the editor, to special correspondents, or in response to surveys and questionnaires initiated by the press organs have long been recognized as one of the most legitimate and interactive exchanges of information that existed in Soviet society.[55]   Both legal and officially encouraged, letters to the Soviet press represent a classic example of what James C. Scott called "Truth Spoken to Power."[56] The "Truth" here is the notion that sometimes a subordinate member of a stratified society would abandon, in full or in part, the normally accepted public rules for interaction and tell a higher-ranking member of the hierarchy how the subordinate truly felt. For members of a traditional subaltern group (e.g., slaves), the emergence of such "Truth" could be a dramatically dangerous event. Soviet letter writing was rarely so dramatic, and certainly carried less danger, yet the basic principle still applied often. A brief example of one published interaction between specialists and a member of the Soviet elite demonstrates many of the aspects of the domination-resistance paradigm and its applicability here.

In October 1981, Mikhail Suslov, Politburo member and chief ideologist of the CPSU, addressed a group of higher-school social science teachers. In an address filled with standard elements of the public ideology of the Brezhnev era,[57] Suslov condemned the "still-persistent inclination toward scholastic theorizing" as "one of the major obstacles in the development of the social sciences." He then called upon them to devote themselves to training specialists capable of assisting the Party and government in resolving specific "concrete" problems of social and economic development, specified in the five-year plans and resolutions of the 26th CPSU Congress.[58]

In contrast to Suslov's elite view of "theorizing" as an obstacle to development and progress, rank-and-file engineers and sociologists complained in several sources that the lack of support for research and theoretical development with which they were faced made their jobs more difficult and lowered their prestige.   This lowered prestige, in turn, reduced their effectiveness in solving the very concrete problems that Suslov favored.

Writing at about the same time as Suslov was condemning social scientists for an overemphasis on theorizing, five industrial sociologists wrote a letter to *Pravda* complaining that industrial managers ignored their research and recommendations in attempting to resolve productivity problems.[59] Specifically, the sociologists noted that their studies revealed that the lost work time due to medical problems and time spent resolving them was much greater than time lost due to violations of worker discipline. Yet, they noted, most enterprises devoted a great deal more time, energy, and expense to discipline problems. The complaints of the sociologists were not directed toward enterprise managers alone. They also decried the lack of government support in publishing the results of research. Specifically, they noted that a study of job categorization, so significant that it represented a "handbook" (*nastol'naia kniga*) of factory sociology, had been compiled at the laboratory of the "Red Proletarian" machine-tool factory in Moscow. Yet this study had never been published for wide dissemination, with the result that any sociologist who desired to use it had to travel to Moscow and copy the original. In closing their letter, these authors declared, "It's long been time to let them [sociologists] have status commensurate with their contribution to technological, economic and social progress, [to let them] complete the necessary research articles and elaborations."

Thus, both Suslov and the sociologists who wrote this letter focused upon the same phenomenon—the need to apply social science knowledge to the resolution of specific problems. But Suslov saw the solution in the greater subordination of social science to theories of Marxism-Leninism and Party control and believed that the emphasis of scholars on research was an obstacle to progress. The sociologists, on the other hand, sought increased autonomy and support for themselves and their colleagues and perceived the organizational constraints and Party restrictions that confronted them as major obstacles. These diametrically opposed viewpoints with respect to the same phenomenon illustrate clearly that, in this instance at least, some educated segments of Soviet society were operating in accordance with a set of beliefs and values that differed from those of the official state ideology.

When elite and subordinate elements of a society view the same phenomena as manifestations of dramatically different facts, a situation of "code-shifting" or "ambiguity" occurs. That is, the two sides attribute vastly different meaning and significance to the sources and implications of the manifestation.

A single example of code-shifting, cannot, of course, be definitive in itself. But a further examination of this example and a comparison with other sources involving professional specialists uncover additional indications of specialists acting in accordance with their own value-system, a system that was subordinate to, yet distinct from, the official elite ideology.

Suslov, as a member of the elite, viewed the problem from a vertical perspective—from the top down. The sociologists, on the other hand, took a more horizontal view, demonstrating both an awareness of, and professional affiliation with, their colleagues throughout the country. The fact that the authors of the letter signed their names and formal academic titles (all engineers) highlighted an important aspect of their subalternity. They had been formally trained as engineers, yet were working as "factory sociologists." It was, in fact, with other sociologists that they identified themselves and on whose behalf they demanded the status and resources that they believed their profession deserved. This was a horizontal connection that spread well beyond the five authors of this letter. The journal *Ekonomika i organizatsia promyshlennogo proizvodstva* published an article making similar complaints in March 1979. That piece noted that factory sociologists were "limited by lack of proper educational opportunities" and called for "formal staff positions for industrial sociologists, without which the job will continue to be performed in the 'disguise' of other positions."[60]   These complaints clearly represented an attempt to establish or expand the "space" in society for sociologists and sociology. This in itself is a significant manifestation of perceived subalternity on the part of these specialists.

Such a horizontal perspective may be indicative of a tendency that was classified by Scott as characteristic of subordinate social groups. This is the element of "mutuality." Scott's "mutuality" is a logical consequence of an awareness of one's opponent that inspires a sense of association or cohesion among identifiable members of a subordinate group, receiving its initial impetus from the subordinates' desire to protect themselves from the efforts of the elite to isolate them from each other.[61]   The failure of the state to publish the sociology "handbook" described earlier and Suslov's insistence upon the primacy of Marxist-Leninist theory in the work of social scientists may have represented—or perhaps more importantly, may have been perceived as—such an effort at isolation.

The sociologists were not alone in recognizing and challenging barriers to the growth of independent ties with their peers. Other specialists likewise pressed for increased horizontal emphasis by focusing upon the status and prestige of their profession. Engineers, geologists, teachers, and others repeatedly made mention of issues of status and prestige when they expressed grievances in the press. Specific instances of these expressions are examined in detail in later chapters. The case of the sociologists as presented here should make clear the applicability of domination-resistance and elite-subordinate paradigms to the relationship between the Soviet state and the young professionals targeted by this study, as manifested in the Soviet press.

The process by which letters and petitions were encouraged and in the Soviet era accepted bears a striking resemblance to the traditional Muscovite and Imperial Russian handling of communications from society and is discussed in great detail in a subsequent chapter.

As indicated earlier, the interpretive nature of this study precludes any notions that it is intended to be "comprehensive" or "scientific" as those terms are normally understood by social scientists. Rather, as a historical study, it attempts to develop a more humanistic portrait of young specialists' lives in the Brezhnev era. Therefore, it relies upon both contemporary and historical interviews with Russian specialists who came of age in Brezhnev's USSR.[62] Given the limited number of interviews, their utility is primarily as a supplement to the press discussions and archival materials that form the documentary core of this study. Yet they have been invaluable in generating a sense of the social context in which those discussions took place. Many of those interviewed in 1995 were openly nostalgic for the lives that they had led in the 1970s, believing that their lives were better then than now.[63] That same nostalgia was missing from most of the interviewees just four years later. In addition, these now middle-aged specialists seemed generally flattered that a Westerner would be interested in writing the history of their generation. Likewise, they were extremely sympathetic to the fact that written sources of information about their earlier lives are now extremely rare. The combination of these factors made for some fascinating conversations that ranged far beyond the initially limited parameters of the interviews.

The interviews from the early 1970s were likewise far-ranging and unpredictable. While much of the information from those interviews was published in Geyer's *The Young Russians*, that same material viewed from the 1990s as part of the "hidden transcript" of the young specialists has proven invaluable in developing a richer sense of the social context that shaped the discussions.

Valid as letters (both published and unpublished) and articles in the Soviet press have been deemed to be, one must nevertheless be aware of potential biases in these printed sources, as well as in the author's interviews. Not all young specialists wrote letters to the press. Those who chose to do so, in essence, 'self-selected' themselves to be potential sources for this study. Just as critical is the notion that representatives of the regime (Party officials, newspaper editors, etc.) selected, to varying degrees, the published letters. An important consideration of the analysis of both the published and unpublished letters must therefore be the question of why they were or were not made public. This aspect of source criticism is discussed in detail in a subsequent chapter.

In a similar fashion, one must keep in mind that those individuals interviewed by the author, as well as those interviewed by Georgie Anne Geyer in the 1970s, *volunteered* to be interviewed. Again, this "self-selection" may make these subjects unsuitable as representatives of their generation.

SUMMARY

The young professional specialists formed a select, yet subordinate, group in the USSR during the Brezhnev era; select in that they overcame obstacles to gain access to, and complete, higher education and subordinate in that they were excluded from the pinnacles of power by the tenured *vydvizhentsy* who personified Brezhnev's "stability of cadres."

As a heterogeneous, yet discernible, subordinate group, the 12 million young professionals developed a set of unique perspectives, a keen awareness of social and philosophical issues, of "transcripts" that interacted in the public sphere with the perspective of the dominant elite. At those points of interaction, the genuine perspectives of both groups were revealed. The following chapters explore the historical records of those interactions. In so doing, these chapters present the ethos of the young specialists as a unique and vital component in the development of Russian society.

Chapter 1 analyzes in detail Soviet society of the Brezhnev era and the role of the young specialists within the parameters of the "Little Deal." Chapter 2 examines the long tradition of petitioning and censorship in Russian history, and the continuity of those processes in the Soviet era. Finally, Chapters 3 and 4 will address specific aspects of the beliefs, characteristics, and values that formed the "ethos" of the young Soviet specialists.

NOTES

1. Elena Iurevna Zubkova, *Russia after the War: Hopes, Illusions and Disappointments, 1945--1957.* Trans. and ed. Hugh Ragsdale (Armonk, NY: M.E. Sharpe, 1998), 5.

2. Ibid., ix-x.

3. Gregory L. Freeze, *From Supplication to Revolution: A Documentary Social History of Imperial Russia* (New York: Oxford University Press, 1988), 6.

4. David Remnick, *Lenin's Tomb: The Last Days of the Soviet Empire* (New York: Vintage Books, 1994), 330-331.

5. Georgie Anne Geyer, *The Young Russians* (Homewood, IL: ETC, 1975), 6

6. Geyer, 260.

7. A university or institute for higher education is known in Russian as a *"vyshee uchebnoe zavedenie,"* or a *"vuz"* for short (*"vuzy"* for plural) graduation from which earned a Soviet citizen designation as a "specialist."

8. A. Rusov, "Mnogovariantnyi Posudnikov," *Literaturnaia gazeta* 21 September 1977, 12.

9. Censorship was not the only tool used by the regime to channel public opinion. Arrest, emigration, and the allocation of scarce goods to eliminate agitators or satiate the discontented were used as well. This study deliberately avoids the focus on dissident elements and overt agitators against the regime. The use of resource allocation to quell unrest was a widespread Soviet practice worthy of further study but lies outside the direct scope of this work.

10. Freeze, 7.

11. The "Little Deal" is most succinctly described in James R. Millar, "The Little Deal: Brezhnev's Contribution to Acquisitive Socialism," *Slavic Review* 44, no. 4 (Winter 1985), 694-706. The specific aspects of the Little Deal and the specialists' place within it are analyzed in detail in Chapter 2.

12 P.O. Kenkman, E.A. Saar, and M. Kh. Titma assert that 75% of higher education students in Estonia had no work experience before entering higher education. See "Generations and Social Self-Determination: A Study of Cohorts from 1948-1979 in the Estonian SSR," as translated and presented in *The Social Structure of the USSR: Recent Soviet Studies*, ed. Murray Yanowitch, 180-214 (Armonk NY: M.E. Sharpe, 1986), 182, hereafter, Yanowitch 1986. L.F. Liss made an identical assertion about first-year students at Novosibirsk State University in 1970. See Liss, "The Social Conditioning of Occupational Choice," in *Social Stratification and Mobility in the USSR*, ed. Murray Yanowitch and Wesley A. Fisher (White Plains NY: International Arts and Sciences Press, 1973), 224, henceforth, Yanowitch and Fisher. This figure is consistent with William Taubman's description of the student body at Moscow State University (MGU), which said that 80% of freshman students entered the university directly from secondary education, with no intervening work or military experience. Taubman notes that this percentage became the norm starting in the 1965-1966 academic year, when the Brezhnev-Kosygin leadership eliminated Khrushchev-era requirements for incoming university freshmen to have first completed two years of work experience. William Taubman, *The View from Lenin Hills: An American Student's Report on Soviet Youth in Ferment* (New York: Coward-McCann, 1967), 47.

13. The 1973 and 1979 figures were cited from *Narodnoe khoziaistvo SSSR* in M.N. Rutkevich, M.Kh. Titma, and F.R. Filippov, "Izmeneniia v sotsial'nom sostave i

professional'noi orientatsii studenchestva SSSR," in *Sovetskaia sotsiologiia*, vol 2. (Moscow: Nauka, 1982), translated and presented in Yanowitch 1986. The 1984 figure was cited by émigré Soviet sociologist Vladimir Shlapentokh in *Soviet Public Opinion and Ideology: Mythology and Pragmatism in Interaction* (New York: Praeger, 1986), 44.

14. Figures for the total population of the USSR as taken from *Narodnoe Khoziaistvo SSSR* are contained in the Appendix.

15. Rutkevich, Titma, and Filippov, "Izmeneniia" transl. and presented in Yanowitch 1986, 216.

16. Murray Yanowitch, *Social and Economic Inequality in the Soviet Union: Six Studies* (White Plains, NY: M.E. Sharpe, 1977), 79-80, henceforth Yanowitch 1977. See also F. Kuebart's summary of Soviet secondary education in Horst Herlemann, ed., *Quality of Life in the Soviet Union* (Boulder, CO: Westview Press, 1987), 84. Gail Lapidus cited an even lower percentage of secondary school grads, "less than fourteen percent" who succeeded in gaining *vuz* entry, in "Society under Strain: The Soviet Union after Brezhnev," *The Washington Quarterly*, no. 6 (Spring 1983), 35.

17. L.A. Gordon and A.K. Nazimova in Yanowitch 1986 noted that between the 1940s and 1970s the rise in the education level was "significantly more rapid than development of the occupational structure." This led to an "imbalance between people's actual occupations and their occupational ambitions."   L.A. Gordon and A.K. Nazimova, "Sotsial'no-professioal'naia struktura sorvremennogo sovetskogo obshchestva: statistika," as presented in Yanowitch 1986, 11-12. British scholar Geoffrey Hosking asserted that "the dramatic rise in education level has enhanced ferment at all social levels in Russia." Geoffrey Hosking, *The Awakening of the Soviet Union*, enlarged ed. (Cambridge: Harvard University Press, 1991), 4.

18. Rutkevich, Titma, and Filippov noted that approximately 5% of entering classes failed to graduate and concluded that "this does not exert a major influence upon the social composition of the student body." See "Izmeneniia," 1982, in Yanowitch 1986, 215-253, esp. 220. A decade earlier, however, O.I. Shkaratan noted that the children of "less educated or less cultured" parents (i.e., workers or other manual laborers) dropped out of the higher grades at a much more rapid rate than did children of the intelligentsia. See O.I. Shkaratan "Social Ties and Social Mobility," in Yanowitch and Fisher, 289-319, esp. 302-303.

19. This "self-regeneration" of the intelligentsia became an increasingly large source of concern for the regime and a favorite subject of Soviet sociologists late in the Brezhnev era. See A.V. Kirkh and E.A. Saar, "A Causal Model of Youth Mobility," in Yanowitch 1986, 173-179. Mervyn Matthews collated Soviet sociological data describing this and other characteristics of Soviet students in "Soviet Students--Some Sociological Perspectives," *Soviet Studies* (January 1975), 86-108. Victor Zaslavsky summarizes the work of several Soviet sociologists on this issue, especially that of N. Aitov, in *The Neo-Stalinist State: Class, Ethnicity and Consensus in Soviet Society* Armonk, New York: M.E. Sharpe, 1982).

20. M.Kh. Titma "The Influence of Social Origins on the Occupational Values of Graduating Secondary School Students" (1970), as translated and presented in Yanowitch and Fisher, 224. See also O.I. Shkaratan "Social Ties and Social Mobility" in Yanowitch and Fisher, 302.

21. M.N. Rutkevich and F.R. Filippov, "Social Sources of Recruitment of the Intelligentsia" from *Sotsial'nye peremeshcheniia*, 1970, 125-129, as presented in Yanowitch and Fisher 1973, 241-274.   L.F. Liss studied figures for students entering Novosibirsk State University in 1967-1970 and noted that children from families in which both parents had higher education passed their entrance exams at rates varying from a low of 57% in 1967 to 71% in 1970. This compared to success rates of 37% to 43% for children of parents with only a general secondary education. See Liss in Yanowitch and Fisher, 285-286.

22. See, for example, V.N. Shubkin, "On Some Social-Economic Problems of Youth," *Nauchnye trudy, seriia ekonomicheskaia*, no. 6, 1965.

23.   B.K.   Alekseev,   B.Z.   Doktorov,   and   B.M.   Firsov,   "Izuchenie obshchestvennogo mneniia: opyt i problemy," *Sotsiologicheskie issledovannia*, no. 4 (1979), 23-32.

24. Geyer, 1975, 236.

25. Rutkevich and Filippov, joined by M.Kh. Titma, addressed the issue anew in the 1982 study "Izmeneniia . . . ," in Yanowitch 1986, 215-253. They concluded that the disturbing trend toward domination of higher education by the children of the intelligentsia that their earlier study had highlighted had been successfully reversed. They gave no reasons for the change, except for a general comment on the "increasing convergence of Soviet society's basic social groups." Basile Kerblay's figures on the composition of the Moscow student body in 1975-1976 support the Soviet sociologists' claims that the proportion of student slots occupied by children of the intelligentsia was decreasing, though still much greater than their proportion in Soviet society as a whole. See Basile Kerblay, *Modern Soviet Society* (New York: Pantheon, 1983), 163.

26. All statistics relative to the CPSU and Komsomol used here are from "KPSS v tsifrakh," *Partinaia zhizn'* no. 14 (1981), 13-26.

27. Ibid., 15.

28. Ibid., 17.

29. See, for example, James R. Millar, ed., *Politics, Work and Daily Life in the USSR: A Survey of Former Soviet Citizens* (New York: Cambridge University Press, 1987), 28.   Also Aryeh L. Unger, "Political Participation in the USSR: Young Communist League and Communist Party of the Soviet Union," *Soviet Studies* 33 (1981), 107-124, esp. 110-111. Articles in the Soviet national press affirm the notion that not all Party/Komsomol members performed their duties zealously and that many, in fact, viewed their memberships as "pro forma" requirements. See "Komu nuzhna 'zona spokoistviia'?" in *Pravda*, 6 March 1981, 2, or V. Kozhemiako's article questioning the commitment of candidate Party members in *Pravda*, 29 March 1981, 2. That both of these articles appeared at the time of the 26th Party Congress is indicative of the widespread nature of such concerns in official circles. Western works focusing on university students, such as those of Matthews and Taubman cited earlier, portray the attitude of such students toward political activity as "passive indifference" or a "necessary evil."

30. Until about 1965, Soviet sociology was able to recognize only two social classes (workers and peasants) and one social "stratum," that of the intelligentsia. Beginning in the mid-1960s, sociologists gradually expanded the sophistication of their portrayal of social groupings to over three dozen specific types. Occupation (one's

relations to the means of production) always formed an essential component of these groupings.

31.   An excellent, concise description of the subtleties of this classification is found in Michael Swafford, "Perceptions of Social Status in the USSR," in Millar, *Politics, Work and Daily Life in the USSR*, 279--300, esp. 282 -283.

32.   Gordon and Nazimova, "Social-professional Structure of Modern Soviet Society," as presented in Yanowitch 1986, 9.

33. Ibid., 8.   V. Iadov likewise stressed the distinctive nature of both the duties (*dolzhnost'*) and the training (*kvalifikatsiia*) of the engineers whom he studied in *Sotsial'no-psykholoicheskii portret inzhenera* (Moscow: Mysl, 1977).

34.   Vera S. Dunham, *In Stalin's Time: Middle Class Values in Soviet Fiction* (New York: Columbia University Press, 1990), 5.

35.   The original title of this study included the phrase "Ethos of the Young Professional Intelligentsia" and met with vehement and unanimous rejection from the Russians whom I interviewed and other Russians with whom I discussed this subject in Moscow in the spring of 1995.

36.   *Literaturnaia gazeta*, 7 March 1973, 13 noted that, according to the 1973 census, women were overtaking men in higher education.   Twenty-six percent more urban women between the ages of 20 and 30 (born 1940 -1950) had higher education of some sort than men of the same age.

37.   This "feminization" became an often-heated topic of discussion in the Soviet press, several instances of which are explored in detail.

38.   L.F. Liss, in Yanowitch and Fisher, 282.

39.   Geyer, 189-193.

40.   Iadov, 1977, 166.

41.   M.V. Timashevskaia, "Some Social Consequences of a City-Building Experiment," as presented in Yanowitch and Fisher 1973, 137-152.

42.   O.I. Shkaratan, "Social Ties and Social Mobility," as presented in Yanowitch and Fisher 1973, 290.

43. Active measures included such steps as the hiring of private tutors and enrolling in special classes.   Both such active measures and more passive methods of parental influence are discussed in detail later.

44 .Komsomol and Party membership was important to almost every specialist. In many cases, it was essential for their professional advancement.   Detailed examples are discussed later.

45.   The label "Thaw Generation" is borrowed from Ludmilla Alexeyeva.   Her work, *The Thaw Generation: Coming of Age in the Post-Stalin Era*, coauthored with Paul Goldberg (Pittsburgh: University of Pittsburgh Press, 1993), is one of the best firsthand summaries of the experiences of that generation.

46.   For a discussion of how these people, the parents of this study's target generation, survived "the long harsh winter of Soviet conservatism" under Brezhnev, see Stephen F.   Cohen and Katrina Vanden Heuvel, eds., *Voices of Glasnost': Interviews with Gorbachev's Reformers* (New York: W.W. Norton, 1989), esp. 20-21.

47.   "Half-lost" is how Sergei Stankevich described his generation to Hedrick Smith.   Cited in Smith's *The New Russians* (New York: Avon Books, 1991), 26.

48.   For discussions of the withdrawal of Soviet citizens into circles of family and friends in the Brezhnev years, see Vladimir Shlapentokh's *Public and Private Life of*

the Soviet People: Changing Values in Post-Stalin Russia, (New York: Oxford University Press), 1989.

49. See Hedrick Smith, 1991 or David Remnick *Lenin's Tomb: The Last Days of the Soviet Empire* (New York: Vintage Books, 1994).

50. See "Russia after Chechnya: The Rise of the New Right," *The Economist*, 28 January 1995, 21-23. This article described the fierce struggle for influence between those born between 1940 and 1950 who formed the nationalistic core of what Russians called the "party of war," and those born in the last years of the target period, 1950-1957. These latter people, such as Iegor Gaidar, Anatoly Chubais, and Boris Feodorov, were the strongest advocates of reform and emulation of the West. In September 1997, the International Finance and Economic Partnership Institute published a "Who's Who" of Commonwealth of Independent States (CIS) participants in the International Project for Success in Economic Survival and Development. These people are described as "some of the most influential leaders of business and administration in the CIS." Of the 110 individuals listed, only 2 did not have higher education. Of the 106 whose birth dates were given, 70 were born between 1940 and 1958. All 70 had higher education of some sort and therefore qualify as members of the target group. Thus, the generation studied here represents two-thirds of these "influential leaders."

51. See, Rutkevich, Titma, and Filippov in Yanowitch 1986, 223, on the recruitment of specialists to fill positions of heavy responsibility. For a discussion of the transition period from the *"vydvizhentsy"* to the young professionals, see Alexeyeva and Goldberg, esp. 29 -32.

52. Gordon and Nazimova, in Yanowitch 1986, 12.

53. A comprehensive discussion of the notions of the "gap" between words and deeds as a feature of Soviet society and state-society interaction as portrayed in the relevant secondary literature may be found in the Bibliographic Essay at the end of this work.

54. A detailed discussion of the relevance of "subaltern studies" and the applicability of domination-resistance paradigms to Soviet society is also contained in the Bibliographic Essay.

55. Both Western and Soviet scholars have studied the phenomenon of letters in the USSR for over 45 years, all concluding that this correspondence served a variety of useful functions for both the regime and the populace as a whole, as well as for the individuals who wrote the letters. Some of these functions included serving as a "safety valve" for the release of built-up popular frustration, a source of legitimacy and feedback for the regime, and an avenue of genuine participation in political affairs for society at large.

56. James C. Scott, *Domination and the Arts of Resistance: Hidden Transcripts* (New Haven, CT: Yale University Press, 1990), 1-10.

57. Suslov's terminology epitomized key elements of the official "sustaining myth" of the "developed socialist society" in Brezhnev's USSR. Some examples included his references to the desires of "aggressive imperialist circles, especially the USA, to turn the wheel of history back to the times of the 'cold war,' " which he used to add emphasis to his exhortations to Soviet citizens to work diligently to resolve the "large-scale tasks of the construction of communism."

58. For Suslov's speech, see "Vysokoe prizvanie i otvetstvennost'" in *Pravda*, 15 October 1981, 2.

59. The sociologists' concerns were expressed in "Chto zabotit sotsiologa," a letter signed by writers who were officially listed as "engineers" yet who clearly identified themselves in the letter as the "sociologist" in the title that appeared in *Pravda*, 28 December 1981, 2.

60. "Factory Sociologist Is an Important Position," *Ekonomika i organizatsia promlyshlennogo proizvodstva* March 1979, 96-117 as translated and presented in *Current Digest of the Soviet Press* 31, no 35, 6-8.

61. Scott, 118 -128.

62. I interviewed or surveyed 30 members of this group in Moscow in the spring of 1995. In addition, Georgie Anne Geyer has graciously given me approximately 400 pages of handwritten notes from interviews that she had conducted with young Soviets in the early 1970s. Tony Parker's *Voices of Russia* (New York: Holt, 1991) included retrospective interviews with 22 members of this group, conducted in 1990. I spoke with four additional members while in the former Soviet Republic of Georgia in 1997 and surveyed an additional seven members (all émigrés) via Email in 1996-1997. In the summer of 1999, two Russian scholars, Leonid Romanovich Veintraub of the Center for the Study of Russia and the Soviet Union and Elena Iurevna Zubkova, director of the Center for Contemporary History at the Russian State Humanities University, assisted me in making contact with another 37 specialists, most in Moscow but some from Novosibirsk as well. Unless otherwise noted, all interviews were conducted in Russian, and all translations are my own. Portions of 14 interviews were lost in the chaos of the Russian postal system; hence further references to statistics from the interviews use a total of 53 instead of the expected 67.

63. In 1997, while serving as a United Nations military observer in the former Soviet Republic of Georgia, I had the opportunity to interview a handful of additional military and civilian specialists. Given the war-torn conditions in the Abkhaz area where I served, these specialists were especially nostalgic for the stability of the Soviet 1970s. Nevertheless, they were equally enthralled by the freedom of interaction that even a war zone offered them in the post-Soviet era.

1

The Limits of the Little Deal: Young Specialists and the Soviet Social Contract

As would be expected of the Children of Victory, young Soviet specialists of the Brezhnev era entered the Soviet workforce with a sense of pride in their education, a willingness to work hard to advance themselves and their society, and a sense of overall optimism consistent with their legacy as the beneficiaries of the victory over fascism. Leaving behind their relatively sheltered university or institute existence, they came face-to-face with the stark reality of Soviet life. In order to fully understand the ethos of this generation of young specialists, we must further explore the character of the reality that they encountered. What was the nature of the society that the specialists encountered? What impact did they, as a group, have upon society, and what effect did it have on them?

This chapter opens with a theoretical discussion of the Soviet "social contract" of the Brezhnev era. It then compares the theoretical parameters of the contract to the realities of the young specialists' lives. The comparison reveals an inherent conflict between the society proclaimed by the regime's ideology and their everyday lives—a gap between the regime's words and deeds. The tension generated by this gap shaped the ethos of the Children of Victory and undermined their faith in the Soviet system.

In 1985, James R. Millar published a description of Soviet society that portrayed the fundamental "contract" between that society and the regime as a form of "acquisitive socialism." Millar's model was known as "the Little Deal."[1] As described by Millar, the Little Deal had several important characteristics. The first of these was the government's goal of "macrolevel" institutional stability by the avoidance of large-scale political or economic reform. Reform was limited to the "microlevel," that is, at the level of kinship or friendship relationships, where toleration of "petty private enterprise and trade" was permitted.[2] To achieve redistribution of scarce consumer goods while avoiding large-scale reform, the Brezhnev regime allowed market and nonmarket ("reciprocal") interactions at the microlevel. In so doing, it sacrificed ideological tenets in exchange for popular material satisfaction.[3] This resulted in the establishment of a symbiotic "second economy" through which Soviet citizens attempted to satisfy their material needs. While increased freedom at the microlevel was allowed, macrolevel discretion (initiative by economic managers, etc.) was restrained. Overt political dissent was persecuted and generally repressed.[4] In the words of an émigré Soviet sociologist, "the regime stopped trying to control the citizen's mentality, and settled for controlled public behavior."[5] Censorship enabled the regime to control what discussions and behavior would, in fact, be "public."

For the young specialists of the Brezhnev era, the Little Deal was a basic fact of their everyday existence. Much of their attention was focused on "microlevel" exchanges, that is, resolving the struggles of everyday life such as acquiring decent housing, maintaining and improving their standard of living, and enjoying their free time with family and close friends. The "second economy" was well established and accepted as a normal part of daily living. Politics were generally avoided. Thus, the parameters of Millar's model have broad application to the period. But, just as many aspects of the Soviet reality of the Brezhnev era support the concept of the Little Deal, other aspects undercut the acceptance of the Little Deal, especially among the young professionals. This chapter addresses briefly some aspects of Soviet society that conform to Millar's parameters, before moving to a discussion of those aspects of Soviet reality that undermined the legitimacy of the Little Deal.

That the Little Deal and the censorship of disruptive issues were successful to a large degree was apparent in the memories of those interviewed in Moscow. The majority remembered their immediate post-*vuz* years as a time of stability and relative prosperity for Soviet society and a time of optimism for themselves and their peers.[6] Only a much smaller number ever felt the need to complain about any aspect of their lives, and those complaints, as the Little Deal would dictate, dealt primarily with "microlevel" issues. The main concern of the young specialists in those days was the pressing need to find suitable housing for their young families. Other family issues, such as income and day care, also ranked high. Free time was spent with spouses and close friends. Only in the most intimate circles of family and friends were items of politics ever discussed.

One of the most illustrative examples of both the microlevel focus of the new *vuz* graduate and the type of "reciprocal" exchanges expected under conditions of the Little Deal was the housing issue. A majority of the specialists surveyed stated that they lived at least a part of the time in their first post-*vuz* years with their own parents or the parents of their spouse. Most of those said that they were satisfied with their living conditions at that time. However, they also said that they remembered well how strongly they would have preferred their own apartments, and they recalled working very hard to obtain a place of their own.[7]

Throughout 1977, *Literaturnaia gazeta* ran a series of articles about the shoddy workmanship and poor service of new apartments being constructed and the difficulties that tenants faced when trying to make repairs. A critical focus of those articles was the need to bribe or otherwise negotiate deals with construction and repair personnel to do quality work or to make quality repairs to new apartments.[8] These articles harked back to a 1972 piece, that discussed the need to make private arrangements with moonlighters or freelancing workers to get such basic services as plumbing or electrical repairs. [9] The transactions described in these pieces were precisely the "reciprocal" arrangements just mentioned, that is, usually the tenant would exchange some scarce goods or services for the repair work.

    Literaturnaia gazeta also ran a questionnaire in 1978 entitled "Who Stayed Home" to collate readers' experiences on the scheduling and completion of home repairs performed by official service agencies. The editorial staff noted that replies were received from all parts of the USSR and that "not one letter supported the work schedules of consumer services as they exist today." Among the problems cited were workmen who showed up late, "less than sober" or not at all.[10]

    Finally, a similar issue was raised by *Sovetskaia rossiia* in early 1979. That piece, focused on the housing status of young couples, noted a disconnect between responsible officials and the populace. While lip service to improving housing was paid by officials at all levels, a survey of readers' letters noted that 25% of young people filing for divorce did so because they "didn't have a place to live."[11] The same letters complained that no state-owned or private apartments were available and that no locator service existed to help them solve the problem. A Komsomol committee in one district concluded that "hotel-type" apartments were "too primitive" and ordered that construction of this type should be discontinued, despite the fact that 90% of those surveyed would gladly accept such accommodations. The article closed by noting, "Sociologists who specialize in the problems of young people believe we need a basic study of the relationships between the young family on the one hand and society and labor collectives on the other."[12]

    While the precise level of young specialists' participation in the housing debate is impossible to accurately determine, the housing issue was clearly important to them. The myriad "reciprocal exchanges" in which they and other Soviet citizens engaged to acquire housing services provide a clear example of the regime's toleration of acts that were technically illegal in order to allow some level of consumer satisfaction. Thus, the housing discussion of the 1970s provides some confirmation of the validity of Millar's Little Deal parameters. Of greater relevance here is the fact that an issue of such widespread concern remained beyond the state's ability to solve over a period of at least the seven years covered by the articles just discussed. One can be sure that this gap between the daily reality and the official proclamations of the state was discussed around many a kitchen table in Brezhnev's USSR.

    The state's willingness to allow expanded freedom of action at the microlevel dramatically reshaped the role of the family in Soviet life. Gail Lapidus termed this reshaping "the virtual revolution in Soviet attitudes towards the family," which resulted in a "family centered value system" that assigned the family a central social role, enhancing its income, privacy, and leisure opportunities and capabilities. [13] Shlapentokh and Millar agreed, with the former declaring the family to be "the first, or one of the first, priorities of Soviet citizens since at least the middle 1960's."[14] Millar called the state's willingness to permit the expansion of the "household's" gain as "the critical element" of the Brezhnev-era social contract.[15]

Immediately after the focus on one's family came one's *kruzhki*, or circles of friends. These were normally composed of colleagues from work or from one's school days. Commonality of interest was the deciding factor, not geography. When asked with whom they socialized, all of the specialists surveyed recalled spending the bulk of their free time with family members or colleagues. None mentioned neighbors as key associates, except in those cases where the neighbors were also colleagues.

All Soviet citizens belonged to a formal *kollektiv*, defined variously as a "goal-oriented complex of persons who are organized and who possess the organs of the *kollektiv*" or as a "contact group built on the socialist principles of association."[16] Soviet citizens, by the 1970s, did not define themselves in accordance with the *kollektiv's* goals, but, instead, they did so in accordance with their own sense of individual morality. This morality was defined by their selection of heroes and by the judgment passed upon them by their own, self-selected community, be that a sports club, a professional group, or simply their own circle of family and carefully chosen friends. Often, this individualism was expressed through the accumulation of certain possessions or the adherence to a certain style of fashion or action.[17] The distinction between the official *kollektiv* and the circle of associates and relatives by which individuals defined themselves and their ethos is critical to an understanding of the young specialists and of Soviet society. This study develops the various aspects of this distinction in detail.

Some of Geyer's interviews in the early 1970s provide additional insight into the microlevel focus of the young specialists.   When she discussed free-time issues with a group of young mathematicians in Moscow, they told her that they intentionally avoided politics to concentrate on " a pure personal life." They "do not want to be compromised by politics," so all activities focused on their personal lives.[18]   Thus, they were very inward-looking.   In Geyer's assessment, their withdrawal "helps the regime...but it is not what the regime wants. It means a lack of spiritual spark from much of the group that should be the creative guiding force here."[19]

The notions of the family as the basic economic element for Soviet citizens of the Brezhnev years and of the "circle" of close friends and associates as the fundamental social element conform to Millar's Little Deal parameters. A much more detailed discussion concerning the family, friends, and free time of the young specialists is found later. For now, this chapter seeks confirmation of the second of Millar's major parameters, that of the "symbiotic" second economy.

The fact that a second or "counter" economy flourished in the Soviet Union under Brezhnev has been widely noted and studied. This parameter of Millar's Little Deal is undisputed. Therefore, this chapter focuses on a particular example of a young specialist's experience. In describing his experiences "On the Other Side of the Counter," a 24-year-old store manager used examples of "reciprocal" exchanges that individuals might make to highlight choices that he faced in his professional life. Clear in his writing was the assumption that everyone knew exactly what he was talking about. Equally clear was the notion that "reciprocal" arrangements had gone beyond the limits that the Little Deal would proscribe, if the regime had its way.[20] A. Artsibashev, a 24-year-old graduate of the Sverdlovsk Economics Institute, was dismissed from his position as manager of a delicatessen in 1975. Because he was one of five young specialists fired in his region, and because the Komsomol was actively encouraging young people to specialize in economic management ("Youth, go into the services sphere," was a current Komsomol slogan), he became the focus of a *Komsomolskaia pravda* investigation. In telling his story, Artsibashev began by candidly describing how his *vuz* education had little relevance to the demands of his profession.

"The first advice I heard from experienced people was: 'Forget what you learned. Trade has its own rules.'" In short, the two basic rules were that, in order to accomplish anything, "you have to first of all find a loophole in the system of surrounding connections." The key to this was the second rule: "Once they find out you are a store manager, everyone wants some scarce goods." Artsibashev described his situation in looking after the needs of his store and its staff as analogous to that of any Soviet citizen. "Anyone who's ever had his own apartment repaired even once knows what it is to call a plasterer or painter. They don't just come to our store [upon request]. They say: 'if you could come up with some scarce goods. . . .'"

The fact that Artsibashev used such an analogy testifies to the widespread nature of the second economy and the commonplace nature of the "reciprocal" transactions that were often necessary to obtain needed services. In this way, his story provides clear evidence that the young specialists of his time were well acquainted with the precepts of the Little Deal. More ominously, from the state's point of view, Artsibashev's story reveals how "reciprocal" exchanges had clearly passed beyond the realm of private, individual, "microlevel" relations into the official business realm. Artsibashev himself realized this when he described the methods that managers used to get things done: "I could name names, but the relationships [that facilitate work] are formed in such a way that it's sometimes difficult to decide what comes within legal norms and what borders on the criminal code. . . but I don't want to keep silent."

This study returns to Artsibashev's story when discussing the professional values and beliefs of the young specialists. But the spread of questionable economic practices beyond the "microlevel" of individual exchange to the business level was not the only situation in which Soviet society, in particular, the young specialists, adopted the precepts of the Little Deal in a fashion that altered the basic parameters of the implicit contract. In complying with the third of Millar's basic precepts, the avoidance of political dissent, young Soviet specialists exceeded the probable expectations of the state.

Georgie Anne Geyer concluded her 1975 study of the young Russians by noting that most of them "believe that many of their society's values are good ones . . . a majority seems to have faith in the future."[21] But, for young specialists, this basic satisfaction with official social values was matched not only by the desired avoidance of overt dissent but by outright political apathy. Like the young mathematicians whom Geyer cited earlier, young specialists were intensely focused on private issues and deliberately avoided broader ones.

Even when specifically questioned or confronted with issues having broad implications, young specialists (at least, in public) avoided even indirect political commentary. One young specialist, referred to only as Boris Ivanovich, typified this response. Boris was a young engineer who employed an advanced cybernetic control system on his projects. A *Literaturnaia gazeta* correspondent who was studying the implementation of such systems throughout the USSR interviewed him. The correspondent noted Boris Ivanovich's extraordinary success, held him up as a model of the promising young Soviet engineer, and asked for his opinion as to why that system had not been adopted for widespread use. In reply, "Boris Ivanovich merely shrugged his shoulders. For him, such a question doesn't exist. He's an engineer, and does his own engineering work."[22] Within the context of the interview, the reporter's question clearly had political implications. Boris Ivanovich's response, or lack thereof, enabled him to avoid involvement in any political issues, despite the temporary celebrity that this particular issue created for him.

As Boris Ivanovich demonstrated his acceptance of the Little Deal's political restraints by his silence, another young specialist, V. Kocheshev, was more explicit in his basic acceptance of political parameters. A design engineer and 1974 graduate of Moscow's Bauman Higher Technical Institute, Kocheshev complained in a 1978 letter to *Pravda* that for three years he had been used by his factory as an "auxiliary housekeeping worker" to dig ditches, paint, gather trash, and so on. Yet he added the following caveat to his complaint: "Don't think that I'm against participating in the city's upkeep or cleaning the factory grounds, if everything is done in moderation." [23] He was committed to the basic tenet of Soviet society that all must pitch in and help but did not openly raise the political issues that logically related to such officially sanctioned use of specialists.[24]

Both Boris Ivanovich and V. Kocheshev had the opportunity to raise political issues in their dealing with the press. Yet both avoided doing so, despite the clearly political agendas of the reporters with whom they were dealing. Both clearly understood the Little Deal restriction against overt political dissension. In avoiding political affirmation as well, both demonstrated the apolitical nature of their generation of specialists. Given the relatively privileged position of the Children of Victory, this apolitical disposition deserves additional scrutiny.

Of course, it is possible that Boris Ivanovich deliberately downplayed his true feelings. The same could be true for any opinions expressed in published materials or in interviews with Soviet citizens during the Brezhnev era, such as those of Geyer. Archival materials indicate that many young specialists did express their feelings about issues with political overtones. It is likely that just such expression prevented the publication of their opinions, as will be discussed in the next chapter.

None of the specialists interviewed indicated that they had ever questioned the legitimacy of the Communist Party of the Soviet Union (CPSU) as the locus of all real power. Of the 35 who said that they had considered the question of whom to turn toward if they had needed any help with an issue or problem, 21 specified the Party. While approximately 40% of those questioned declared their "negative" feelings toward the CPSU's *nomenklatura* system of sponsorship, an even greater number declared themselves "neutral" or "indifferent" to the system. They thus placed themselves in solidarity with the apolitical stance of Boris Ivanovich and V. Kocheshev.

A possible explanation for the specialists' lack of interest in politics may be found in the words of one of their number, who by 1995 was a professor of sociology at Moscow State University (MGU). "No one thought the system would collapse so fast. Everyone thought of the system as being eternal."[25] Two trends in the respondents' answers may indicate that the young specialists believed that this "eternal" system neither required nor desired their involvement. Eighty-five percent of the respondents felt that they had no voice in determining the interests of Soviet society in the 1970s. That is, they felt that the system functioned without them. At the same time, over 75% considered their outlook on life at that time to be optimistic. This "voiceless" optimism reflects their understanding of the true nature of the system as well as their expectations that the system would continue to function with its parameters intact. Within those familiar parameters, they could pursue happiness.

This is not to say that the young specialists played no role in the collapse of that "eternal" system. As this study demonstrates, their optimism inspired efforts to attempt to improve and "humanize" the system. Expectations for improvement stemmed from their optimism and led to their frustration. Within that dynamic process, young specialists developed (as did other Soviet citizens) an ethos that prepared the way for the emergence of new priorities, such as privacy and democracy, following the Soviet collapse.[26] Reasons for both their understanding of the system and such expectations of the system's durability may have stemmed from the fact that the Children of Victory were very much the products of that system.

Only 4 of the 53 specialists surveyed had never been members of either the Komsomol or the Party.[27] Forty of the 53 had fulfilled some sort of military service, usually reserve officer training in connection with their university program.[28] The specialists were enrolled in the organizations, but in keeping with the desire for privacy of the young mathematicians and the apolitical positions of Boris Ivanovich and V. Kocheshev, their membership was passive and quite often, in name only.

Klara Paramova, a lecturer in foreign languages, joined the CPSU in 1975 at the age of 24. When asked about her reasons for joining the Party, she candidly admitted: "In those days. . . there was no doubt that if you wanted to get on it would be a great advantage to you to be a Party member." The competition for jobs teaching at a vuz was intense, and membership could make the difference. "Yes, I am saying precisely that joining the Party was for me entirely a calculated way of furthering my career. It had nothing at all to do with ideals."[29] Two other specialists described other types of such pro forma membership.

Art critic Vadim Koronov, born in 1945, related that he joined the Party as a "present" for his army officer father and thereafter remained a member as a "memorial" to his family. He recalled, "I was a good party candidate. . . . Let me say as well because it's true that I enjoyed it. . . . I was doing it entirely because I wanted my father to see."[30]

Yet a third variant of the pro forma membership in the Party was described by Philip Andreyev, by 1991 a professor of English who, like Koronov, was born in 1945. "I am a born Communist, in the same way that people in other countries are born Roman Catholics, born Quakers, born aristocrats, born paupers or whatever label they may wish to use."[31]

Each of the preceding examples is retrospective, declared by specialists interviewed in 1991. Yet both foreign and domestic observers of the young specialists noted the same type of passivity during the Brezhnev years. Georgie Anne Geyer noted that despite their universal Komsomol preparation, "young Russians are very turned off by the Komsomol scene. . . . They just go through the motions. They criticize it because it's so dull."[32]

D. Skudaev, the head of the Philosophy Department at the Chita State Medical Institute, levied a more detailed criticism of Komsomol activists. In an article for *Komsomolskaia pravda*, Skudaev decried lack of assertive action by Young Communist League (YCL) activists. He noted that the YCL had introduced topics of special interest to young people, leading to a marked increase in student interest in Komsomol discussions. But he then declared that the YCL propagandists were consistently proving themselves unable to satisfy that interest. "Not so much in the lectures per se. Assembling the materials presents no difficulties. But immediately following the talk come the questions. . . ." He noted that answering those questions was "incredibly difficult" for passive propagandists, those same passive ones who don't take action when they see problems such as foreign jeans for sale at an exorbitant price.[33]

Skudaev's criticisms could be directed to the young specialists as a group. While they seemed to support the basic values of the Soviet myth, that support was largely passive.[34] They accepted the parameters of the Little Deal as a basic rule of their existence but, even within the framework of that acceptance, the foundations of some dissatisfaction developed. The gap between words and reality in the housing situation, the growth of reciprocal economic transactions beyond the family "microlevel," and specialists' avoidance of open political dissent via avoidance of nearly all genuine, active political involvement—all of these undermined the effectiveness of the Little Deal.

CONTRADICTIONS OF THE LITTLE DEAL

The previous discussion confirmed that Millar's three basic parameters of the Little Deal (the microlevel focus, the second economy, and the avoidance of overt political dissent) were, in fact, concrete aspects of the Soviet reality faced by the young specialists. As noted within that discussion, however, young specialists' manner of acceptance of those parameters generated some phenomena that undermined the Little Deal as a genuine social contract at all three levels. The discussion now turns to more specific discussion of how the process of undercutting the Little Deal occurred on each level.

The same specialist who described the expectations of the "eternal" nature of the Soviet system also discussed one of the most critical shortcomings of that system that every specialist faced at the personal level. "Everyone, including me, thought that the Soviet system was not very efficient, human, or humane, if you wish. It was not very efficient in terms of giving advancement to talented people, rather blocking them than supporting them."[35] While this blockage was not a stated goal of the regime, macrolevel stability certainly was. The "stable cadres" who distinguished the Brezhnev era from Khrushchev's turbulent times looked a lot like a glass ceiling from the perspective of the young specialist. The social position of those doing "highly skilled mental work" was, by the 1970s, the" most stable position of all" in Soviet society.[36] Because of the lifetime tenure that Brezhnev's cadres enjoyed, "many highly educated young people have minimal opportunity for advancement."[37] That this lack of opportunity created a tension within Soviet society was described by Vladimir Shlapentokh as a problem of "higher aspirations and lower opportunity. . . the bureaucratic stagnation caused by Brezhnev's stabilization closed an outlet of energy for the young."[38]

In extreme cases, young specialists reacted to this frustration of their aspirations by "dropping out" of society. The young researcher-turned-cabdriver discussed in the Introduction is one such example. Others took less drastic, yet similar, actions. Iuri Ivanovich Bulgakov, born in 1942, graduated at the top of his institute's mathematics class early in the 1960s. By 1971, he was working at a "third rate job in a government office."[39] Iurii Ivanovich had once violated the political parameter of the Little Deal and made a statement in defense of a young poet whose work had earned the displeasure of the regime. In that way, his case was atypical of the young specialists. Nevertheless, his place of work illustrates an intermediate avenue—safe, voluntary, "it's a living" underemployment—by which the specialist could deal with frustration; but one not so drastic as that of Posudnikov or others who took to manual labor.

Most young specialists, however, did not "drop out." Fifty-one of those 53 surveyed indicated that they had achieved at least some professional aspirations during the Brezhnev years. Ranging from earning an additional academic specialty, to publishing their own books or articles or defending their candidate's dissertation, the aspirations achieved indicate that while the stability of cadres may have slowed progress and inspired frustration, it did not completely prevent such progress, but even a young specialist who managed to advance to the top of his field was not immune to frustration.

Alexei Lebedev, a 1968 graduate of the Moscow Physical-Technical Institute, described his career as advancing through "all the scientific positions from the very bottom to the very top."[40] Not until he reached the top of his profession did he feel any sense of acute frustration. As he stated, "My problems began when I achieved the top scientific position in my Institute and saw that I mean [*sic*] nothing, nothing in the scientific policy of 'my' institute!"[41]

Lebedev's case, like Bulgakov's, represents an extreme. The critical element in his situation is that his frustration began when his expectations were no longer satisfied by the reality that he faced in his daily professional life. Lebedev was exceptional in that his expectations were largely satisfied until he had advanced quite far in his professional career. But the confrontation between reality and expectation was a common experience for all of the young specialists of the Brezhnev era. The level of expectation determined the nature of the confrontation, and the expectations of the Children of Victory were quite high.

One of the defining characteristics of the Soviet society in which the Children of Victory came of age was the promise of social mobility. Both Soviet and Western observers noted that the key to such mobility was the achievement of higher education.[42] Thus, the Soviet citizens targeted here could look back on the lives of their parents and grandparents and witness almost uninterrupted material, social, and intellectual progress, even given the cataclysmic destruction of the World War II. As the recipients of higher education, they could expect that such progress would continue in their own lives and those of their children. These individual, microlevel expectations had, by the 1970s, begun to have an impact well beyond the microlevel. Geyer best summarized the situation: "To a great extent, it [the Soviet educational system] worked; they have created a far more educated, far more cultured individual. But they are now [1975] at the point that they have succeeded so well on that minimal level that they are reaching the level where *the person—and the person's desires, are affecting the state.*"[43]

That influence was clearly manifested at the highest political levels. The Five-Year Plan (FYP) announced at the 24th Party Congress in 1971, in contrast to earlier plans, raised expectations among the young due to its promise of a forthcoming emphasis on the high-tech production of consumer goods.[44] The same Party Congress, in its draft plan for 1971-1976 called for 9 million specialists with higher or specialized secondary education.[45] These two precepts, the "words" of the regime in their most public form, could only add to the optimism of the young specialists and further increase their expectations for "deeds" to match. The failure of those deeds, particularly in the economic realm, would lead to both economic and political frustrations, which would further undercut the legitimacy of the Little Deal.[46]

The economic frustrations of the young specialists (and the rest of Soviet society) are perhaps the easiest to describe. They were certainly among the most frequent subjects of complaints in the Soviet press. As specifically concerns the young specialists, the primary areas of frustration centered upon pay (more precisely, pay scales), working conditions, corruption, and shortages of goods and services.

When the infamous Posudnikov (researcher-turned-cabdriver described in the Introduction) left the scientific research institute where he worked, he described himself as "no fool who would stick to the duties of a junior research assistant for 105 rubles per month with no chance of defending his candidate's dissertation."[47] Posudnikov's dissatisfaction with his wages was not so much centered on the absolute quantity of rubles that he earned but on the relative amount of his paycheck compared to those of others and the lack of opportunities to supplement his income.

One of the consequences of official Soviet glorification of the working class was the pronounced reduction of wage differentials between simple workers and those of educated employees. In fact, "the steadily diminishing ratio of engineering-technical wages to those of manual workers was the most clearly established trend in Soviet occupational wage structure." [48] This trend was certainly not lost on the young specialists.

A series of letters to *Pravda*, written in response to an article concerning "earned and unearned rubles," included the declaration of one specialist that the "correlation of pay for the work of specialists and workers not only definitely undermines the prestige of engineering-technical work, but even is the reason for the decline of interest in obtaining higher education."[49] While this particular reader's assessment of the level of interest in higher education is contradictory to both Soviet and Western studies, his concern for the specialists' prestige was quite widely shared. Anecdotal accounts from specialists were reported in the same article. Some of these reported instances of diploma-bearing engineers transferring to workers' jobs to gain wages and benefits. This phenomenon of underemployment was not unique to the late Brezhnev years but had been a problem for some time.

In a series of articles in 1971 and 1972, *Literaturnaia gazeta* discussed the hidden costs to the state of the education of diploma-bearing specialists in comparison to the actual practice of their employment. In the second article of that series, many young engineers reported that "they were not able to receive work in correspondence with the specialty indicated by their diplomas. . . . It was proposed to them to fill vacancies, but often these duties did not demand an engineer's qualifications."[50] Filling workers' billets that paid as much or more as the normal billet for a junior researcher may properly be considered more a problem of prestige than of pay, but the fact remains that many young specialists were forced to do precisely what Posudnikov had willingly done. Just how many young specialists were forced to do so is unclear. But the significance of the issue is underscored by the fact that it generated a large number of letters and petitions from young specialists to the press and Party. Early in 1976, *Pravda* submitted a summary of readers' letters to the Central Committee in response to the draft Party Program for the "Basic Direction of the Development of the Soviet Economy, 1976-1980" for the 25th CPSU Congress.   Prominent within the summary were letters criticizing the draft program for its lack of specificity in addressing the training and assignment of engineers and technicians. The draft called for 9 million total graduates, without specifying the relative proportions of specialists and technicians.[51] The letters cite this lack of specificity as the obvious cause of the imbalance between numbers of specialists and numbers of technicians.[52] Most significantly, the problem remained unsolved, and the expectations of these unfortunate young specialists remained frustrated, for at least the nearly 10-year period between these articles.

Even some of those specialists who did find a job corresponding to their education level were not satisfied with their income. One way for an engineer to supplement his standard income was to earn an incentive bonus for exceptional performance or creativity (such as an invention). But even such bonuses, lauded as stimulating creativity by the same *Literaturnaia gazeta* article that detailed the fate of those less fortunate specialists, were criticized as inadequate. The problem was that a prizewinning engineer could expect a 30-50-ruble prize and then "could hardly count on another single prize in the next two years."[53]

While paychecks and pay differentials contributed to the economic frustrations of the young specialists and undermined the Little Deal, a significantly larger number of the Children of Victory complained about their working conditions. These complaints most often centered upon concerns with the job placement system, actual physical hardships imposed by the work environment, shortages of equipment, and the restriction of creative opportunity.

The same 1972 articles in *Literaturnaia gazeta* cited earlier to discuss the widespread "underemployment" of young specialists to fill technician and even workers' billets proposed changes to aspects of the planning and hiring system. But nearly 10 years later, *Pravda* told the story of Alexei Lobanov.[54]   Alexei was a young electrical engineer who did well enough at the *vuz* to be granted "the right to choose his future work." Alexei said that he took a job at an enterprise that advertised for an electrical engineer because it was a union-level enterprise, and he thought that he would "find a solid basis for professional growth and broad perspective." However, "they gave him drafting work that even a first year student could handle." Alexei said: "I tried to search for and to suggest interesting solutions, but they brushed me off." Alexei was told to do "what they want done and the administration will do the thinking." Alexei left that post and had, at the time of the interview, spent a year working as an "adjuster" (*naladchik*) in a machine building plant—a worker's job.

The article went on to describe other such examples, including statistics showing large numbers of engineers filling workers' slots in one geographic area while enterprises in other areas were desperately short of the same engineers. The author of the article blamed three causes: first, poor treatment of newly arrived specialists by enterprises (lack of creative work, no housing, poor wages); second, arbitrary determination of numbers of engineers/specialists requested— determinations that often changed while the specialists training to fill them were still in *vuzy*; third, the failure of republic and union ministries to develop and present a scientifically based method of ordering specialists, despite the fact the USSR Council of Ministers ordered them to do so by the end of 1978. Alexei's complaints of filling a worker's billet and being denied creative opportunities were common to many other specialists, as discussed further later.

While Alexei felt that he had been denied adequate career opportunities, other young specialists had complaints that were even more basic. Physical well-being, not just creative potential, was the concern of several groups of teachers, including some young specialists whose letters were summarized in the teachers' newspaper *Uchitel'skaia gazeta* in August 1979. It seems that the teachers, all working in the northern part of European Russia or Siberia, were unable to get local officials to assist them in acquiring adequate supplies of heating fuel for the coming winter. [55] Several teachers' letters complained about the insensitive attitude of local officials toward assisting the (mostly female) teachers in locating, loading, and transporting fuel. The reporter who wrote the article, I. Kolesnikova, noted, "The local Soviet and the principal seem to have forgotten that the Law on Public Education mandates greater concern for teachers."[56]

The patterns demonstrated by this article—a collective summary of complaints followed by blame leveled toward local officials and the citation of a relevant law or decree—were quite common in the Soviet press and are more fully analyzed in subsequent chapters. For the moment, another similar example strengthens the argument that hardships imposed by working conditions contributed to the undermining of the Little Deal in the eyes of the well-educated young specialists.

In the summer of 1973, a series of articles in *Literaturnaia gazeta* attempted to answer the question of job assignments for young forestry management specialists. The articles appeared under the title "No Further than the Garden Ring [Road]."[57] Here *Literaturnaia gazeta* sought to explain why 90% of the recent graduates of a forestry-management *vuz* had taken jobs in urban Moscow—and not in the forests of the USSR. This, despite the pleas of the USSR Forest Ministry, which complained that over the previous five years, only 43% of all the forestry-management specialists trained in the Russian Republic had actually taken jobs working in the nation's forests. The second article was actually a letter of response to the question by the rector and the Party committee secretary of the Moscow Forestry Institute. They noted that "for years, young specialists, assigned to forest areas without apartments, have lived wherever they had to, taking corners wherever they could. Therefore we must review the system of payment for their work and improve their living and productive conditions in the most basic ways. In addition to decent apartments, foresters must be supplied with modern transport and means of communication."[58]

The most damning portion of the discussion, in terms of undermining the young forestry engineers' faith in the economic aspects of the Little Deal, was the reporter's note that "the Ministry's orders on the business of young people who have forestry experience remain on paper, since regional administrations fulfill the Ministry's orders at a rate of twenty to twenty-five percent."[59] This was followed by ministry assessment that "the article objectively reflects the situation. . . ."[60]

Once again, the "words" of an official organ were unmatched by "deeds" in the real world. That regional bureaucrats failed to implement central policies was perhaps not surprising when considering the Byzantine world of the Soviet bureaucracy, but such disconnects could only weaken the young specialists' faith in the extant social contract. Even more critical damage was done to that faith when the young specialists perceived that the gap between the regime's words and the deeds that they witnessed was caused not by bureaucratic inertia or confusion but by outright corruption.

In many ways, "as corruption led to labor demoralization, the second economy supplanted the first."[61] Such was the assessment of the declining productivity of the Soviet workforce in the 1970s by an émigré Soviet sociologist. Demoralization and allegations of corruption were evident in both the published and unpublished petitions and statements of young specialists of the time.

Unpublished complaints and petitions, taken from archival sources, tended to focus on issues of major consequence to all elements of Soviet society, not just to young specialists. But young specialists' letters concerning shortages of basic staples, such as meat and milk, and complaints about the dismal state of Soviet medical care illustrated their high level of demoralization. Many of the Children of Victory apparently faced these problems with a sense of incredulity that such problems could exist in their USSR.

In a June 1976 letter to *Komsomolskaia pravda*, V.A. Berannikov, a 28-year-old graduate of a juridical institute wrote:

Beginning in 1967 and right up to today, you could only rarely buy meat in the stores of our city. The basic trade in the commodity took place in the market, where the price of a single kilo was between 4.5-5 rubles. Can it really be fair, that in a major city like Kuibyshev, that this product, which is so important in life, is only very rarely in stores? This was also the situation with eggs, herring and oranges. There's only one way to eliminate these shortages—work together. And in this work, one must not forget that everything is done by human hands—and that all of these people have needs: a place to live, a variety of food products, clothing and mainly—attention.[62]

Liuda Rostovtseva was a 25-year-old accountant-economist and mother of a four-month-old when she wrote to *Komsomolskaia pravda* in December 1975 about the impossibility of finding any milk, including fresh, dry, or condensed. She opened her letter by identifying herself as a Komsomol member since 1966 and noted that she had been recognized as a "shock worker."[63] She further noted that people regularly stood in line for four to five hours only to be told that the stores had not received their milk quota and that such problems had been ongoing since June (more than six months).[64]

An important aspect of these shortages in shaping the young specialists' ethos was that both of these letters were written at the time of the 25th Congress of the CPSU. Five years earlier, *Komsomolskaia pravda* had submitted similar collections of letters in the pre-Congress period of the 24th Party Congress with the comment that "many letters complain of shortages, especially of meat, which demonstrates the hard facts of disgrace and irresponsibility which our readers meet."[65] In other words, the state had been unable to solve these problems despite the passage of more than five years. Despite the fact that these letters were never published, the shortages and the failure of the Party and state to resolve them undermined the young specialists' willingness to accept the Little Deal as a long-term contract. Berannikov's reference to basic human needs—including the need for attention—and Rostovtseva's identification of herself as a Komsomol member and "shock worker" represented ironic appeals to some of the official "myths" of Soviet society. The irony would not have been lost on press and Party officials reading their letters. Nor would it on readers of the paper, which may be why the letters remained unpublished. Much more likely, however, the letters were not published because they described critical shortages of essentials—shortages that might have roused public anger had they appeared in the press.[66]

Shortages of goods were not the only major problems shaping the specialists' ethos. Along with other Soviet citizens, they were confronted daily with the disastrous state of one of the best "benefits" of Soviet society—free medical care. By the mid-1970s so many letters were received in editorial offices that newspapers forwarded "bulletins" of complaints, petitions, and suggestions to the Central Committee. Medical ethics, doctors' accountability, equipment and drug shortages, and issues of basic sanitation were all major concerns. Patients' right to choose their doctor, the training of doctors, and many other issues concerning medical care were raised. There was much discussion of medical issues published in the Soviet press, but the bulletins in the archives reveal vast quantities of unpublished material, centered on very serious deficiencies.[67]

As their disillusionment grew, some young specialists moved beyond irony to blunt allegations of corruption in describing shortages of goods and services. A young specialist wrote anonymously to *Komsomolskaia pravda* in February 1976 about food shortages, poor living conditions, and the corruption of the local Party chief in Kazan, whom the author accused of "keeping the best for himself."[68] While the author violated the traditional form of petition by remaining anonymous, he did explain his motive for his outburst—his new status as a father led to his impatience and led him to name those whom he believed responsible for the problems. Less specific, indirect allegations of corruption were often included in published sources.

Returning to the story of fired delicatessen manager A. Artsibashev, whose summary of his frustration with the world of trade was cited earlier: "I could name names, but the relationships [that facilitate work] are formed in such a way that it's sometimes difficult to decide what comes within legal norms and what borders on the criminal code. . . but I don't want to keep silent. The atmosphere in some organizations of trade in our city is intolerable, it gives rise to nepotism and lends itself to abuse."[69] Young specialists certainly were not the only Soviet citizens to criticize such practices, but Artsibashev highlighted a particular frustration of the educated specialist when he concluded that "workers' relations should be based on real business principles, not on the buddy (*preiatelskikh*) principles."[70] Artsibashev's education had exposed him to "real business principles."[71] He knew how business should work and was frustrated by the fact that Soviet trade did not operate in a scientific manner. This contradiction between principles and reality, between "words and deeds," was often the first step in the disillusionment of the young specialists. Even more than most other elements of Soviet society, young specialists had some knowledge of world standards of performance within their respective fields and craved additional information about how those standards were achieved and maintained.[72] Often these desires were motivated by the desire to resolve a problem or improve the functioning of the Soviet system. The frustration of the specialists' desires to build a working system in the USSR led to their disillusionment. Such disillusionment was frequently accelerated when the government's inability or unwillingness to provide goods or services demanded by the public led to the public's finding other ways to fill the gap. Then, if the public sector found such a means of providing goods or services, and the stopgap measure had political repercussions, the resultant disillusionment and frustration could overcome the apolitical inclinations of the young professionals.

An example particularly close to the interests of young specialists was that of "tutoring services." As the official education system became widely perceived as inadequate for preparing would-be *vuz* students for entrance exams, private tutors filled the gap.[73]

G. Belouzova, the director of a social service agency, first raised this issue by complaining that, while her agency had successfully organized tutoring services from 1967 to 1969 to meet ever-growing public demand, the services were outlawed in the Russian republic early in 1969.[74]   The Republican-level Ministry of Education declared that such services "upset the work of public schools and diverted teachers from their basic activity."   G. Belouzova stated in her letter that "many citizens are sending bewildered questions" about the discontinuation to the agency.

The official response, by V. Strezikozina, the head of the Programmed Method Department of the RSFSR Ministry of Education, was extremely patronizing, citing tutorial services as violations of the Soviet Constitution, which says that all types of education should be free and as contrary to the basic official policy that all Soviet citizens have the right to an equal level of education.[75] Strezikozina further decried the fact that tutorship made the education level received dependent upon the family's financial situation and blasted the notion of putting such services into the control of a non-Ministry of Education department as a violation of two 1918 laws on the principle of unified schools in the USSR.

V. Strezikozina concluded by noting that tutorship was popular because of the "existing inadequacies in the work of general education secondary schools and the *vuzy*, inadequacies which are not yet fully eliminated." She criticized *vuzy* for raising entry requirements from the specified levels due to intense competition and said that raising standards of secondary schools was the "obvious" alternative to paid tutoring services.

The editorial staff of *Literaturnaia gazeta* openly stated that it "cannot agree" with V. Strezikozina's arguments and criticized secondary schools for providing equal preparation in all subjects, without the chance to specialize or increase coverage in those subjects most critical for admission to a *vuz*. Finally, the staff promised to return to the subject "in connection with the gap which exists for everyone . . . between the possibilities of the secondary school and the demands of the *vuzy*."

The promised follow-up did not appear in *Literaturnaia gazeta*, but the problem obviously didn't go away. *Komsomolskaia pravda* four years later decried the fact that "[the tutor] has become a sign of the times, a status symbol about which parents brag among friends. Tutoring service has become a 'business,' in many cases setting up 'assembly line' tutoring sessions to make large amounts of money."[76]

Like V. Strezikozina, *Komsomolskaia pravda* noted, "Tutoring disrupts and counteracts the state's social policy in education." But the article then went on to ask, "Is this [tutoring] necessary especially because, acting as a middleman between the secondary school and the higher school, as a third 'independent' link in education, the tutor really does help some people? It is common knowledge that the [preparatory] courses now in operation cannot absorb the enormous number of people who would like to enroll in them."

Komsomolskaia pravda published a summary of readers' responses less than one month later. Those letters indicated that the practice of tutoring was "both widespread and expanding."[77] Many readers submitted proposals for development of alternatives to tutors proposed in the January article. One reader commented that "practically all the country's major newspapers have discussed the need to change the system for evaluating the work of schools . . . . At present, pupils from the first grade through the graduating class know quite well that their 'twos' and 'even threes' will cause more unpleasantness for their teachers than for themselves." Komsomolskaia pravda closed out (and brought the discussion full circle) by publishing the response of one reader who proposed "that the system of tutoring be officially organized, possibly through a consumer services firm" (like the one in Literaturnaia gazeta that started the discussion!).

Young specialists took full part in discussions such as this, which had direct bearing on their lives and those of their children. By the last five years of the Brezhnev regime, such discussions had progressed beyond the mere suggestion by readers of alternative solutions to social and economic problems. Two brief examples suggest how far that progression had gone.

In 1974, the state instituted a program under which persons could turn in scrap paper for recycling. In exchange, they would receive coupons that they could exchange for books that were otherwise hard to acquire. Many of the books of the exchange lists were genuinely popular titles by Western authors, though some less popular titles by Soviet authors were always included as well. A summary of the program's effectiveness (or lack thereof) was run in Literaturnaia gazeta in December 1977.[78] An official reply from the director of the USSR State Committee responsible for the program, which understated the problems with the program, was placed in contrast to a report from a Literaturnaia gazeta correspondent in Novosibirsk.

The correspondent summarized the problem with the exchange: "The timing was off. Publication dates are indefinite, records are kept by quarters. . . the element of chance intrudes." As a result, people were unable to trade their scrap for the titles they wanted from the list, and the coupons ended up on the black market, while volumes of books sat on shelves until the end of their scheduled "quarter" in the program, when the black market coupons fetched a higher price. In frustration, the correspondent noted:

At present we have a setup that has opened a loophole for speculators—because we created shortages. What great masters we are at creating shortages, sometimes out of nothing! Is it because we tried to combine an experiment in procuring scrap with a mission of enlightening people? The original idea was to attract scrap collection by offering popular, entertaining books. Why don't we confine ourselves to offering three or four of these entertaining books. . . in sufficient quantities, instead of loading the list with additional, less popular titles?

As with the meat shortages described earlier, the problems in publishing popular literature had also arisen much earlier, according to archival sources. In March 1972, Pravda provided the Central Committee with a series of letters from readers on this same subject. These letters were used as part of the agenda for a conference of ideological workers conducted by the Central Committee in June 1972. One of the participants in that conference advised the Central Committee, "Young people follow official explanations for the shortage of literature particularly closely."[79]

Such questions concerning examples of the state's recurring inability to satisfy demand led to open sarcasm and questioning of the system and called into question both the optimism and apolitical tendencies of the young specialists. This was especially true of shortages such as the following one, which no amount of censorship could hide from public knowledge.

According to a 1979 *Literaturnaia gazeta* article, the ongoing shortage of eyeglasses in the country (covered in a long series of *Literaturnaia gazeta* articles since 1973) "is so serious that it has been taken up by the USSR Council of Ministers. Innumerable ministries, committees, departments, services, institutes and institutions are involved in some way. . . that's why dozens of decisions and resolutions have been adopted and hundreds of orders and instructions issued. But most of the decisions have remained on paper."[80] *Literaturnaia gazeta* again opened this discussion in 1981 - 1982 with the sarcastic column "Where did Martyshka get her glasses?" and a follow-up of the same title.[81] The June 1982 article published a new official response from the Ministry of Medical Industry. *Literaturnaia gazeta* stated, "We publish this new official response with satisfaction. It seems that even the readers will like the business-like response in which we are informed about the punishment of those guilty ones, and which sets forth an active program of resolution which doesn't prolong the eyeglass problem." The article details the dismissal and reprimand of responsible figures in the medical equipment industry, lists current and proposed production figures, declares a special change in emphasis in the production of eyeglasses, and introduces plans to import needed supplies of both lenses and frames from abroad. Ultimately, however, the damage caused by such shortages was already done, as the public turned to the second economy and the black market to satisfy demand.[82]

SUMMARY

In keeping with the theme of this chapter, it is important to note that the irony, sarcasm, and open questioning of key elements of the planned central economy demonstrated earlier can hardly be termed "apolitical." The Little Deal, while tolerated as a basic fact of daily existence, was not accepted as a long-term social contract either by the population as a whole or by young specialists in particular. As the "gap between words and deeds" grew—and unpublished materials on the problems of food supply and medical care reveal the gap's true size—specialists tried to help solve society's problems via proposals and petitions to the Party and press. The popular press was a legal and public forum for such discussions. While clearly limited in scope and manner of expression, the public discussion in the press forum became the one place in Soviet society where alternative opinions could be safely expressed. This public discussion was paralleled by censored proposals to the Party. This study now turns to more detailed discussion of censorship and press discussions, and to a deeper analysis of the ethos of the young specialists themselves.

NOTES

1. James R. Millar, "The Little Deal: Brezhnev's Contribution to Acquisitive Socialism," *Slavic Review* 44, no. 4 (Winter 1985), 694 -706, henceforth, Millar 1985. Interestingly, Dutch writer Karel Van Het Reve described Soviet society in strikingly similar, if more specific, terms in 1979, in the introduction to *Dear Comrade: Pavel Litvinov and the Voices of Soviet Ctizens in Dissent* (New York: Pitman, 1979), v. Van Het Reve declared, "In the 1960's, the Soviet regime's interior policy has pursued two main objectives: first, that in public nothing be said, insinuated, shown, sung, performed, acted or printed, broadcast or shown on television, that had not been previously approved by authorities; and, second, that all be quiet: no arrests, no noisy propaganda campaigns, no alarms, no demonstrations, no terror, no big changes, no Stalinism, no denunciation of Stalinism."

2. Millar 1985, 695.

3. That is, many of these reciprocal exchanges were illegal in terms of Soviet law. Ibid., 697.

4. Ibid., 697.

5. Vladimir Shlapentokh, *Public and Private Life of the Soviet People: Changing Values in Post-Stalin Russia* (New York: Oxford University Press, 1989), 31 -32, henceforth, Shlapentokh 1989.

6. Thirty-nine of the 53 specialists surveyed by the author described their basic outlook at that time of their lives as "optimistic."

7 Thirty of the 53 said that they lived in the apartment of their parents or in-laws. Half of those 30 said that such an arrangement caused dissatisfaction or frustration (50%). In contrast, only 6 of those 23with other living arrangements expressed similar dissatisfaction (26%).

8. This was especially true of *Literaturnaia gazeta* articles "Ne skupis'" khoziaika," 5 January 1977, and two articles under the title "Firmennaia ulybka" in *Literaturnaia gazeta*, 12 October 1977, 12 and 2 November 1977, 11.

9. "Kto stuchitsia v dver'," *Literaturnaia gazeta*, 23 August 1972, 2.

10. *Literaturnaia gazeta*, 10 May 1978, 12.

11. *Sovetskaia rossiia*, 14 February 1979, as translated and cited in *Current Digest of the Soviet Press*, 31 no. 8, (1979), 13.

12. Ibid. Unfortunately, the article cited only letters from "young people" without giving any background as to their precise age and education levels.

13. Gail Lapidus, "Society under Strain: The Soviet Union after Brezhnev," *The Washington Quarterly* no. 6, (Spring 1983): 42.

14. Shlapentokh 1989, 166 -167.

15. Millar 1985, 703.

16. Oleg Kharkhordin, *The Collective and the Individual in Russia: A Study of Practices* (Berkeley: University of California Press, 1999), 90 -91.

17 Ibid., 355 -357.

18. Georgie Anne Geyer, Research Notebook No. 1, 1971, 80.

19. Georgie Anne Geyer, *The Young Russians* (Homewood, IL: ETC, 1975), 147.

20. A. Artsibashev, "Po tu storonu prilavka: Ispoved' byvshego rukovoditelia," *Komsomolskaia pravda*, 14 March 1975, 2. *Komsomolskaia pravda* correspondent S. Troitskii followed Artsibashev's story with a report on his interview with the province

manager of the food stores for which Artsibashev worked and his own analysis of the situation. All of the following quotations are taken from this discussion.

21. Geyer, 1975, 269.

22. A. Smirnov-Cherkezov, "Podavaite zaiavleniie, Boris Ivanovich: spornye zametki na besspornuiu temu," *Literaturnaia gazeta,* 2 February 1972, 10. This article earned a follow-up report by the editorial staff and an official reply from the deputy chairman of the USSR state construction agency in *Literaturnaia gazeta* on 31 May 1972, 11.

23. "Grabli dlia. . . konstruktora," *Pravda,* 4 June 1978, 2.

24. The reporter who followed up on his complaint, however, did do so. A further analysis of this article, and the 25 December 1978 article in *Pravda* that followed it, as well as other discussions of menial labor by young specialists, appear later.

25. Professor Nikita Pokrovsky, a 1973 graduate of MGU's Philosophy Department, interviewed by the author, tape recording, Moscow, Russia, 16 March 95.

26. Kharkhordin, 357, noted that the self-selection of one's own circle helped prepare the expectation of privacy that emerged in post-Soviet Russia.

27. Thirteen of the specialists surveyed had become full Party members. All but one of the remaining 40 had "automatically" become Komsomol members by virtue of their status as *vuz* students.

28. Only 2 of the 53 were career soldiers.

29. Klara Paramova, interview by British journalist Tony Parker, in *Russian Voices* (New York: Holt, 1991), 212.

30. Vadim Koronov, interview Parker, 219.

31. Philip Andreyev, ibid., 230.

32. Georgie Anne Geyer, Research Notebook No. 1, 1971, 79.

33. D. Skudaev, "Komy nuzhna 'zona spokoistviia'?" *Komsomolskaia pravda,* 6 March 1981, 2. Questions posed to propagandists (those representing the YCL and others) and the propagandists' consternation in dealing with those questions, described in archival sources, present fascinating insight into the young specialists' ethos, as addressed in detail later.

34. Kharkhordin noted that, by the mid-1980s, the "mutual surveillance" that guaranteed that Soviet citizens would adhere to the notions and goals of their formal *kollektivy* and hence, of Soviet society had become "thoroughly routinized," with citizens loyal only to the forms, not the content, of Soviet myths. Kharkhordin, 309.

35. Professor Nikita Pokrovsky, interviewed by the author, tape recording, Moscow, Russia, 16 March 95.

36. O.I. Shkaratan, "Changes in the Social Profile of Urban Residents," 1982, as translated and presented in Murray Yanowitch, ed., *The Social Structure of the USSR: Recent Soviet Studies* (Armonk, NY: M.E. Sharpe, 1986), 116. See also P.O. Kenkman, E.A. Saar, and M.Kh. Titma, "Generations and Social Self-Determination: A Study of Cohorts from 1948-1979 in the Estonian SSR," in ibid., 189.

37. Geoffrey Hosking, *The Awakening of the Soviet Union,* enlarged ed. (Cambridge: Harvard University Press, 1991), 69.

38. Vladimir Shlapentokh, *Soviet Public Opinion and Ideology: Mythology and Pragmatism in Interaction* (New York: Praeger, 1986), 155,158.

39. Geyer, *The Young Russians,* 144 -147, and Research Notebook No. 2, 64-65.

40. Alexei Lebedev, interview by author, E-mail, English 26 August 1995.

41. Ibid., (emphasis in original).

42. N.A. Aitov, "The Dynamics of Social Mobility in the USSR" as presented in Yanowitch 1986, 254 -270, asserted that among the young in the 1970s social mobility was up to five times greater than their parents had achieved over 25 years. O.I. Shkaratan in

1970 posited that the key to social mobility was higher education. See Murray Yanowitch and Wesley A. Fisher, eds., *Social Stratification and Mobility in the USSR* (White Plains, NY: International Arts and Sciences Press, 1973, 311 -312.

43. Geyer, 1975, 236, (emphasis in original).

44. Geyer, Research Notebook I, 51. Her interviews indicated that the young persons were just as excited about the regime's promise to import technology from abroad to produce consumer goods as about the actual production of the goods themselves.

45. This is the figure cited by the editorial staff of *Literaturnaia gazeta* in the introduction to an article entitled "Slol'ko stoit inzhener," *Literaturnaia gazeta,* 10 March 1971, 10-11.

46. As the figures in the Appendix show, 4.18 million students graduated from *vuzy* in those years, less than half the projected number. Logically, the remainder should have graduated from specialized technical schools. As discussed later, this was not necessarily the case.

47. "Mnogovariantnyi posudnikov," *Literaturnaia gazeta,* 21 September 1977, 12.

48. Murray Yanowitch, *Social and Economic Inequality in the Soviet Union: Six Studies* (White Plains, NY: M.E. Sharpe, 1977), 30. The same study noted also that from 1956 to 1970 the highest Soviet income levels held steady, while the lowest gradually increased, 24-25.

49. "O rubliakh zarabotannykh i nezarabotannykh," *Pravda,* 17 November 1980, 7. The original article that inspired this summary of readers' letters was "O ruble zarabotannom," *Pravda,* 24 May 1980.

50. "Besplatno--dorozhe: Eshche raz o tom, skol'ko stoit spetsialist," *Literaturnaia gazeta,* 23 February 1972, 10. This article followed up on the *Literaturnaia gazeta* article entitled "Slol'ko stoit inzhener," *Literaturnaia gazeta,* 10 March 1971, 10-11.

51. "Specialists" refers to those with higher education, while "technicians" designates those with a specialized secondary (vocational) education.

52. *Tsentr khraneniia sovremennoi dokumentatsii* (Center for the Preservation of Contemporary Documentation); henceforth, TsKhSD. Fond 5, Opis 69, Delo 495, Listok 1-15, especially L. 7-10. All subsequent references to Russian archival material appear in this format, with the following abbreviations: F= Fond: record group; O= Opis: inventory; D= Delo: volume; L= List: page.

53. *Literaturnaia gazeta,* 23 February 1972, 10.

54. "Paradoksy raspredeleleniia: vysshaia shkola: zakaz na spetsialista," *Pravda,* 14 November 1981, 3.

55. "Poka ne grianuli morozy," *Uchitel'skaia gazeta,* 21 August 1979, 2.

56. Ibid.

57. "Ne dalee sadovogo kol'tsa. . . ," *Literaturnaia gazeta,* 4 July 1973, 11 and 22 August 1973, 10. These articles constitute another of the "discussions" at the core of this study and are examined in much greater detail later.

58. *Literaturnaia gazeta ,* 22 August 1973, 10.

59. Ibid.

60. Ibid.

61. Shlapentokh, 1989, 70.

62. TsKhSD F5, O68, D387, L291-2. The text of the letter was included in a summary of letters from *Komsomolskaia pravda* to the Central Committee.

63. Such identifications were a regular part of the traditional petitioning process, the evolution of which is discussed in detail in the next chapter.

64. TsKhSD F5, O68, D387, L204.

65. TsKhSD F5, O63, D90, L10-11.

66. More detailed discussion on the censorship process addresses the issue of public anger in the next chapter.

67. See TsKhSD F5, O67, D180, L35-178 for such bulletins from 1974. Both published and unpublished petitions regarding medical care are discussed in more detail in later chapters.

68. TsKhSD F5, O63, D90, L22-24.

69. *Komsomolskaia pravda*, 14 March 1975, 2.

70. Ibid.

71. Obviously, the principles of business for the manager of a Soviet state store differed dramatically from those learned in Western business schools, but Artsibashev would have been taught the "official" methods of bookkeeping, inventory, labor practices and so on. Obviously, those clashed with the reality that he encountered.

72. By virtue of their educations, young specialists, especially in scientific and technical fields (even more so than in the services sphere used as an example here), gained initial exposure to world standards. Their craving for additional information, their frustration when that information was not available, and the consequences of that frustration are discussed in more detail later.

73. As previously discussed, the pressure to gain admission to a *vuz* became increasingly intense during the course of the Brezhnev era. Passing entrance exams became the critical point of passage into the intelligentsia class, whereas failure to do so would "condemn" one to life in the working class.

74. "Repetitorstvo zapreshcheno?" *Literaturnaia gazeta*, 22 December 1971, 12. G. Belouzova's letter appeared under this title with an official response by officials from the Russian Republican Ministry of Education and editorial commentary by the *Literaturnaia gazeta* staff.

75. Ibid.

76. "Repetitor udachi?" *Komsomolskaia pravda*, 17 January 1975, 2.

77. "Repititor bez illiuzii,' *Komsomolskaia pravda*, 6 February 1975, 2.

78. "When the 'Count' [of Monte Cristo—a genuinely popular work] Comes Barreling," *Literaturnaia gazeta*, 21 December 1977, 12, as translated and presented in *Current Digest of the Soviet Press*, 29, no. 51 (1977), 18-19.

79. TsKhSD F 5, O64, D78, L29.

80. "Shortage on the Bridge of the Nose," *Literaturnaia gazeta*, 14 February 1979, 13, as translated and presented in *Current Digest of the Soviet Press*,, no. 14, (1979), 16.

81. "Gde dostala ochki martyshka? Ochkariki ostalis' nedovol'ny!" *Literaturnaia gazeta*, 30 June 1982, 13.

82. Unpublished sources reveal just such a process concerning spare parts for cars and motorcycles, as indicated in a summary of letters from *Pravda* to the Central Committee in February 1972. See TsKhSD F5, O64, D78, L17-24.

2

Petitioning, Censorship, and the Stifling of Social Initiatives in the USSR

A seminal characteristic of the ideology behind the Russian Revolution was the notion that men (and, by implication, governments) proved their worth in the process of "revelation by deeds." An individual's actions, not his or her words, were the concrete manifestations of his or her true nature. Lenin adopted this notion from the character of Rakhmetov in Chernyshevsky's *What Is to Be Done?* and made it part and parcel of the Bolshevik legacy.[1] Soviet citizens judged the nature of the regime based upon its actions, which, from the outset, were often at odds with its words. As mentioned in Chapter 1, the reality of Soviet life in the 1960s and 1970s contrasted greatly with the regime's artistic formulations of just what "developed socialism" should be. While this was not a new phenomenon (Soviet films of happy, prosperous collective farmers in the 1930s contrasted sharply with the poverty and sometimes the starvation that ravaged the countryside), the high expectations and optimism of the young specialists inspired equally high levels of frustration when reality confronted Soviet oratory. As the "gap" between the words and deeds of the Soviet regime grew throughout the Brezhnev years, so did a corresponding gap between the regime and the society that it sought to govern. In 1991, Moshe Lewin described the increasing divergence between the elite and masses of post-Stalin Soviet society as part of the evolution of a more "civil" society in the USSR, increasingly sophisticated and dynamic. His primary emphasis remained on the nature and policies of the Soviet political system, the "command-administrative" system established in the 1930s. For Lewin, this top-heavy state system failed to adapt to the changing nature of the society that it ruled and "kept losing its capacity to solve problems, and hence to rule."[2] At the same time, Lewin noted that Soviet society "perpetually transformed itself into a diverse and restive 'civil' society," capable of developing solutions to problems. Lewin used the term "civil" society without precisely defining his conception of that society. The contextual implication was that nongovernmental entities were becoming increasingly sophisticated and capable of problem solving, without necessarily developing the corresponding opportunity to do so. The young specialists at the heart of this study formed part of one such entity. Soviet specialists tried to solve problems via proposals to Party and press. Such proposals continued the ancient Russian tradition of petitioning, and the regime both accepted and encouraged such efforts. The state, however, also censored many such proposals to enhance the short-term stability of the Little Deal. Censorship guaranteed the escalation of pressures and frustrations in Russia's increasingly educated and dynamic society. These pressures shaped the ethos of the young specialists and ingrained in them commitments to practicality and moral principles in their lives and aspirations.

Citizens' petitioning for redress of grievances and government censorship of public information represented two distinct traditions in Russian and Soviet history. This chapter briefly traces the historical evolution of each process and the relationship between them. By the Brezhnev era, the unique development of the Soviet press meant that the interaction between censorship and petitioning formed an important aspect of Soviet society. Some young specialists actively participated in this interaction, writing letters or requesting information. On a larger scale, the process itself had either a direct or indirect influence on the development of all young specialists.

Petitioning and censorship formed a nexus of interaction that was an integral part of Russian, not just Soviet, history. Within the specific context of this study, the essence of censorship is repression of social initiative by the state for the purpose of maintaining stability. The more broadly defined notion of censorship, of which this specific aspect is but part, is discussed in more detail. Over centuries of evolution, this nexus was surrounded by a complex set of notions, rules, and "transcripts" by which both society and state were bound. When those rules were violated or changed, the pressures and frustrations that the petitioning-censorship nexus controlled could, and did, explode in violence.

PETITIONING IN TSARIST RUSSIA

From the earliest days of Russian history, Russian supplicants of all ranks placed their petitions for redress of grievances at the mercy of the benevolent leader. Soviet leaders continued this tradition and made the petitioning process a critical tool for the assessment of public opinion. Both tsarist and Soviet petitioners had to conform to a framework—an evolving set of written and unwritten rules—for their petitions to be successful. This section briefly examines major trends in the evolution of the Russian petitioning process from its Muscovite roots through the reign of Nicholas II. The section that follows compares Soviet petitions to this Muscovite and Imperial framework.

By the mid-sixteenth century, the petition (*chelobitnaia gramota*, literally, "forehead-knocking charter") had become so regularized as to represent a unique literary 'genre' that included specific, stylized elements.[3] Formalized, elaborate petitions were directed to the tsar himself and evolved as the Muscovite government became more bureaucratic and less personal. Petitions in earlier times were much simpler and shorter, especially those directed to local or lower-level officials and to nongovernment figures (e.g., petitions to landlords from their serfs). The social status of the petitioner also influenced the format of petitions. Petitions had become such a normal part of Muscovite culture and government that Ivan IV established a Petitions Chancery in 1551 for their administrative handling. By that point in the sixteenth century, two distinct types of petitions had developed.

The first type represented the traditional request for redress of grievances. The second, instead of a request for redress of grievances, actually offered advice to the tsar on foreign policy and the selection of domestic officials.[4] This "advisory" petition established the precedent of a subject's using the petition forum to advise the ruler on the solution to political and social problems.[5]

Taken together, these types of petitions contained elements that became standard in petitions throughout Russian and Soviet history. While the relative importance of various elements changed over time, the fact remains that Soviet petitions from the Brezhnev years contained the same elements as did tsarist petitions from the sixteenth century. An analysis of those elements provides important context for the subsequent comparison and analysis of Soviet petitions themselves and for the "rules of engagement" of the petitioning process in the Soviet period.

In describing petitions as a unique form of "literary genre," Dewey and Kleimola identified three fundamental sections as standard elements of the regular petition. The first section, the opening, typically comprised sentences that exalted the addressee, while humbly identifying the petitioner. This "upward allocution," the emphasis of the gulf in status between humble petitioner and exalted tsar, became a standard element of formal petitions to the tsar.[6] The second section set forth grievances, named offenders, or otherwise spelled out the problem at the core of the petition. Given the specific nature of each petition, this section was normally the most varied and individualized. Dewey and Kleimola noted that this second section sometimes also included suggestions that the addressee might benefit from granting the request. Finally, the third section represented a conclusion that normally included pleas for mercy and threw the petitioner on the mercy of the addressee.[7]

Obviously, some differences existed between those petitions that sought redress of grievances and those that offered advice. Nevertheless, the form of the petitions remained the same. The unique characteristics of those petitions that were advisory were more closely associated with the author than with the format of the petition itself. Certain very specific rules of engagement developed for advisory petitions as well.

In the first place, righteous advice to the tsar was seen as the obligation of all loyal servants as individuals, not as members of any political or social organization. Righteous servants were to be abjectly subservient to the autocrat yet were obligated to speak out against injustices that might damage the autocrat's authority. The Patriarch Germogen, whose calls roused the people to action against the foreign invaders and domestic pretenders during the Time of Troubles, epitomized such a righteous servant.[8] Vital to the notion of giving advice was that this was an obligation of the righteous individual, not of a certain social class.[9] This meant that any citizen could offer advice, regardless of his or her origin, education, or position.

Just how vital were these "rules of engagement"? At the intuitive level, it would seem obvious that deviation from accepted protocol would doom the supplicant's petition to failure or cause the addressee to turn a deaf ear toward the writer's advice. However, failure to follow established patterns actually had far more dire outcomes and occasionally led to violence, disorder, and death. Such failure could be the fault of the petitioner for exceeding or violating accepted parameters, or failure could be the fault of the addressee, even the tsar, who had certain reciprocal obligations under the rules of engagement as well.

In 1648, when returning from a pilgrimage, the young Tsar Alexis Mikhailovich broke with long-standing tradition and refused to personally accept petitions. His actions and those of several high-ranking officials triggered massive riots that destroyed large parts of Moscow. The riots also forced the tsar to hand over one official to the mob for execution and to relieve (at least temporarily) other allegedly corrupt officials from their posts.[10] Precisely why Tsar Alexis refused to accept the petitions remains a matter of historical speculation. But it is possible that the tone and format of the petitions were significant factors. Alexis' rejection of these militant petitions marked a significant watershed in the evolution of Muscovy, from a highly personalized, religion-centered autocracy, to a bureaucratic, impersonal, and increasingly secular state. This change was formalized in the *Ulozhenie* of 1649, which mandated that petitions be submitted via bureaucratic channels, instead of being directly presented to the tsar.[11]

Of course, establishing legislation to regulate the handling of petitions did not immediately lead to the smooth transition from personal autocracy to bureaucratic administration. Adhering to the traditions that obligated the tsar to reciprocate by at least receiving their petitions, the citizens of Muscovy continued to attempt direct access to the tsar in circumvention of the bureaucrats. The belief in the goodness of the tsar, in contrast to the evil of the boyars (and later, bureaucrats), remained a significant social factor in Russian history at least until 1905. Part of this notion held that the tsar, as *batiushka,* or a father figure, was obligated to look after the welfare of his subjects.[12]

While the tradition of petitioning was well established in pre-Petrine Muscovy, the advent of the private printing press and the newspaper eventually set the traditions of petitioning on a path into the realm of the censor. Censorship did exist in Russia before Peter's time. Books were banned and information controlled. That censorship lies outside the focus of this study. Given this study's focus on censorship of social initiative, attention here is more appropriately devoted to censorship following the advent of the press. Russia's first newspaper appeared in 1703 at the direction, and sometimes under the personal editorship, of Peter the Great.[13] Yet that periodical was designed to disseminate news and information from the regime to its subjects, not solicit information from them. Not until Catherine the Great legalized private ownership of printing presses did suggestions, proposals, and opinions from Russia's subjects appear in a public forum. The fates of N.I. Novikov (arrested in 1784) and Alexander Radishchev (arrested in 1790), two of the first to take advantage of Catherine's policy to express their ideas in print, are well known. Of course, neither Radishchev's *Journey from St. Petersburg to Moscow* nor the materials for which Novikov was imprisoned were petitions in the classic sense. Radishchev's book, however, certainly represented the criticism of the extant order and included both implicit and explicit proposals for change. In this sense, it foreshadows the Soviet-era proposals.

Catherine's fear that the ideals of the French Revolution would reach the restive masses of Russia overcame her intellectual affinity for Western philosophy. Ironically, Catherine, who had allowed expansion of private printing, initiated Russia's "first comprehensive system of censorship" in 1796, shortly before her death. [14] Designed principally to fight the "French infection," Catherine's censorship system was nevertheless classified as "mild."[15]

With equal irony, Nicholas I, the "Iron Tsar," whose censorship laws of 1826 earned the sobriquet the "cast-iron statute,"[16] nevertheless revised those laws in 1828 and presided over the "golden age" of Russian literature. Russian music, theater, and science also blossomed during Nicholas' reign.[17] However, like Catherine before him, Nicholas feared the spread of revolutionary ideas to the Russian masses, and his reign was difficult for the periodical press after the French "July Days," the subsequent Polish revolt of 1830-1831, and especially the revolutionary outbursts of 1848.

Each of the three rulers Peter I, Catherine II, and Nicholas I, envisioned their literary policies (including the censorship for Catherine and Nicholas) as a means to educate or guide the Russian people. Catherine and Nicholas understood that, if democratic or revolutionary ideas reached the Russian masses, the autocracy would be undermined. As a result, they sought to control via censorship the amount and content of popularly available information, especially information that might incite or rile the masses.

Formal petitions, including complaints or denunciations, remained largely private correspondence between supplicants and officials for most of the Imperial period. Citizens could, and did, make complaints, suggestions, and denunciations to local officials or to the tsar himself. In stark contrast to the letter and spirit of the 1649 *Ulozhenie*, yet in keeping with the Muscovite tradition, Paul I kept a yellow box in front of the Winter Palace, into which anyone could drop a complaint or denunciation. Citizens who became aware of treasonous or potentially seditious speech or action were required to submit a denunciation under pain of death. [18]

Russians from every social class (and even foreigners living in Moscow) continued to submit petitions addressed to the tsar throughout the nineteenth century. Those petitions remained remarkably consistent with the traditional aspects of petitioning evolved from Muscovy. The humility of the supplicant, his (or her or their) declarations of fealty and obedience to the Tsar, the "upward allocution" in style designed to dramatize the gulf between his lofty stature and the petitioner's lowliness were all regular components of nineteenth-century petitions.[19] One important difference developed in the 1860s, when the state began to circulate drafts of proposals or legislation for public comment. This conscious effort to bring society into the decision-making process, even if only in an advisory role, raised popular expectations and bolstered the legitimacy of the monarchy, at least temporarily.[20]

At the end of the tsarist era, one petition brought together each of the aspects of the petitioning tradition, censorship, the dangers of "riling" the people, and the ruler's responsibility to hear the pleas of his subjects. The "Most Humble and Loyal Address" to Nicholas II carried by Father Gapon on 9 January 1905 contained the three basic elements of the *chelobitnaia* described earlier and was written in full expectation that the tsar would receive it and respond to alleviate the suffering of his loyal subjects.[21] Gapon's missive reflected the still-present belief among many in Russia's lower classes that the country was ruled by the benevolent *batiushka* tsar. The notion that the tsar would intervene on his subjects' behalf if only he was aware of their suffering was clearly implied in the text of the petition, which began: "Sire, We the workers and inhabitants of St Petersburg . . . come to thee, O Sire, to seek justice and protection." When Alexis Mikhailovich failed to accept the people's petitions in 1648, Moscow burned. When Nicholas' troops fired upon the icon-bearing crowds that followed Gapon, they killed much more than those physically present. They murdered the myth of the innocent Good Tsar, separated from his people by corrupt or incompetent boyars or administrators.[22] Thus, Bloody Sunday did much to undermine the legitimacy of the autocracy and paved the way to revolution.

The notion of appeals and advice "from below" thus formed a critical aspect of Russian state-society relationships for centuries before the advent of Soviet power. The notion that any citizen could appeal to the authorities or propose solutions to problems remained a deeply ingrained characteristic of Soviet society. Just as the tsars had to deal with challenges arising from the petitioning process, including satisfying the people's perception that the tsar was obligated to at least receive their petitions, Soviet leaders also found petitions to be both boon and bane.

PETITIONING IN THE SOVIET PERIOD

Clearly relevant to this discussion is the study of domination and resistance conducted by James C. Scott, which places great emphasis on the disguised expressions of their beliefs inserted into historical sources by the subordinate elements in stratified societies. When Scott's methods are combined with the specifically Soviet insights of sociologist Vladimir Shlapentokh, they seem to hold great promise indeed.

In his 1990 study *Domination and the Arts of Resistance*, Scott argued that groups that occupy a subordinate status within any society must measure and restrain their responses in the presence of members of the dominant group. Such self-restraint inspires a sense of frustration. This frustration, in turn, leads subordinates "to create and defend a social space in which offstage dissent to the official transcript of power relations may be voiced" behind the scenes.[23] In Scott's terminology, this "offstage dissent" represents a "hidden transcript" that can provide insight into the beliefs, feelings, and functions of the subordinate group.

In analyzing Soviet society, Vladimir Shlapentokh concluded that "due to the pressure to conform to official interpretations of reality, facts and feelings in contradiction with the official view tend to be suppressed . . . they accumulate, increasing pressure . . . awaiting an opportunity for a release."[24] Clearly, Shlapentokh's "suppressed facts and feelings" would seem to indicate the presence of "hidden transcripts" within Soviet society.[25]

Scott asserted that the hidden transcripts of the subordinate and of the elite came into contact in a "zone of constant struggle" in the public domain, where both hidden transcripts were constrained and modified by accepted public parameters.[26]   The advent of the newspaper and private printing press in Imperial Russia set the tradition of petitioning into "constant struggle" with the censor.   The collision between petitioning and censorship in the Soviet era represents the key nexus where Lewin's "sophisticated and dynamic" society confronted the "command-administrative" system. Subsequent sections of this study show that the relationship between petitioning, censorship, and Soviet society was interactive.   Society, through its petitions and other manifestations of "public opinion," had a definite and (in historical hindsight, at least) measurable impact upon Soviet governments from Lenin to Brezhnev, including Stalin's state during the worst trials of terror and war.   Likewise, the state shaped popular opinions through both passive censorship (restriction of what was published) and active aspects of information management (staging discussions or selectively allowing the publication of particular letters, etc.). The role of this interaction in forming the ethos of the young specialists of the Brezhnev era and their subsequent role in shaping Soviet society form the bulk of the subsequent chapters.

As noted, the most prominent and accessible "points of interaction" between the people and the elite of the Brezhnev era were the discussions of social issues in organs of the Soviet press. Both legal and officially encouraged, letters to the press represent a classic example of Scott's "Truth Spoken to Power" and are the most solid evidence of the growing dynamism of Soviet society. The regime accepted and encouraged this interaction, even after it drove the dissidents underground in the early 1970s.

Just as tsarist petitioners had to conform to accepted protocols for seeking redress or in giving advice, the process of letter writing during the Soviet period involved certain protocols or "rules of engagement." The most important of these was that letters that contained any explicit or implicit criticism of elite policies were acceptable only if a single individual or a group of colleagues from one organization authored them. Only single sources of criticism were accepted by the Soviets: single, in keeping with the notion that righteous individuals could offer advice to the tsar and that petitions were legitimate if forwarded by a local collective, but not on behalf of an entire social class. Petitioners could represent themselves as individuals or as a specific work collective but could not claim to speak for any broad segments of society.

That the Soviet regime attempted to restrict, or at least regulate, the growth of horizontal, unofficial ties among social and professional groups has been widely noted. In his study of letters of complaint by Soviet citizens, Nicholas Lampert described the "cardinal rule" of Soviet petitioning: petitioners must act alone or with others from the same organization. Any attempt to cross institutional boundaries could "create a direct challenge to the legitimacy of the state." Lampert deduced this "rule" from the study of cases where the KGB had taken action against petitioners who attempted collective action. While those petitioners came from diverse occupations and were united only by their frustration with the petition system, Lampert's work clearly demonstrates that the isolation of petitioners and restriction of horizontal mutuality were an important characteristic of the petition process. [27]

Related to this requirement was the restriction on the acceptable scope for complaints. Criticism was considered acceptable so long as it was directed at a *specific*, preferably localized problem. In essence, each of these limitations had its source in the application of the old Lenin dictum of "criticize, but don't generalize."[28] Ilia Suslov, a former editor of the "Twelve Chairs Club" humor column in *Literaturnaia gazeta*, spelled out specific "issues" that represented such prohibitions. His comments are particularly relevant here. Despite the fact that they were specifically addressed to the content of Soviet fiction and newspaper columns, they apply to letters and petitions as well.   According to Suslov, problem areas included indications of generational conflict, ethnic problems, economic shortcomings, and predominance of negative attitudes, shortages of optimistic attitudes, alcoholism, and "generalizations." "Generalization—this is the most awful word. Do not generalize. This is the chief principle of Soviet censorship." Additional concerns that had bearing on letters and petitions included: allusions to Party vacillation, criticism of Party bureaucrats in the higher echelons, and hidden support for dissident thought. Suslov also noted that issues concerning or raised by citizens with Jewish names could lead to trouble with the censor.[29]

The organs of the press that received letters treated them very seriously, as did the regime and the letter writers themselves. Soviet correspondent Vitali Vitaliev described the gravity of work in the letters department of *Literaturnaia gazeta*:

As soon as a letter arrives at the editorial office . . . it ceases to be just a scribbled piece of paper—it becomes a document and is taken under control. A special filing card is provided for each, and a number assigned. On the cards . . . our letters department sums up the contents in a few sentences. Then the letter is forwarded to one of the other departments, depending on the subject. A copy of the card goes into the special card index, soon to be joined by an official reply from the organization to which it was forwarded, or by a resolution.[30]

Both published and archival sources corroborate Vitaliev's description of the control mechanism and the seriousness with which all parties viewed that mechanism. British correspondent Jonathan Steele published an interview with the head of the letter department of *Pravda* about the handling of letters in the *London Guardian*,[31] which, when compared to Vitaliev's portrayal, demonstrated the standardization of letter-handling procedures among major Soviet newspapers. The common element in the administrative handling of letters was the completion of "control cards" concerning each letter for submission to organs of the Party and state.[32] Summaries of letters to press and Party organs now available in archives include such filing cards for the newspapers *Komsomolskaia pravda, Trud,* and *Pravda* and the journal *Kommunist*. The summaries of letters from other periodicals include references to the tracking number and the disposition of the cards. Archival records indicate that copies of the tracking card, bearing the assigned number of the letter and the routing of its distribution, including its final disposition, were sent as postcard "receipts" to the authors of letters. In several cases, letter writers who were displeased with the bureaucracy's response to their missives attached the tracking card to a second letter to complain about its impersonal or bureaucratic nature.[33]

The standardized tracking schemes employed by so many different press organs implied that a higher authority closely followed the letters. Archival sources confirm that the Central Committee of the Communist Party of the Soviet Union (CPSU) did indeed view citizens' petitions as a serious matter.

It was a common phenomenon in the Soviet period for letters intended for the Party to be sent directly to journals and newspapers, regardless of the publisher. This process was interactive, as it was also likely for letters addressed to journals and newspapers to be forwarded to Party officials. In many cases, letters would travel for review between Party and press offices until the final resolution or filing of the case. The Soviet public clearly understood this and regarded the submission of petitions to Party or to the press as a routine fact of Soviet life.[34] The routine of this process was similar to, and had its historical precedent in, the submission of petitions "through channels" originally demanded by the *Ulozhenie* of 1649, developed in the aftermath of the 1648 disaster.[35]   Did the discussion forum provided by this press-Party-people interaction constituted a uniquely Soviet version of "civil" society? Not if one adheres to the traditional notion that a civil society is one in which nongovernmental actors directly influence state actions or policies, as Moshe Lewin's discussion implied at the outset of this chapter. After all, the newspapers and journals were tools of the same Party that ran the state.   But it was certainly an important aspect of Soviet society, and its characteristics are important enough to merit brief discussion here.

"Alternative" opinions existed in Brezhnev's USSR. An "alternative" opinion was one that differed from either the stated policy or de facto practices of the official regime. The petition cycle served as a means of expression for such alternative opinion that was public, legal, and accepted by both society and the regime.   Viewed in this way, the opinions and suggestions of petitions differed in critical ways from the alternative opinions voiced by the generation of Soviet "dissidents" beginning with the Siniavskii-Daniel trial of 1965. While the petitions and demonstrations that the dissidents presented were legal in accordance with the Soviet Constitution, they were not tolerated by the regime, which drove the dissident movement underground in the 1970s. Likewise, while the *samizdat* (self-published and covertly hand-circulated) publications circulated in the USSR did contain the nucleus of alternative opinion, they failed to meet the test of legality and acceptance. In contrast, petitions that avoided any connotation of political challenge were accepted and apparently seriously evaluated by the regime. This notion of *avoiding political challenge* while proposing a course of action that may modify or contradict an officially adopted petition represented a critical distinction between the submission of an alternative opinion for consideration and the open political challenges posed by "dissidence." Clearly, the two phenomena are related, but the *difference* is critical. The petitioners at the heart of this study sought to work within the system, while the dissidents wanted to change it.

Several examples of how seriously the Central Committee (CC) viewed citizens' petitions follow. The director of a Cheliabinsk production enterprise sent a letter to the CC complaining that a publication about shortcomings in planning that had appeared in *Pravda* and *Izvestiia* had criticized two section leaders from his enterprise whose sections were, in fact, not part of the problem. Attached to his letter was a copy of a subsequent Central Committee directive to the editors of the newspapers to correct the error.[36] The newspapers made the correction. The Central Committee directive was not published; therefore, it was not likely done for public appearance. Rather, it appeared to reflect a genuine concern for accuracy on the part of the Central Committee.

A memorandum, prepared by Iu. Skianov, deputy director of the Central Committee Propaganda Department in early 1971, served as an additional indicator of the seriousness with which the Central Committee considered readers' letters. Skianov recorded that "material from *Komsomolskaia pravda*, prepared per request of the Propaganda Department's newspaper section, was used during the preparation of information to the CC CPSU about workers letters addressed to the XXIVth Party Congress." [37]

One reason that the regime took letters so seriously was the fact that it often viewed newspapers as conduits of information from the population to the Central Committee. The Central Committee, in its turn, used this feedback when directing the activities of Party governmental and economic organizations. For example, the newspaper *Sotsiologicheskaia industriia* complained, late in 1969, about the "inattentiveness of ministries and administrations to the newspaper's declarations," which resulted from readers' inputs. Specifically, *Sotsiologicheskaia industriia* sent to the CC copies of formal and cursory replies to *Sotsiologicheskaia industriia* from the road-building ministry.[38] Shortly thereafter, *Sotsiologicheskaia industriia* submitted a series of proposals to the CC regarding the draft of the party program for the upcoming 24th Congress (1971). These proposals were direct and open and often used readers' input to describe genuine economic difficulties faced by various industries. For example, one proposal called for an increased role by the "engineer-technician cadres in production—raise their role as organizers of production and leaders of scientific and technical progress."[39] By calling for increased participation by professional specialists in the planning of economic production, *Sotsiologicheskaia industriia* sided with the specialists against the professional planners of GOSPLAN (the centralized Soviet State Planning Commission). *Sotsiologicheskaia industriia*, just prior to the 34th Congress in 1971, submitted to the Central Committee detailed reports on questions raised by readers concerning the draft program for the Congress and analysis of government agencies' responses.[40]

Again in 1980, *Sotsiologicheskaia industriia* experimented in increasing readers' input and feedback to the CC. It set up mailboxes at industrial enterprises, construction sites, scientific institutions, and so on, with the invitation to employees to pose questions about their interests and problems, which were then directed to the appropriate ministries or agencies. These issues were then discussed at meetings with leaders of economic organizations set up by *Sotsiologicheskaia industriia*. According to the records, "At those meetings, detailed, open discussions occurred about those things which worry people." *Sotsiologicheskaia industriia* took these steps in response to CC directives on "improving ideological education work."[41] Six specific meetings were recorded in the archives, all of which had "full houses" of 250-620 people in attendance.[42] Frequently, the meetings raised issues of poor work by central ministries and agencies in handling local problems.[43] Local authorities were not spared criticism either. Because so many of the complaints concerned construction of living quarters, transport systems, and cultural institutions, *Sotsiologicheskaia industriia* concluded that "we can tell that local party, economic and soviet institutions are still weakly engaging problems of planning the social development of collectives." [44]

In many cases, follow-up actions by the CC or its designated agents to investigate allegations from letters are included in the archival fond with the letters. A review of letters submitted by *Komsomolskaia pravda* for the period December 1974 through September 1976 included detailed reports on several investigations into complaints made to *Komsomolskaia pravda* from December 1974 to April 1975.[45] In two of the four cases documented, the investigators (who ranged from an army lieutenant general, to a *Komsomolskaia pravda* reporter, to the head of a local Party executive committee) found the allegations to be justified, and corrective action was taken. In the third case, the reporter assigned to investigate declared that, after investigation, he determined the complaint to be unfounded. In another, the local Party official and the local Komosomol director, who together conducted the investigation, reported that the problem had previously existed, but repairs had been made to address it, and the situation was now "normal." Especially striking was the investigation into a meat shortage reported in a letter from Stavropol Krai. In this case, the head of the local Party executive committee declared, "At the present, we cannot fully meet the demand of the population or organize uninterrupted sale of these items because of reasons which were decreed from above." It was never unusual for local Party authorities to blame their problems on the center, but, of course, such allegations never appeared in the public arena.

Another indication of the seriousness with which the leadership viewed letters and one that supports the notion that published letters were, in fact, genuine is found in a 1969 review of readers' letters conducted by the editorial staff of *Kommunist*. That collection included the original (usually handwritten) letters and the typed, edited version of the letters that were actually published in the journal. Comparison of the original and edited versions indicates that letters were edited for length and construction, but *not* for basic content.[46]

The volume of letters received by Party and press organs was astounding. Archival sources are incomplete,[47] yet those that are available testify to the massive participation in the letter-writing process by the Soviet population and to the growth of that participation over time.   The journal *Sotsialisticheskaia industriia* reported to the Letter Department of the Central Committee of the CPSU that it received 12,838 letters from readers in 1970, 81,509 in 1978, 187,057 in 1981, and 186, 483 in the first eight months of 1982.[48]   The more narrowly focused journal *Chelovek i zakon* received 50,000 letters in its first year of publication (1971), 132,500 in 1974, and 46,501 in the first quarter of 1976.[49]   Such a dramatic increase in number of letters received was consistent in both specialized journals and daily newspapers as well.   Over a six-month period in 1975, *Pravda* averaged over 30,000 letters received per month.[50]   Television and radio outlets also received large numbers of letters.   In the second quarter of 1974, Soviet Central Television and Radio received over 26,500 letters.[51]   Smaller, more specialized journals received smaller, yet significant, quantities of letters.[52]   In all cases, these letters included complaints, questions, and proposals or recommendations.

Each journal and newspaper reported on its work with readers' letters to the Letter Department of the Central Committee of the Party.   While those reports differed in format among the various reporting agencies (e.g., some broke the letters down by subject, some by the occupation of the author), the archival material available supports the notion expressed by Vitaliev that the regime took these letters and petitions very seriously indeed.

Brezhnev-Era Petitions

Several petitions from the late Brezhnev era demonstrate the continuity of the petitioning process with that of the tsarist past, in both the petitioner's obligation to adhere to accepted parameters and the Party's assumption of the tsar's obligation to receive and address the people's grievances and issues.   The first two petitions were written not by the young specialists at the heart of this study but by prominent citizens, whose public stature and fame generated sufficient attention to ensure that the archival records of their petitions would be exceptionally detailed and thorough.   The likelihood that the author's social prominence may have influenced the petition format is also explored.   The specific background of each petition is *not* the critical issue here.   What is important is that the detailed archival records demonstrate important aspects of the interactive nature of the petitioning-censorship process. The records of the debate and discussion regarding these two petitions allow for a detailed comparison to the tsarist petitions.   Following the discussion of the "famous" citizens' petitions, this study examines petitions from young specialists that demonstrate similar characteristics, even though the archival records of those petitions are less complete.

In March 1982, four leading Soviet aviators wrote a letter the Central Committee of the CPSU requesting public Soviet recognition of the achievements of aircraft designer Igor Sikorsky.   The petition itself demonstrates the Soviet evolution of the traditional model for a petition. The routing and handling of the petition demonstrate the interactive nature of the relationships between Party and press, which was typical of many Brezhnev-era petitions, as well as the seriousness with which the petition was treated.[53]

Soviet-era petitions rarely followed the step-by-step sequence of the tsarist "genre" but nevertheless included all the same elements, albeit in different order. As did their tysarist predecessors, Soviet petitioners exalted the "addressee" of their petitions.   No longer focused upon the flattery of an individual autocrat (although homage to Lenin's memory sometimes bordered on the same type of flattery), this exaltation instead glorified Soviet power or, at least, associated the author with that power.   References to the October Revolution, to the victory over fascism, or to the superpower status of the USSR all served as modern versions of the traditional exaltation found in tsarist petitions. Whereas tsarist petitions directed their "upward allocution" to the person and power of the tsar, Soviet petitions recognized the "objective realities" of Soviet power and the inevitable victory of socialism. Petitioners often used the myths of such "objective realities" to highlight the shortcomings of corrupt or incompetent officials.[54] Such use of the official "myth" of the regime to point out problems is typical of subordinate elements of hierarchical societies when they interact with the elite in a "public transcript" such as a newspaper.[55]

The emphasis on the author's humility characteristic of tsarist petitioners was considerably toned down in the Soviet period. Instead, either the signature block or opening paragraph of the petition identified the petitioner in terms of his or her standing relative to Soviet power. For example, "member of the Communist Party since 19XX" was a frequent and concise method of placing the petitioner's status in the appropriate context.

The 1982 petition on behalf of Sikorsky clearly demonstrated both the "upward allocution" of glory to Soviet power and the self-categorization by the petitioners. Therefore, it satisfied, Soviet-style, the traditional requirements of the first part of the petition "genre," which called for exaltation of the addressee and humble identification of the petitioners.

All four of the signatories of the Sikorsky petition were decorated Heroes of the Soviet Union.[56] Their own status within the hierarchy of Soviet power was therefore immediately apparent. Having been recognized as among the most diligent and capable builders of socialism, the petitioners could dispense with any other focus upon themselves and instead could turn immediately to the "upward allocution" of glory to Soviet power. While they could dispense with "humility" because of their status, that same status may have "forced" them to more fully comply with the traditional petitioning format and the "myths" of Soviet power.[57] They did so by noting that some of Russia's most prominent figures did not understand the true nature of the October Revolution and therefore left to live abroad. Despite their lack of understanding, the best of these émigrés maintained "respectful" relations to the Soviet Union. The composer Sergei Rakhmaninov, author Ivan Bunin, and ballerina Anna Pavlova were listed as examples. The world recognized each of these native Russians as a leading talent in his or her respective field. The petitioners asserted that "their honor and talents remain accomplishments of the motherland" and deserve recognition by "memorial placards, the founding of museums and the distribution of publications." [58] They then described Sikorsky as a "world-renowned aviation designer" whose development of the world's first helicopter and the multiengine aircraft *Ilia Muromets* "carried the genius of Russian aviation thought into the annals of world aviation design."[59] Sikorsky, the petitioners asserted, asked Lenin himself for permission to emigrate after the revolution, so that he could continue his design work away from the ravages of the civil war. Lenin, they wrote, "sadly agreed."[60]

Having identified themselves within the context of Soviet power, demonstrated their "objective" understanding of the October Revolution, and invoked Lenin himself as a supporter of Sikorsky,[61] the petitioners successfully concluded the first part of the traditional petition. They next turned to the "second" classic element: description of their request and the identification of those "offenders" who opposed them.

The aviators noted that, despite the fact that Sikorsky "always demonstrated respect for the USSR and dreamed of returning" and that he "saw his design work as just another blow against Hitler in alliance with his motherland," his name was never mentioned in any positive context in the Soviet press.[62] They characterized the pride that the nation should have in Sikorsky's achievements and the press' failure to facilitate growth of that pride as a "dual relationship." The term 'dual relationship' appears frequently as a Soviet euphemism for situations involving inaccuracy, with the implication that the actions of some individual or agency are incorrect (not necessarily intentionally so). In Sikorsky's case, the dual relationship was characterized by praise for his early work (done in Russia) versus condemnation of his later work in the United States. The aviators proposed the rehabilitation of Sikorsky's name as an aviation inventor and designer, to be recognized by the erection of memorial plaques at appropriate locations and the publication of Sikorsky's design work inside the USSR.

The third element of the classic tsarist petition normally included pleas for mercy or a statement of what benefit to ruler or to the regime would be gained by approving the petition. Pleas for mercy appealed to the personal intervention and benevolence of the tsar. Citizens did send personal requests or appeals to Brezhnev. One such situation is discussed in the next example. High-level appeals, however, tended to emphasize the good of the state rather than the benevolence of the leader. To this end, the aviators took full advantage of the tense international situation of the time.

Alluding to the United States' defense buildup of the early 1980s, the petitioners reminded the reader, "Now, while US militarism fans the flames of the Cold War . . . is a good time to recognize Sikorsky. [Doing so] will help defeat those propagandists abroad who falsify history."[63] They concluded their petition: "We ask the Central Committee of *our* Party to examine our request to publicize material about this leading compatriot, to end the current dual relationship with him."[64] In so doing, the aviators reaffirmed their own status within the hierarchy (decorated Heroes, Party members), reemphasized the culprit (the "dual relationship"), and asserted that the USSR could only benefit from granting this request in its ongoing propaganda competition with the United States (which was not going well at the time). While the petition itself is important as demonstrating the applicability of the traditional model for a petition, equally important are the routing and handling of the petition as indicators of the importance of petitions in general from the perspective of the regime.

Like many petitions in the Brezhnev era, the aviators' request was addressed to a monthly journal, not directly to any politician. The petitioners, nevertheless, addressed their letter to the Central Committee of the CPSU. As shown in the discussion on the interactive nature of petitions to the press and Party, this was actually quite common. It was also in keeping with Russian tradition. Even after the *Ulozhenie* demanded that all petitions be submitted through channels, many of those received by the bureaucracy were still addressed to the tsar. In this particular case, the letter was intended as an item to be shared and discussed in public, as consistent with the authors' goal of widespread propagandizing of Sikorski to restore his name. The authors asked the editorial staff to support their request. The particular journal in question was published under the auspices of the Central Committee, so it was a logical choice.

A second case study demonstrated the continuity of the "rules of engagement" and consistency in the handling and routing of Soviet-era petitions. Aspects of this case study go beyond these points, however, and demonstrate the relationship between the petitioning process and the censorship apparatus within the USSR. Once again, the particular details of the petitions themselves are secondary to the insight into the petitioning process provided by the detailed records available. Two petitions submitted by the eminent Soviet war correspondent and author Konstantin M. Simonov between 1966 and 1979 came into direct conflict with the Soviet censorship apparatus. The actions and reactions of both the regime and Simonov illustrate another critical aspect of the petition cycle.

In January 1979, Konstantin M. Simonov appealed to the Central Committee of the CPSU to establish an archive of military memoirists. His proposal followed the classic patterns of petitioning, including all three of the basic elements. [65]   In his opening section, Simonov, who, like the aviators, needed no introduction to the authorities, demonstrated "upward allocution" in the exaltation of Soviet power and in the understatement of his own position within that hierarchy.

Simonov noted that, "despite the vast work already done by the Party, State and society," some important questions concerning the Great Patriotic War remained to be solved.[66] He then requested that the Central Committee examine one such "burning question with which we 'literati' who work with the history of the war have collided for a long time."[67] Simonov, a six-time winner of the Stalin Prize, former director of the Union of Soviet Writers, and former editor of the journal *Novy mir* and the newspaper *Literaturnaia gazeta*, was certainly more than just one of the anonymous "literati" who worked with the history of the war. He was, in fact, a critical part of that "vast work already done by the Party, State and society." He wrote the "standard" works of Soviet fiction regarding World War II[68] and directed the television documentary series *Soldiers' Memoirs*, which brought the stories of the winners of the *Slava* (Glory) order to the Soviet public. His popularity and reputation peaked in the 1960s yet remained significant at the end of the 1970s. Clearly, his petition's opening corresponded to the finest traditions of the petitioning process.

The second section of his petition, as expected, described the problem and identified obstacles: no state repository existed for the personal memoirs of World War II veterans, and valuable material was being lost as those veterans aged and died. As a result, those memoirs ended up in private or uncoordinated collections. Simonov therefore proposed creation of a central archive under the control of the Defense Ministry's Main Archive to which veterans could voluntarily submit personal memoirs. Simonov identified obstacles to the creation of such a repository by suggesting that certain conditions be applied to the new collections. Specifically, he argued that the new repository should not be a department of the Central Archive of the Ministry of Defense but an attached section (*pri arxiva*) working on a different principle basis than the other sections. Further, the announcement of the repository's establishment should underscore that it was established for personal, eyewitness accounts of veterans, that it not be obligated to publish all or parts of the material, and that memoirs kept in the repository would not be viewed as official documents or used for official purposes (verification of service time, etc.). Each of these conditions was clearly designed to overcome obstacles or opponents that Simonov believed his proposal would encounter.[69]

In the final section of his letter, where Simonov would be expected to flatter the addressee, plead for mercy, or assert the advantages of his proposal to the state, he does all three. He gave two primary reasons for his request. The first provided some flattery to the Central Archive of the Ministry of Defense (TsAMO). Simonov noted that TsAMO "has enormous experience, as I know from fifteen years close work with the organization." Such experience was critical because the repository's "address must inspire confidence in the veterans so they will send their material. TsAMO does." The second reason was a combination of a plea for expediency (more appropriate for an open forum than mercy) and an assertion of the utility of the suggestion. "Act now: the youngest veterans are now in their 60s—most are older. These materials MUST be taken into a state repository." [70]

Simonov's petition thus satisfied all of the requirements of the traditional petitioning process. Nevertheless, it was ultimately denied because of concerns by the Ministry of Defense regarding control of the memoirists' materials.[71] The notion of controlling access to, and hence the dissemination of, historical material—that is, its censorship—is even more critical to the second of Simonov's petitions included in this case study.

The second Simonov petition with relevance to this discussion actually was submitted earlier, in 1966. In October of that year, Simonov sent a letter directly to Brezhnev regarding action by the censorship agency, GLAVLIT,[72] on his book, *100 Days Of War*. This case study demonstrates important aspects of the relationship between writers and censor in the USSR and includes discussion of self-censorship by Soviet authors.

As noted, in the mid-1960s, Konstantin Simonov's official reputation was soaring. His novel *The Living and the Dead* was released in 1962 and quickly became the standard work on the opening days of World War II.

Simonov was no stranger to the Soviet elite. In 1966, the journal *Novy mir* (of which Simonov was a former chief editor) prepared to publish excerpts from his latest work, *100 Days of War: Memories of those Who Perished in 1941.*[73]

After initial approval by the recently appointed chief censor, P.K. Romanov, Simonov was forced by Romanov to seek additional approvals from the military archives and from the military censor. Simonov made the cuts suggested by the military censor. After two more weeks, Simonov, frustrated by the delays, turned to the Party Culture Department. He then received an invitation to visit the censor, who suggested a series of changes and cuts, which Simonov made. The work was printed. After printing, Romanov changed his mind and decided to forbid publication.[74] Simonov, in turn, complained to the Central Committee, and the book was sent to the publisher. It was not, however, ever issued. In October 1966, Simonov wrote a personal letter to Brezhnev, asking for his intervention and pointing out that the 1956 Party decree on the Stalin cult was still in force and that his work corresponded "with the spirit of this decree."[75] He apparently never received a direct answer, but on 24 November 1966 the Central Committee of the CPSU issued a memorandum that stated, "No reason exists to review GLAVLIT's (Romanov's) decision."[76]

His comments to Brezhnev indicated that, obviously, Simonov believed that his portrayal of Stalin's role in the opening months of the war was the critical issue. In a case of self-censorship,[77] Simonov sought to avoid, or at least minimize, his direct criticism of Stalin and the state in his commentary that accompanied the soldiers' memories in *100 Days*. According to the Central Committee official tasked with preparing a recommendation on the fate of the work, Simonov "emphasized that the correspondent's notes from the time reflect only superficial perceptions of the facts, their incorrect integration, and are based on the unknown causes of the military tragedy."[78] That is, Simonov focused on the perspective of individual soldiers, who obviously could not view the events of 1941 from any broad perspective. This was the same measure that he used in writing *The Living and the Dead*. In that novel, whenever a soldier questioned the preparedness of the Red Army or Soviet state for the outbreak of war, he was reminded or warned by another character that he could not possibly know what was going on elsewhere on the front and therefore should avoid such criticism. Simonov's emphasis on the personal, individual nature of the veterans' memoirs in the case study also highlighted the narrow scope that he associated with those documents. Simonov clearly understood the sensitivity of criticism of Stalin (Khrushchev's forte) in the context of the new Brezhnev-Kosygin regime's efforts to distinguish itself from Khrushchev and altered his work to make it more palatable.

The censor obviously understood this sensitivity as well. In its year-end collection of notes on works published in 1966, GLAVLIT noted that Simonov's *100 Days of War* classified the Red Army's lack of readiness in 1941 as the result of Stalin's oppression of 1937-1938, referred to the 1939 Molotov-Ribbentrop pact as the result of Stalin's desire for power, and raised the issue of Soviet society's complicity in placing "broad power in the hands of one individual." [79] This would have placed Stalin in the same category as Hitler in terms of lust for power and raised uncomfortable questions about "complicity" at all levels of the Soviet political and social hierarchy. Therefore, from the censor's viewpoint, the decision was clear-cut.

The issue may have been closed for GLAVLIT, but it certainly remained an open wound for Simonov. In 1971, he made comments to West German media calling for the publication of Alexandr Solzhenitsyn's novel *August 1914* and publicly questioned whether the expulsion of Solzhenitsyn from the Writers' Union was the best "educational measure" for that writer.[80] According to the censor's report, Simonov commented further that Lenin had initiated censorship in the USSR specifically to prevent the publication of "counterrevolutionary, mystical and pornographic literature." Agreeing that censorship was necessary to achieve these purposes, Simonov then insisted that "when censorship departed from this framework of limitations, to me, it is no longer at all in the same [Leninist] spirit."[81] Simonov then stated that when the censor withheld his own work, he (Simonov) "conducted [himself] as a communist and turned to the Party. I am convinced that I will be proven correct."[82] Despite Simonov's declared faith in the Party, his comments provoked high-level response from GLAVLIT, which declared that his remarks in effect "denounced" Soviet censorship and could serve as the basis for a "new anti-Soviet campaign" in the West centered on the "persecution of Solzhenitsyn."[83]

Neither Simonov nor the prominent aviators in the Sikorsky petition were members of the target cohort of this study. But the high-profile nature of their cases guaranteed a level of archival documentation that demonstrates the continuity between Soviet petitioning and its tsarist predecessor and provides insight into the functioning of Brezhnev-era Soviet censorship. The rough parallel between prominent Muscovites and prominent Soviet citizens may account for their strict adherence to the norms of petitioning. Just as Russian peasants' petitions to local landlords or authorities tended to be less formalistic and more direct, those of young Soviet specialists tended not to be so formal. Petitions from unknown young specialists naturally did not command the same level of caution or coverage in terms of archival documentation. Nevertheless, two such petitions may now be examined in light of the insight from the high-profile cases. Despite their brevity and bluntness, they demonstrate much of the same adherence to the petitioning tradition and format as their more famous contemporaries.

As mentioned in the previous chapter, Liuda Rostovtseva was a 25-year-old accountant-economist when she wrote to *Komsomolskaia pravda* in December 1975 about the impossibility of finding any milk in her home city of Karatau in Dzhambulsk oblast. Her petition naturally did not receive the level of detailed description in the records that Simonov and the aviators earned, yet it is nonetheless critical, as it, too, demonstrates the traditional elements of the Russian petition.

Respected editorial staff of *Komsomolskaia Pravda*,
Writing to you is a Komsomol member (since 1966) from the city of Karatau. I am twenty-five years old, and I work as an accountant-economist in the Karatau branch of Gosbank. I've been recognized as a Shock Worker of Communist Labor. Right now, the

truth is, I'm on maternity leave, my young son is four months old. I suppose it's possible that things must be this way, I don't know, but I think there has to be a way out. In our city, it's a major problem to get any kind of milk. People start to stand in line at six in the morning and not rarely they stand there until ten or eleven o'clock in vain. The stores explain that the quota of milk has not been distributed to them. It's like this all over our city. By the way, these problems with milk began in June. And for some reason, there's no dry or condensed milk either. You can't ever get even the slightest bit of milk.[84]

Rostovtseva immediately established her place in the Soviet social hierarchy (a Komsomol member, shock worker, specialist, and young mother), described the problem that she faced, and levied a certain amount of blame (the distribution system) without raising any direct political challenges. Despite a bit of dissembling ("I suppose it's possible that things must be this way, I don't know"), she nevertheless maintains her optimism ("but I think there has to be a way out.") Like her more famous contemporaries, she complied with the basic parameters of petitioning and with Suslov's caution to avoid a "predominance of negative attitudes," even when addressing such a dramatic economic shortcoming.

In a letter to *Komsomolskaia pravda* dated September 1975, a young teacher in Ordzhonikidze who identified herself only by her family name, Medveda, asserted, "I've never written a letter to a newspaper before, but having read some articles in your paper about dealing with parents I decided to write." She then complained that the director of her school and the head teacher (she named them) force other teachers to collect money from students' parents "for repair of classes and corridors. They even force [us] to equip classes with textbooks and to buy curtains to spread in the windows—all of this at parents' expense."[85] And this despite the fact that "money is released to the appropriate factory director in sufficient quantity. It's likely that this money gets 'spread out' on its way to the school, having organized for all the teachers and their families a banquet at a restaurant that corresponded to the completion of repairs. I'd like to know if someone could check up on all of this and limit this shameful levy from parents. Believe me, I don't write for any ulterior motive."[86]

While Medveda is less direct, she also assumes her humble place in the Soviet hierarchy by using just her last name and openly noting her inexperience ("never written a letter before"), her acknowledgment of the newspaper's leading role ("having read some articles in your paper"), and her simple honesty ("I don't write for any ulterior motive"). She also conforms to the parameters of petitioning by acknowledging the authorities' power: "I'd like to know if someone can check up on all of this." At the same time, she does implicitly challenge those authorities to comply with the regime's official ideology "and limit this shameful levy from parents" (emphasis added).

Rostovtseva's charges of economic shortcomings and Medveda's allegations of corruption were not published in the Soviet press, despite their compliance with the parameters of petitioning. Suslov's comments and the likelihood that their letters would undermine the Little Deal,[87] provide some insight into why their letters were not printed. But it remains appropriate here to return to the question of how letters were selected for printing or were kept unpublished.

Speculation regarding the extent and procedures of Soviet censorship was common in the West during the Soviet era. Some insight has been gained since the Soviet collapse by interviews with former officials of GLAVLIT. Together with archival data on cases such as these, it is now possible to compile a more accurate portrayal of the relationship between censorship and petitioning and their combined role in shaping both "hidden" and "public" domains of Soviet society.

Censorship

The "rules" of the petitioning process shaped the information sent to both tsars and Soviet leaders "from below." Both tsarist and Soviet officials developed procedures and techniques for the selective dissemination of information that originated in petitions (as well as, of course, information from other sources). Soviet authorities used this controlled release of information as a tool to demonstrate the regime's responsiveness to the needs and desires of the people and to stimulate public feedback on issues of concern to the regime. This selectivity, or censorship, has been the subject of much debate and speculation. Even the post-Soviet availability of archival material and access to former censorship officials has only partially clarified important questions about the censorship process. What were its parameters? How did they change over time? Were specific guidelines defined, or merely general rules of operation? Who established such definitions?

An intriguing source that demonstrates continuing confusion as to the true nature of Soviet-era censorship is an interview with one of GLAVLIT's chief officials, Vladimir Solodin. Born in 1931, Solodin served in GLAVLIT from 1961 to 1991 and was the senior censor after two or three Kremlin appointees (officially director of GLAVLIT's Fourth Department for "Artistic and Political Literature"). He referred to himself as the "highest professional" in the agency and was commonly, but unofficially, referred to as the "Chief Censor."[88]

According to Solodin, GLAVLIT's charter required it "not to allow into print any matter which consists of state secrets, or other secrets protected by the law, as well as matter which disinforms public opinion."[89] By his own admission, the phrase "disinforms public opinion" gave the censor key latitude that "allowed us to put any material in this category." Solodin denied the existence of any specific "lists of forbidden themes." Almost immediately, however, he qualified his position on "forbidden" themes by mentioning certain "categories" that were prohibited. The state policy of socialist realism, for example, demanded exclusive domination of art and literature, so Dali, Picasso, and others "did not have the right to exist." After ensuring compliance with such "canonistic views," Solodin insisted that his agency's overall guiding principle was, "Don't rile the people for nothing."[90]

Clearly, Solodin's vision of censorship was dramatically broader than the Leninistic approach cited by Simonov. Soviet writers understood the world in which they operated and often practiced the type of self-censorship demonstrated by Simonov.[91] Nevertheless, the "broader vision" of the censor was the source of frequent conflict between Soviet writers and the censorship. It was, after all, that "broader vision" that determined what would remain hidden or what would be public knowledge in Soviet society.

For example, in April 1968, E. V. Iakovlev was fired as editor of the journal *Zhurnalist* for allowing publication of "photographs and reproductions of pictures with a modernistic and naturalistic character."[92] Iakovlev's dismissal certainly fits with Solodin's comments about the application of socialist realism but simultaneously undermines the notion that the censorship was effective in preventing the publication of questionable or unacceptable items. That notion is reinforced by the fact that Iakovlev's firing was followed in January 1969 by a Central Committee decree on the "Increase of Responsibility for the Ideological Level of Published Materials and Repertoires by Leaders of Print, Radio, TV, Cinematography Organs and Institutions of Culture and Art."[93] That decree cited "circumstances of sharpening ideological struggle between socialism and capitalism" as making adherence to the guidelines of socialist realism more vital than ever. It then condemned the fact that "some leaders of publishing houses, print organs, radio, television, cultural and artistic institutions do not take measures necessary for the prevention of ideologically mistaken work, work poorly with authors and display pliancy and lack of political principle in deciding questions about the publication of ideologically vicious materials." Instead of properly fulfilling their responsibilities, the decree accuses some leaders of passing that responsibility on to GLAVLIT.[94]

While this example tends to lend credibility to Solodin's position, other archival information contradicts his statements that no specific "lists of forbidden themes" existed. The State Archive of the Russian Federation (GARF) contains an extensive collection of formerly classified files dealing with GLAVLIT and its functions. Some of those documents represent just the type of list denied by Solodin. For example, in July 1971, P.K. Romanov signed a set of "GLAVLIT's Operative Censorship Instructions," which included nine specific "prohibited" items. Some of the prohibitions dealt with topics of a potential military or national security nature (the prohibition against mention of Soviet soldiers participating "as volunteers in national liberation movements against American and other aggressors, a prohibition on any mention of Soviet orbital rockets, of an underground neutrino station and a "chemical-pharmaceutical factory" under construction, or about naval traffic in the North Sea), but others clearly did not. Any mention of "natural disasters" was prohibited without prior approval of GLAVLIT, as was information about participation by Israeli and Spanish representatives to the Congress of Presidents of International Association for the Security of Industrial Property, which was held on the territory of the USSR. Finally, any "works, reviews or other information which positively characterize" the Bulgarian writers V. Petrov, D. Asenov, E. Manov, or J. Radichkov were prohibited.[95] Obviously, a significant body of subjects existed that the state did not want to address in the public domain.

But where was that information recorded, and how did it change? According to émigré Soviet author Leonid Finkelstein, every author and editor was familiar with a thick green book kept by the censor that listed all the information that was forbidden for publication. Officially entitled "Index of Information Not to Be Published in the Open Press," Finkelstein joked that it was familiarly referred to as the "Talmud."[96]

Assertions like Finkelstein's and the specificity and diversity of topics in Romanov's instructions directly challenge Solodin's assertion that no lists of forbidden themes existed. The last paragraph of Romanov's list noted, "Earlier operative orders (except those of 7 July 1971) may be considered as no longer in force."[97] Obviously, Romanov's instructions of 12 July were not a unique or exceptional occurrence. Just as obviously, instructions on what material could or could not be published changed from time to time, and the censorship office updated the literary community. Finkelstein noted that censors would regularly attend "seminars" so that they could stay current with any changes in what was or was not permitted for publication.[98] The prohibition on mention of natural disasters seems especially damning of Solodin's credibility. If avoidance of mention of disasters was such a natural example of "don't rile the people for nothing," why did Romanov include it in these operating instructions?

Even Solodin's categorization of himself as the "chief censor" must be qualified by noting that Romanov was still signing specific lists of prohibitions nearly a decade later, in the midst of Solodin's tenure. One such list, signed in January 1980, includes the same wide variety of very specific topics as the 1971 list. Some military or state secrets, such as the deployment of Soviet military units in the Mongolian People's Republic or the construction of yet another "chemical-pharmaceutical factory" in the Primorskii krai city of Partizansk would be expected to appear in a document classified as "secret." But some of the other specific prohibitions, such as the banning of Frederick Forsyth's novel *The Day of the Jackal* (and any reviews, excerpts, or commentaries about the novel), the prohibition of publication of statistics on the costs of the Soviet filmmaking industry, the number of Soviet citizens who watched foreign films, and the amount paid to foreign cinema firms for those firms' "favors" in filming scenes on Soviet territory certainly do not seem to deserve the same level of security protection and appear to be nothing more than the lists of prohibited themes that Solodin denies.[99] This same list included qualified prohibitions (permission required) on discussion of unidentified flying objects and the search for valuables allegedly pilfered by German occupation forces in the western USSR during World War II.

One potential explanation for the specificity and simultaneous variety of the censorship orders is that they were reactive, rather than proactive. The prohibitions relative to discussion of the Soviet cinematography industry in January 1980 directly parallel a series of questions raised in *Literaturnaia gazeta*. From June through December of 1977, *Literaturnaia gazeta* ran a series of eight articles that analyzed the Soviet theater industry. The articles placed particular stress upon the ever-rising costs of the "theater arts." Noting that this was a worldwide phenomenon, *Literaturnaia gazeta* asserted: "In bourgeoisie countries, it has been met mostly by raising the price of tickets." But the newspaper dismisses this as an option in the USSR. "Tickets within the means of all represent a historic achievement of the Soviet theater. So subsidies are essential and must inevitably increase."[100] The similarity between the newspaper's questions about the theater and the censor's prohibitions regarding the film industry suggest the strong possibility of a cause-and-effect relationship.

In similar fashion, an issue that Solodin highlighted as one of the "bad things" that he had done as a censor may have also represented the state's response to society's criticism. Solodin noted the virulent opposition by the Soviet intelligentsia to the regime's plans to divert the flow of the great Siberian rivers from north to south. In his words, "Hundreds of articles, scores of books were written on this topic. GLAVLIT closed all of this. This theme was opened up only when it was determined that there simply would not be enough money for this project. This was a campaign of great scale, and we eliminated all the articles, books, notices."[101] What Solodin did not mention was that, in 1976, public debate on the merits of the project was commonly highlighted in the pages of *Literaturnaia gazeta*.[102]   So long as the debate centered on matters of scientific or engineering practicality, it continued. By the end of the year, however, questions were being raised about the ecological consequences and whether the project should continue, instead of just whether or not it could be done.[103] GLAVLIT'S termination of the discussion kept ideological issues out of public discussion, just as the prohibition of commentary "in financial terms" about Soviet cinematography eliminated questions about the balance between financial irresponsibility and ideological necessity in subsidizing ticket prices and productions. In this way, the changing of the "Talmud" list of what was and was not permitted for discussion, the Party could, through GLAVLIT, control public discussion so that it did not get "out of hand" and challenge the regime's authority.

As noted earlier, the notion that the censorship represented the regime's response to issues raised by Soviet society is critical in the context of this study. Equally critical is the fact that, as demonstrated by the "hundreds of articles, scores of books" that Solodin's office had to reject on the Siberian project, Soviet citizens and society did not stop developing and working on ideas just because the regime would not allow their public discussion. Thus, the censorship represents one point of ongoing interaction between the regime and society, not merely the "top-down" or one-sided type of interaction typically associated with censorship. Just as the Imperial Russian government had before it, the Soviet regime also initiated or solicited public discussion of certain issues. Alexander II's decision to solicit public opinion and potential solutions to the problem of serfdom and other reform issues in the second half of the nineteenth century shaped both the reforms themselves and Russian society in its expectations. Likewise, for the Soviet era, an analysis of the types of issues to which the censor responded and a review of some of the public discussions that the regime initiated can provide insight into the nature of the issues and ideas that were of vital interest to Soviet society.

Literaturnaia gazeta was one newspaper that played an active, preemptive role in the collation and expression of public opinion. The newspaper frequently issued surveys on topical issues, soliciting readers' feedback. In other cases, *Literaturnaia gazeta* established recurring sections on specific issues, publishing new articles and letters under a continuing rubric.

These rubrics became some of the most popular portions of *Literaturnaia gazeta* and likely surveyed issues that the Party considered important. Several examples follow.

In 1970 and 1971, various articles and surveys in *Literaturnaia gazeta* focused attention on the education, training, and utilization of specialists. *Literaturnaia gazeta* published a survey in July 1970 that asked scientific workers and engineers to give their opinions on "how to better organize their research work, to raise its effectiveness to the fullest possible extent."[104] The implication would appear to be that the extant system of utilization of scientific workers was not as well organized or efficient as it should be. *Literaturnaia gazeta* followed up one year later with an analysis of readers' responses.[105] In the overall conclusion to the survey analysis, the editorial staff concluded that the time had come to develop "an all-embracing criteria of scientific productivity that one way or another takes into account expert evaluation [i.e., the judgment of specialists]."[106] This followed the specific notation of the low opinion among survey respondents of the quantity of specialists' publications as a perceived indicator of productivity. This low opinion stood in contrast to the fact that such quantity of publication was a critical factor in the extant system of "evaluation of scientific workers in competitions, attestations, the awarding of stipends, et cetera . . . even in the dissertation defense." The implications of this system for the young professionals are discussed in a subsequent chapter. Its relevance here is that this call for change in 1970-1971 compares unfavorably to the regime's progress in solving this problem. The theme of poor employment of scientific workers in general and young specialists in particular appeared repeatedly in articles from the later 1970s and early 1980s. This theme, in fact, became one of the most prominent expressions of young specialists' frustration.

Closely related to the employment of scientific workers and equally relevant to the milieu in which the ethos of the young specialists developed was a series of articles, letters, and discussions that *Literaturnaia gazeta* ran throughout 1974 that focused on the qualifications and compensation of persons holding academic titles. The discussion participants concluded that the extant system of certification was too broad and cumbersome to be effective, with lax standards and "shenanigans" abundant.[107] Two months after the final *Literaturnaia* piece on the subject, *Pravda* announced the state's response to this problem (no direct correlation to this article series was specified).[108] After review by the CPSU Central Committee and the Council of Ministers, the certifying body was moved from the USSR Ministry of Higher and Specialized Secondary Education to the USSR Council of Ministers. In some sense, at least, this action may be seen as the response of the state to popular opinion on an important subject.

Despite this "action," issues of compensation and qualification of scientific specialists continued to be discussed as problematic. Once again, the gap between words and deeds was made apparent and lent evidence to the fact that the state itself could not solve this problem. The issue was raised again in 1979 in *Pravda*. "The Higher School, the Diploma and Economic Accountability" decried the inefficient use of young specialists and the false perception that their education was free of cost to society. It proposed specific solutions to the problem.[109]

Two years later, *Literaturnaia gazeta* raised the qualification issue once more in a letter from L. Orlov, a candidate of technological science, who proposed scrapping the "candidate's" degree and making the Soviet doctoral degree coincide with the Western style.[110] Orlov noted that his proposal was "not original. The idea has been 'in the air' for long time, and was expressed in the press, including *Literaturnaia gazeta,* during the discussion of reforming the academic certification process that took place several years ago." *Literaturnaia gazeta* initiated another survey as to whether the educational classification system should be changed, thereby bringing the discussion full cycle in seven years.

One cannot help but wonder at the frustration that must have been felt by many of the thousands who responded to the 1974 survey when the debate continued throughout the next seven years without any significant resolution or improvement. Clearly, public discussion of issues could remain impotent as an agent for change. Nevertheless, the popularity of such discussions remained high. Society continued to openly debate problems and to propose solutions, indicating that even potentially impotent discussions remained valuable as outlets for the formation and expression of public opinion.

Two other such discussions are indicative of the perceived utility of such expressions and therefore deserve mention here. In 1974, *Literaturnaia gazeta* initiated a new rubric entitled "If I Were the Director . . . ," which encouraged readers to submit suggestions for new ideas, new ways of doing business, new ways of organizing "capabilities of society."[111] Three years later, *Literaturnaia gazeta* summarized the success of this column: "over 8,000 readers have contributed 17,000 suggestions."[112] The paper assembled 800 of the proposals in the form of a bulletin, which was submitted to the USSR Council of Ministers for action. After listing examples of the wide-ranging proposals and citing the adoption of several, the article concluded, "The 'If I Were Director' department of the newspaper demonstrates the constitutionally guaranteed democratic participation of Soviet citizens in managing the affairs of state," referring again to the new Constitution.

The article appeared under a text box citing Article 49 of that new Constitution as saying: "Each citizen of the USSR has the right to bring to state organs and social organizations proposals about the improvement of their activities, and to criticize shortcomings in their work."[113] This citation served the purposes of both the newspaper and the regime. For *Literaturnaia gazeta*, it asserted the notion that, despite the impotence of some discussions, letters to the press did constitute a legitimate expression of opinion that could have some impact. For the state, recognition of the legitimacy of the popular petitioning process served to enhance the legitimacy of both the new Constitution and the state itself.

But some discussions indicate that the petition process was viewed as more than just a "safety valve" or tool of legitimacy for the state. In "From Worker to Minister, Stages of Growth," a genuine debate occurred on the question of legal regulation of the appointment process by which Soviet executives earned their posts.[114]   Composed of articles, letters, and discussions running from November 1975 to November 1977, this series debated the following questions: What qualifications should be required for management executives?   Should subordinates have a role in selecting their managers?   Are managers best appointed from within an organization or from outside?   "Should we have legal regulation of executive appointment?"[115]   The discussion was wide-ranging, including serious questions about the extant system of selection, which was regarded as disorganized, with rampant nepotism and cronyism as prominent features.   The state's solution to this problem was announced in *Izvestia* on 22 November 1977: the creation "under the USSR Ministry of Higher and Specialized Secondary Education [of] an interagency council for the advanced training of managerial personnel and specialists."[116]   *Literaturnaia gazeta* formally closed its discussion of the topic in November 1977 by summarizing readers' proposals and attributing the "great response" to this topic to the fact that "the discussion concerned deep public interests."[117]

This discussion generated a myriad of proposed solutions from readers. The creation of a "council" to study and solve the problem was not one of those proposals.   The sterility of the state's response would seem to indicate yet another case of impotence on the part of the newspaper and its readers, given their inability to implement any of the proposals put forward.   Once again, the state's inability or unwillingness to resolve problems stifled those dynamic initiatives of society that might have done so.   But the newspapers and society continued to solicit and develop such initiatives on many different issues. Obviously, such initiatives could not have been pursued without at least the passive acquiescence of the state, and the proactive nature of Soviet censorship made it likely that at least some of these discussions were initiated or encouraged by the regime.

From "chief censor" Solodin's perspective, the primary function of the censorship was to maintain order in the country and the stability of society. "We knew very well that our society is very prone to losing its balance, to going to pieces, to ending up in a bloody Russian coup."[118]   He blamed these tendencies on the level of material poverty and on nationalistic tensions. From his viewpoint, the collapse of the USSR was not due only to one man (Gorbachev) but to the unfettering of society's desire for change. [119]   The censorship preserved order and stability by channeling society's initiative or by stifling that initiative through the restriction of information that might "rile up" the people. The "filtering" effect of the censorship could be changed over time, as the authorities decided to increase or decrease the flow of information to the public. The censorship could thus evolve according to Party politics, specific directions of the leadership, the personalities of censorship officials or petitioners themselves, or even what the people focused upon as a current issue. Solodin describes how the censorship suppressed information about the 1962 shooting of demonstrators in the city of Novocherkassk and prevented this incident from sparking widespread unrest.   The censor's actions reduced a potentially inflammatory incident to the level of an unsubstantiated rumor for most Soviet citizens.

Unpublished letters in Russian archives reinforce Solodin's assertion that controlling information in accordance with the notion "don't rile the people" was a genuine interest. The subject matter of the unpublished letters is strikingly different from that of letters actually published in the Brezhnev-era press.

As noted, newspapers and journals regularly submitted summaries and reviews of materials received from readers to the Central Committee for review. One of the most significant reviews declassified to date reviews unpublished letters submitted to *Pravda, Komsomolskaia pravda*, and *Sel'skaia zhizn'* between December 1974 and September 1976.[120]

Some of the letters in this collection were complaints against individuals who abused their positions or comments about less-than-optimal working conditions. Such letters were relatively routine, and many were published. However, the vast majority of letters in this collection deal with much more systemic problems, which would have undoubtedly "riled" the people of the USSR if they had been published. Complaints of massive food shortages, transportation system breakdowns, and homelessness among working citizens and Soviet army soldiers on active duty are among the most dramatic in the collection. They were received from all areas of the USSR, including such high-profile areas as the Komsomol and army camps of the Baikal-Amur Mainline.[121] Issues less frequently mentioned but just as inflammatory included the failure of local authorities to maintain schools, problems of environmental pollution, and black marketeering.[122] Problems with the Soviet medical system, including lack of drugs, poor training level of doctors, and lack of access to care also appear frequently. The medical system was a topic of discussion in the open press, but the unpublished letters indicate that the problems were far more serious and widespread than any open sources indicated.[123] Several young medical specialists working in a Moscow hospital wrote one specific example of such a letter.

Our collective at Moscow Hospital Number 67 is "headed" by a pseudo-scholar, scoundrel and maybe even an addicted, drunken debaucher, 'Professor' G.S. Iumashev. . . God only knows how he got this duty. He has basically closed off all access to his office. We have already written to the Medical Institute Director and the Minister of Health, all in vain. We'd write to Brezhnev himself, but we can't wait any longer.[124]

Isolated cases of alcoholism or corruption, however, were only some of the aspects of the Soviet medical system that drew the ire of its citizenry. One especially valuable collection of letters regarding the medical industry includes reports from *Literaturnaia gazeta* and *Izvestiia* from 1974.[125] The *Literaturnaia gazeta* staff noted that letters were in response to an article published 1 May 1974 entitled "People's Health and Medical Advances" and the accompanying "reply" of academician V. Mikhailov, minister of health.[126] "The goal of these bulletins is to inform leaders of the Party and Soviet organs about critical observations and proposals contained in our mail." [127] The letters were most likely not published due to the sensitive nature of the topic and their extreme specificity in dealing with shortcomings in the Soviet medical system.

One such letter came from G. Sudarenkova, a specialist in her 30s who described how, after "working as an engineer for nearly 15 years," she fell ill with depression. She complained that her first doctor treated her rudely and inattentively. After relocating to another city, she received proper, professional medical care. Sudarenkova's complaint raised the issues of doctors' ethics and accountability. She alleged that the "social aspects of our medical system" were defective when a doctor could arbitrarily abuse or mistreat a patient with no fear of accountability. "Who answers for such activity by a doctor?" she asked. She then concluded, "Our doctors are afraid of statistics," in terms of both their success rates in treating patients and patients' satisfaction with their doctors.[128] Her letter was followed by several others expressing dissatisfaction with the availability and quality of mental health care, noting in one case, "No treatment is available in our area (Saratov) for nervous disorders, despite the fact that we have a lot of medical Research Institutes."[129] The final letter in this particular bulletin took the minister of health to task for his comments in *Literaturnaia gazeta*, which, according to the young engineer who wrote the letter, "contradict state comments in earlier articles from *Literaturnaia gazeta*," specifically a piece from *Literaturnaia gazeta*, no. 17, 1972, which he quoted in great detail to support his position.

The minister of health, B.V. Petrovskii, sent a response to *Literaturnaia gazeta* concerning the bulletin on 29 August 1974, in which he noted, "The significant number of letters and the questions they raise (homeopathy, organization of medical service system, emergency care, etc.) are being studied by the corresponding agencies and will be used in planning improvements to our medical service to the population."[130] This was followed by a similar bulletin from *Izvestiia* dated August 1974 that noted, "Every month we receive an average of 400 letters with complaints about treatment, institutions, or medical personnel" and that "complaints about medical issues occupy seventh place out of thirty-two in *Izvestiia*'s problem mail."[131]

Izvestiia's review mainly comprises commentary interspersed with letters and letter excerpts. The letters are mostly complaints and center on five issues: insufficient planning or poor organization of the medical care system's material base, the low level of service in rural areas, shortfalls in organization of preventive care for mothers and children, the weak medical transport system (ambulances), and violations of medical ethics, along with complaints regarding the low level of qualification or irresponsibility of doctors.

In commentary at the end of the review, *Izvestiia*'s editor noted, "Every month, from all parts of the USSR, we get these letters. Many readers take up one of two basic positions: they call for an expansion in the number of facilities in the medical care network, or they call for an increased level of care."[132]

Follow-up material in the *fond* gives some indication that the Party took the feedback from these bulletins seriously. A Central Committee memorandum dated 17 October 1974 and signed by S. Trapeznikov, director of the Science and Scholarly Administration Section of the Central Committee, indicated that the "letters demand concrete action" and noted that "on 10 September 1974 the Central Committee had adopted a resolution "on measures of further development of the medical industry." Trapeznikov added that "the

Council of Ministers is now reviewing the issue, especially that of ambulances. In addition, the Ministry of Health is drawing up its activity for tenth Five Year Plan."[133]

A noteworthy contemporary source indicates that the newspapers were not the only agencies deluged with questions about the medical care system. In the second quarter of 1974, Soviet Central Television and Radio received more than 26,500 letters from citizens. Four thousand (15%) dealt with the medical care system. Fully 14,400 dealt with alcoholism and thus had clear implications for the health care and support system.[134]

An article that may or may not have been designed to inspire a public response generated the medical surveys. As mentioned earlier, the Soviet regime, like its tsarist predecessor, often openly solicited citizens' input concerning major issues via letters to the press. One favorite method was to publish a "draft" program for Party Congresses or some other major document, such as the 1977 Constitution. Once the "draft" was published, readers would be invited to comment—and comment they did.[135]

In a summary of letters received by *Komsomolskaia pravda* in the period leading up to the 24th CPSU Congress in early 1971, the editorial staff stressed to the Central Committee: "We feel it necessary to direct attention to those letters whose authors raise one of the most pointed questions about our ideological work—the upbringing of the current generation in the spirit of proletarian internationalism, and the spirit of respect for the nationalistic feelings of fraternal peoples. What is most unsettling is the growth of nationalistic antagonism which occasionally becomes acute."

After citing specific examples from a number of such letters, the editorial staff concluded, "In many letters, one can sense that their authors don't know what they should do . . . where to direct their efforts." Hence a letter from Dushanbe complaining about ethnic nationalism concludes with the words:

How is it possible in our country, in the most just of nations, to tolerate this? Can it be that we, coping with external enemies, cannot bring order, cannot do that which is necessary so that people may sleep peacefully at night? I can't put my signature here, but I want my letter to end up in the hands of the hope of the people, in the hands of our Communist Party, in whom we believe. I want this letter to reach the Central Committee. It is impossible to tolerate further such disgrace.[136]

When such letters were received, the newspapers were open and direct in their reporting to the CPSU. Their summaries often included sensitive, unvarnished issues. In its *Spravka* of letters received in May 1976, *Pravda* reported to the CC that readers "as always, sent many letters about further economic development, noting how enterprises are forced to use reserves to fulfill plans, and readers suggest that the failure to update plant machinery leads to problem with plan fulfillment, and question why such updates are not being made."[137]   The same *Spravka* includes extensive summaries of letters complaining about food shortages, especially of meat.[138]

SUMMARY

In preventing the publication of such inflammatory materials, the censorship certainly upheld the principle of "don't rile the people." As such, it upheld the short-term stability of the Soviet state. But the vast extent of the problems guaranteed that the majority of the population would develop some knowledge of these problems, at least at their own local level. The failure of the state to solve the problems, as well as the limitations upon, and apparent impotence of, any meaningful discussion of potential solutions, guaranteed the escalation of pressures and frustrations generated by an increasingly dynamic, well-educated society.

The process represented by Soviet society's continuing analysis of the problems that it faced and the development of potential solutions to those problems despite obstacles such as the censorship should be viewed as analogous to a fluid stream. Educated, trained, and sophisticated elements of Soviet society naturally sought to confront problems of economic, social, and technological development. Their energy and motivation inspired an impetus toward the solution of Soviet problems. Like a stream of water, this impetus grew along channels where it met less resistance. In those social spaces where such growth was blocked, the movement sought other channels or stopped. But, if stopped (e.g., the public discussion on the Siberian rivers), the pressure exerted by the energy and motivation of certain social elements continued to build and seek new outlets (e.g., the hundreds of books and articles still written and submitted to the censor). The specific details of how this process contributed to the evolution of Soviet society during the Brezhnev years and its consequences for Russian history are discussed elsewhere. What is critical here is to keep in mind the interactive nature of the relationship between petitioning, censorship, and Soviet society. Specialists tried to solve problems via proposals to Party and press. Such proposals continued the ancient Russian tradition of petitioning, and the regime both accepted and encouraged such efforts. The state, however, also censored many such proposals to enhance the short-term stability of the Little Deal. Censorship guaranteed the escalation of pressures and frustrations in Russia's increasingly educated and dynamic society. These pressures shaped the ethos of the young specialists and ingrained in them commitments to practicality and moral principles in their lives and aspirations. The specific development of this ethos is the subject of the next two chapters.

Petitioning may be seen as one element of society's efforts to confront and solve problems. Its long-standing traditional roots and its well-evolved methodology gave it special standing in Soviet society. Acceptable to both the public and the regime, the processes of petitioning and censorship represented unique elements of Russian/Soviet society. Those processes, like the tsar's obligations, were reciprocal, with both society and regime bound by the parameters of the processes. While those parameters may not have comprised a society that was "civil" in the Western sense, they were a vital element in the functioning of the Soviet state and society in which the young specialists lived.

NOTES

1. Oleg Kharkhordin, *The Collective and the Individual in Russia: A Study of Practices* (Berkeley: University of California Press, 1999), 269 -270.

2. Moshe Lewin, "Russia/USSR in Historical Motion: An Essay in Interpretation," *Russian Review* 50 (1991), 250.

3. This is the central thesis of Horace W. Dewey and Ann Marie Kleimola, "The Petition as an Old Russian Literary Genre," *Slavic and East European Journal*, Volume 14, no. 3 (1970), 284-301.

4. Ibid., 289.

5. Dewey and Kleimola cite A.A. Zimin, comp. and D.S. Likachev, ed. of "Sochineniia i. Peresvetova," Moscow, 1961, 27 as crediting Peresvetov with the creation of the advisory petition as a literary genre. Dewey and Kleimola, 289.

6. Dewey and Kleimola, 292.

7. Ibid., 287.

8. Daniel Rowland, "The Problem of Advice in Muscovite Tales about the Time of Troubles," *Russian History* 6, Part 2 (1979), 259-283.

9. Ibid., 275. It is important to note one distinction between petitions that sought redress and those that offered advice. While advice was offered by individuals, petitions seeking redress were often collective, representing the grievances of a particular group of townspeople, servitors, and so on. Such collective petitions in Muscovite Russia are discussed in detail in Valerie A. Kivelson, *Autocracy in the Provinces* (Stanford, CA: Stanford University Press, 1996).

10. The most detailed analysis of this event is Valerie A. Kivelson, "The Devil Stole His Mind: The Tsar and the 1648 Moscow Uprising," *American Historical Review* 98, no. 3 (June 1993), 733-756, henceforth Kivelson 1993.

11. Kivelson 1993, 755. It is very important to note that, despite the *Ulozhenie's* proscriptions, tsars and emperors continued to receive and in some cases (notably, Paul I) personally solicited direct petitions. As late as January 1905, many Russian citizens considered a direct petition to the tsar as the ultimate source of redress.

12. The best English description of this "myth" of the Good Tsar is Daniel Fields, *Rebels in the Name of the Tsar* (Boston: Houghton Mifflin, 1976), 1-29.

13. Robert K. Massie, *Peter the Great: His Life and World* (New York: Ballantine Books, 1980), 392. See also Sidney Monas, *The Third Section: Police and Society under Nicholas I* (Cambridge: Harvard University Press, 1961), 135.

14. John T. Alexander, *Catherine the Great: Life and Legend* (New York: Oxford University Press, 1989), 324.

15. Marc Raeff, *Understanding Imperial Russia* (New York: Columbia University Press, 1984), 106.

16. Monas, 139. W. Bruce Lincoln, *Nicholas I: Emperor and Autocrat of All the Russias* (DeKalb: Northern Illinois Press, 1989), 236.

17. Lincoln, 238. Fascinating insight into the censorship of Nicholas I is available in Helen Saltz Jacobson, ed. and trans., *Diary of a Russian Censor: Aleksandr Nikitenko* (Amherst: University of Massachusetts Press), 1975.

18. See Monas, 35, for a description of Paul's petition box. Political crimes (*slovo i delo*) were the direct purview of the tsar, at least from the time of Alexis Mikhailovich (Monas, 30-37).

19. Gregory L. Freeze compiled a sampling of petitions from all Russian social classes in the 1860s as part of *From Supplication to Revolution: A Documentary Social History of Imperial Russia* (New York: Oxford University Press, 1988), 101-196.

20. Ibid., 101-102. This proactive insertion of issues into the press for public discussion was also continued in the Soviet era.

21. Many works examine the events of Bloody Sunday. The most complete in English is Walter Sablinsky, *The Road to Bloody Sunday: Father Gapon and the St. Petersburg Massacre of 1905* (Princeton, NJ: Princeton Unversity Press), 1976. References here to the petition itself are taken from the translated text of the petition in that work, 344-349.

22. An excellent, concise description of the impact that Bloody Sunday had on the faith of the masses is found in Orlando Figes' *A People's Tragedy: A History of the Russian Revolution* (New York: Viking, 1996), 177-180.

23. James C. Scott, *Domination and the Arts of Resistance: Hidden Transcripts* (New Haven, CT: Yale University Press, 1990), x-xi. Scott discusses the impulses generated by such frustration in more detail on pages 26-35.

24. Vladimir Shlapentokh, *Soviet Public Opinion and Ideology: Mythology and Pragmatism in Interaction* (New York: Praeger, 1986), 128. In the introduction to this book, Shlapentokh even went so far as to recommend methods for deciphering the "hermeneutics" involved in assessing the official ideology of the USSR, xv-xx.

25. The notion that Soviet citizens, especially those of the 1960s and 1970s, held personal beliefs that stood in contrast to their public actions has been frequently acknowledged, though rarely explored. A few examples of the many sources that acknowledge this dual nature of Soviet society include Boris Kagarlitsky, *The Thinking Reed: Intellectuals and the Soviet State, 1917 to the Present* (London: Verso, 1988), 181-215 ; Robert C. Tucker, *Political Culture and Leadership in Soviet Russia: From Lenin to Gorbachev* (New York: W. W. Norton, 1987), 184; Nicholas Lampert, *Whistleblowing in the Soviet Union: A Study of Complaints and Abuses under State Socialism* (New York: Schrocken Books, 1985), 59-60, 85 as well as Vladimir Shlapentokh, *Public and Private Life of the Soviet People: Changing Values in Post-Stalin Russia* (New York: Oxford University Press, 1989), 97-98.

26. Scott, 14-15.

27. See Lampert, esp. 67-68 and 133. James R. Millar noted the Brezhnev regime's efforts at controlling unofficial interactions above the "microlevel" of family and kin in "The Little Deal: Brezhnev's Contribution to Acquisitive Socialism," in *Slavic Review* 44, no. 4 (Winter 1985), 694-706. Vladimir Shlapentokh describes the "privatization" of Brezhnev-era Soviet society in *Public and Private Life of the Soviet People*.

28. Mark S. Rhodes describes the application of this Leninist dictum in "Letters to the Editor in the USSR: A Study of Letters, Authors and Potential Uses" (Ph.D. diss., Michigan State University, 1977), 10.

29 Suslov made his comments at a 1983 conference on "Soviet Direction of Creative and Intellectual Activity," held at the Kennan Institute for Advanced Russian Studies in Washington, DC. See Marianna Tax Choldin and Maurice Friedberg, eds., *The Red Pencil: Artists, Scholars and Censors in the USSR* (Boston: Unwin Hyman, 1989), 150-151, henceforth Choldin 1989.

30. Vitali Vitaliev, *Special Correspondent: Investigating in the Soviet Union* (London: Hutchinson, 1990).

31. 29 July 1980, 6.

32. Stephen White, Mark Rhodes, and V. Bogdanov and B. Viazemskii each describe the submission process of these "control cards" to organs of the Party and state. See Stephen White, "Political Communications in the USSR: Letters to the Party, State and Press," *Political Studies* 31 (1983), 43-60, esp. 54, Rhodes, 44, V. Bogdanov and B. Viazemskii, *Spravochnik zhurnalista* (Leningrad: 1965), 271.

33. For examples of the summaries, see RTsKhIDNI F599, O1, D516 (for the journal *Kommunist*), F614, O2, D39, L30-35 (for the journal *Agitator*), or TsKhSD F5,

O69, D390, L16-27 (*Komsomolskaia Pravda*), F5, O67, D180, L32-178 (*Literaturnaia gazeta*).

34. Between 1995 and 1999 I interviewed 62 Russian citizens who graduated from institutes of higher learning between 1964 and 1984. Some believed that letters published in the press were "staged," by the regime; others felt them genuine. But all recognized the letters and the discussions that they generated as a normal part of Soviet life.

35. Kivelson, "The Devil Stole His Mind," 754-756.

36. TsKhSD F5 O69 D390 L27-31.

37. The memorandum was signed Iu. Skianov, Deputy Director, Propaganda Department, 24 February 1971. It summarized and provided commentary on letters received during the "pre-Congress" period when the regime solicited public opinions in preparation for the 24th Party Congress. TsKhSD F5, 063, D90, L19.

38. RTsKhIDNI F638 O1 D21 L20-23.

39. RTsKhIDNI F638 O1 D21 L30.

40. RTsKhIDNI F638 O1 D21 L47-85.

41. RTsKhIDNI F638 O1 D21 L93-94.

42. Ibid., 94.

43. RTsKhIDNI F638 O1 D21 L20-23

44. RTsKhIDNI F638 O1 D21 L98.

45. TsKhSD F5 068 D387, L28-31.

46. RTsKhIDNI F599 O1 D342, L39.

47. The collections and summaries of letters that I found in Russian archives in the summer of 1999 had been declassified since May 1995. Summaries for some years were available, while others were not. The declassification process is ongoing, though apparently haphazard.

48. RTsKhIDNI F638, O1, D 21, L125.

49. TsKhSD, F5, O69, D415, L10-14. *Chelovek i zakon* summarized the subject of letters received as "40% complaints, 50% questions and 10% proposals."

50. According to TsKhSD F5 068 D387, the following were the statistics on letters to *Pravda* in 1975: March: 49,467 (L40); June: 38,272 (L52); July: 31,117 (L108); August: 27,250 (L120); September: 29,093 (L133); October: 32,007(L171); November: 32,757 (182); December: 42,165 (L196).

51. TsKhSD F5 O67 D133 L 9-32. As discussed elsewhere, this collection was especially useful, for it broke down letters by subject and quantity. Over 14,400 (54%) dealt with the problem of alcoholism.

52. *Agitator* received 1,831 letters to the editorial staff in 1974, yet took that mail just as seriously. The editorial staff of *Agitator* directly answered 1,128 of those 1,831 letters. RTsKhIDNI F614 02 D39 L33. *Sovetskaia kultura* experienced more than a 50% increase in the number of letters received from 1973 to 1981 (14,665 to 22,768) RTsKhIDNI F630 O1 D38 (1973), D46 (1981).

53. The document summarizing the Central Committee decision to reject the petition indicated that the issue was reviewed by the KGB, Defense Ministry, Academy of Sciences, and the editorial staff of the popular science journal *Tekhnika—Molodezhi* at the request of the CC. The inclusion of the journal is indicative of the interactive nature of the petition cycle and was typical of the archival petitions that I reviewed.

54. An excellent, concise summary of the "myths" or "stories" that shaped the way Soviet citizens understood life may be found in Sheila Fitzpatrick, *Everyday Stalinism, Ordinary Life in Extraordinary Times: Soviet Russia in the 1930s* (New York: Oxford University Press, 1999), 8-11.

55. The notions of "public" and "hidden" transcripts are Scott's. See Scott, 18-23.

56. The petitioners included three winners of the order of Hero of the Soviet Union: M.Gallai, test pilot; Colonel-General of Aviation M. Gromov, test pilot and professor; G. Hofman, writer. The fourth was a bearer of the order of Hero of Socialist Labor, Academician O. Antonov, general designer. Note that their job titles were just as important a part of their self-categorization as their designation as "heroes." The petition itself and the Party documents associated with it are found in TsKhSD F5, O88, D14, L3-8.

57. Members of elite elements of a society must more strictly adhere to the public transcript of that society. Scott, 2-15, 18.

58. Ibid., L 5.

59. Ibid.

60. Ibid.

61. Invocation of Lenin in the form of a quotation or, as in this case, an assertion of his personal involvement was a normal part of petitions written in the Brezhnev era, especially petitions to Party officials. Such invocation provided both the petitioner and respondent a common vocabulary for use in their "public transcript."

62. TsKhSD F5, O88, D14, L6.

63. TsKhSD F5, O88, D14, L7.

64. Ibid. (Emphasis added).

65. Each of the documents cited here is found in TsKhSD, F5, O76, D12, L3-19. They were publicly printed in Russia in the journal *Otechestvennye arkhiv,* no. 1 (1993), 63-73. My translations are based upon the published documents.

66. Ibid. , 65.

67. Ibid. It should be noted that Simonov's letter, though addressed to the Central Committee, was actually submitted through the Archeological Commission of the Soviet Academy of Sciences. The Academy of Sciences often played a role in the petition process analogous to that of the journals and newspapers. Simonov was the commission's literary secretary; hence, this was a natural forum for submission of his request.

68. His novels *The Living and the Dead* and *Days and Nights* chronicled the opening six months of the war and the battle of Stalingrad, respectively.

69. Simonov's desire for this separation of the memoirs from traditional collections was twofold. In the first place, he seems to have genuinely believed that the situation was urgent and that the memoirs of the rapidly disappearing veterans had to be collected as quickly as possible. Perhaps he was influenced in this by his own rapidly failing health. In the second place, Simonov knew well the Brezhnev regime's sensitivity to potential criticism of Stalin's leadership early in the war.

70. *Otechestvennye arkhiv,* 67 (emphasis in original).

71. The context in which this petition was denied is critical to understanding its rejection. Late in the Brezhnev era, it was no longer acceptable to criticize Stalin, directly or indirectly, as it had been in Khrushchev's time. Therefore, any memoirs that might reflect unfavorably on the Soviet leadership, especially in the opening months of the war, were to be strictly controlled. The memoirs of leading Soviet generals, including Marshal Zhukov, had repeatedly encountered publication problems throughout the Brezhnev era because of such criticism.

72. GLAVLIT is the Russian acronym for the highest censorship agency. The acronym was developed from the original title of the censorship agency, the Main Directorate for Affairs of Literature and Publishing (in Russian Главное Управление по делам Литературы и издательства). This title was applied beginning in 1922 and has been used since to refer to the highest censorship organs of the Soviet Union, regardless of changes in the agency's official title. See "Polozhenie o Glavnom Upravlenii po delam literatury i izdatel'stva," 6 June 1922 in T.M. Goriaeva, comp., *Istoriia sovetskoi*

politcheskoi tsenzury: Dokumenty i kommentarii (Moscow: ROSSPEN, 1997), 35. In August 1966, as Simonov's work was being readied for publication, a decree of the Council of Ministers of the USSR strengthened and renamed the censorship agency as the "Chief Administration for the Preservation of State Secrets in Print" and appointed P.K. Romanov as its head yet kept the common appellation of GLAVLIT. "Postanovlenie soveta ministrov SSSR o glavnom upravlenii po oxrane gosydarstvennyx tain v pechati pre sovete ministrov SSSR (GLAVLIT)" dated 18 August 1966. State Archive of the Russian Federation (GARF) F R-9425, O2, D432, L1.

73. This issue is discussed in detail by Iurii Burtin, "Vlast' protiv literatury (60-e gody)," *Voprosy literatury*, no. 2, (1994), 223-306. Burtin includes Simonov's struggle for the publication of *100 Days* as one of four major clashes between Soviet writers and the censor during the 1960s, 252-267.

74. No archival materials shed light on Romanov's change of heart. Burtin, however, attributes Romanov's withdrawal of his approval to insecurity related to his recent appointment. According to Burtin, Romanov did not want to challenge an author of Simonov's stature on his own but rather sought to collect support from other state and Party figures.

75. Simonov's letter was published in Russian in Burtin, 257-258.

76. Ibid., 267.

77. The phenomenon of self-censorship by Soviet authors is discussed in more detail later.

78. A. Okhotnikov, Recommendation to the Central Committee, 21 September 1966. TsKhSD, F5, O58, D29, L39 as printed in Burin, 253-255.

79. "Spravka GLAVLITA o zamechaniiax k materialam, podgotovlennym k opublikavaniiu v 1966 g." Dated 15 March 1967 and signed by P.K. Romanov. GARF F R-9425, O1, D1261, L11.

80. TsKhSD F5, O63, D146, L24.

81. Ibid.

82. Ibid.

83. Ibid.

84. TsKhSD F5, O68, D387, L204.

85. TsKhSD F5O68 D387 L156.

86. Ibid.

87. As discussed in Chapter 1.

88. Steven Richmond, "The Eye of the State: An Interview with Soviet Chief Censor Vladimir Solodin," *The Russian Review* 56 (October 1997), 581.

89. Ibid., 584.

90. Ibid.

91. For a dramatic, firsthand account of the phenomenon of self-censorship by Soviet writers, see the commentary and discussion of émigré Sovet writers on this subject in Martin Dewhirst and Robert Farrell, eds., *The Soviet Censorship* (Metuchen, NJ: Scarecrow Press, 1973), esp. 5-6, 26-49.

92. "Postanovlenie sekretariata TsK KPSS o zhurnale *"Zhurnalist"* i osvobozhdenii E.V. Iakovleva ot dolzhnosti glavnogo redaktora," 26 April 1968, "Most Secret." TsKhSD, F4 O19 D101 L11 as published in Goriavea, 187-188.

93. TsKhSD F4 O19 D131 L2-6; Goriavea, 188-191.

94. Ibid.

95. GARF F R-9425 O1 D1387 L35-36.

96. Dewhirst and Farrell, 55-58. See also John L.H. Keep, *Last of the Empires: A History of the Soviet Union, 1945-1991* (Oxford: Oxford University Press, 1995), 275-276.

97. GARF F R-9425 O1 D1387 L36.

98. Choldin, 17-20.   As demonstrated in the second Simonov example, sometimes the censor's guidance changed and authors did not find out in advance. Hence, Simonov wrote to Brezhnev that his work corresponded to the Party's 1956 decree on Stalin—but the decree had since been superseded.

99. GARF, F R-9425 O1 D1680 L6-11.

100. *Literaturnaia gazeta*, 28 December 1977, 2.

101. Richmond, 586.

102. See, for example, *Literaturnaia gazeta*, 1 September 1976, and follow-up discussions in *Literaturnaia gazeta*, 17 November 1976.

103. V. Podoplelov and A. Brattsev raise such issues in *Literaturnaia gazeta*, 17 November 1976, 10.

104. "Kak vam rabotaetsia?" *Literaturnaia gazeta*, 15 July 1970, 11.

105. "Kak vam rabotaetsia?' *Literaturnaia gazeta*, 4 August 1971, 10; 11 August 1971, 11; 18 August 1971, 11.

106. "Kak vam rabotaetsia?" *Literaturnaia gazeta*, 18 August 1971, 11.

107. "A kak schitaete vy?" *Literaturnaia gazeta*, 15 May 1974, 13 was a survey published in response to readers' letters on the subject of "attestation" of academic credentials.   Additional letters and readers' responses to the survey were published in "Uchenye i Izheuchenye," *Literaturnaia gazeta*, 5 June 1974, 11 and again under the same title on 12 June 1974, 12.   Additional commentary and letters appeared in "Uchenaia sepen': Pokazatel' kvalifikatsii?   Chek na prediavitelia?"   *Literaturnaia gazeta*, 3 July 1974, 12.   A statistical analysis of the survey results appeared in "A kak schitaete vy?" *Literaturnaia Gazeta*, 10 July 1974, 10 (it cited over 9,000 readers' replies).   The discussion concluded in "Dissertatsii na forume mnenii," *Literaturnaia gazeta*, 11 September 1974, 10.

108. *Pravda*, 9 November 1974, 2 as translated and presented in *Current Digest of the Soviet Press* 26, no. 45 (1974), 10.

109. *Pravda*, 6 January 1979, 3, as translated and presented in *Current Digest of the Soviet Press* 31, no. 1 (1979), 9-10.

110. L. Orlov, "Certification Marathon," *Literaturnaia gazeta*, 18 March 1981, 13, as translated and presented in *Current Digest of the Soviet Press* 33, no. 15 (1981), 13-14.

111. "Esli by direktorom byl ia . . . ," *Literaturnaia gazeta*, 27 March 1974, 12.

112. "Vosem tysiach direktorov!" *Literaturnaia gazeta*, 12 October 1977, 12.

113. *Literaturnaia gazeta*, 12 October 1977, 12.

114. The rubric "Ot rabochego do ministra: stupeni rosta" first appeared in *Literaturnaia gazeta*, on 21 July 1976, 11. But the series was introduced by two other articles: "Kak stat' ministrom," *Literaturnaia gazeta* 5 November 1975, 11 and "Etazh cheshkova," *Literaturnaia gazeta*, 17 December 1975, 11.

115. This question was specifically posed in a letter from engineer F. Grigoriev, *Literaturnaia gazeta*, 16 September 1976, 10.   It serves well to sum up the overall theme of the entire discussion.

116. *Izvestia*, 22 November 1977, 2 as translated and presented in *Current Digest of the Soviet Press* 29, no. 48 (1977), 5.

117. *Literaturnaia gazeta*, 30 November 1977, 10-11.

118. Richmond, 589.

119. Ibid., 590.

120. TsKhSD F5 O68 D327 L 1-327.   Entitled "Reviews of Unpublished Letters from the Post Received by the Editorial Staffs of the newspapers *Pravda*, *Komsomolskaia pravda* and *Sel'skaia zhizn'* in 1975," this collection was declassified on 30 May 1995.   It contains actual letters, not just excerpts, from a wide range of citizens

on many types of topics. Particularly valuable are those from *Komsomolskaia pravda*, which normally include background on the age and education level of the author.

121. Ibid., especially L3-4, 18-19, 21-24, 151-154, 204, 254-262, 289-291.

122. Ibid., L 156, 207-212 (schools), 205-206 (pollution), and 155-156 (black marketeering).

123. Ibid., L 93-96. The extent of the medical system's problems is made even more apparent by collections of documents from *Izvestiia* and *Literaturnaia gazeta* found in TsKhSD F5 O67 D180 L 1-178. These review letters regarding medical care generated by published articles in the newspapers and are scathing in their derision of the Soviet medical system in all parts of the country. *Izvestiia* noted that medical complaints occupied 7th place of 32 in the editorial staff's "problem mail," L169.

124. TsKhSD F5 O68 D387 L93-94.

125. TsKhSD F5 O67 D180 (declassified 4 April 1995), L32-178. L32-34 include commentary from the editorial staff of *Literaturnaia gazeta*, actual *Literaturnaia gazeta* letters on L35-99. Staff commentary notes that "letters were not edited for content, only shortened," L34. Letters from *Izvestiia* occupy the remainder.

126. Based on the evidence available, it is impossible to determine if the article was specifically designed to generate such a large response or if the response was natural.

127. Ibid., L32.

128. TsKhSD F5 O67 D180 L69-74.

129. TsKhSD F5 O67 D180 L84-87.

130. Ibid., L146.

131. Ibid., L169.

132. Ibid., L151.

133. Ibid., L178.

134. TsKhSD F5 O67 D133 L9-32.

135. TsKhSD F5 O63 D90 L1-62 includes a *Komsomolskaia pravda* review of letters from January to February 1971 entitled "The Precongress Period" for the 24th Party Congress (Declassified May 30, 1995).   TskHSD F5 O69 D495 contains collections of letters and summaries of letters from *Pravda* to CC on the draft CC report to the 25th Party Congress on the "Basic Direction of Economic Development for 1976-1980," L1-15, L40-49. "Protection of the Environment," L17-28 and "Medical Services," L29-39 (Declassified May 10, 1995).

136 TsKhSD F5 O63 D90 L18. Similar letters may be found in TsKhSD O68 D387 L1-2. These note that ethnic Moldovans' nationalism makes Russians living there fear for their lives. L81-83 of that same *fond* deal with nationalism in Azerbaizhan and the Caucasus.

137. TsKhSD F5, O69, D390, L50.

138. Ibid., L51-55.

3

Children of Victory, Grandchildren of the Victors: Individual Values

In the summer of 1999, I spent several delightful afternoons discussing the young specialists of the Brezhnev era with Elena Iurevna Zubkova, director of the Center for Contemporary History at the Russian State Humanities University in Moscow. I explained to her how frustrating it had been to develop a sense of the character and beliefs of the specialists as a group. She laughed and said, "That's because we were a generation of individuals," as opposed to the people of the 1960s (Gorbachev's generation), whom she termed "team players." When I suggested that, despite their emphasis on individuality, the young specialists must have had some common beliefs, hopes, or dreams, she suggested that I pose a new question to those whom I interviewed. She suggested that it might be useful to ask members of the group who they thought would be the "best representative" of their generation and then ask them to explain why they chose that person.[1]

The question proved a remarkable tool for getting my subjects to open up and discuss the nature of their individual beliefs and values. Many could not or would not name a specific individual, but all were willing to talk at length about the traits that they believed the ideal representative of their generation should have. A number of characteristics repeatedly appeared as critical in the specialists' mind-set. Svetlana, a specialist in the "automation of technological processes," best summarized the common traits valued by the young specialists: "I cannot name one, but he (or she) should have the following traits: an aspiration toward higher education, the desire to grow, not only in an educational sense, but also in a sense of culture. He should possess a strong sense of human goodness or kindness, and maintain sincere relations [with others]."[2]

Professor Zubkova's notion that the young specialists formed a generation of "individuals" and Svetlana's emphasis on the values of human goodness and sincerity, especially in relationships, appear with striking frequency in both published and archival sources from the Brezhnev years, as well as in contemporary interviews with other specialists. Just as striking as their frequency is the fact that these values are antithetical to the stereotypical "Soviet" emphases on collectivism and interaction based upon scientific or revolutionary principles. Because the emphases on "individualism" and "humanism" represented critical aspects of the young specialists' ethos, it is important to precisely define them here.

Individualism grew largely out of the practical conditions of Soviet life. Oleg Kharkhordin has theorized that one of the dominant features of Soviet society was the development of a "*kollektiv* mentality." This mentality, which emphasized the priority of the goals of the work or school group to which every citizen belonged, was enforced, in Kharkhordin's view, by an all-pervasive system of "mutual surveillance," through which Soviet citizens monitored each other's compliance with the rules of conduct established by the regime.[3] But some of the tools that led to the perfection of this system of mutual surveillance by 1957 had, by the 1980s, given rise to the unintended side effect of an increased emphasis on individuality. The very instruments intended to make Soviet citizens *objects* of mutual surveillance instead led them to assert themselves as active, *individual subjects*, able to select goals of their own and modify their own behavior accordingly.

By 1985, Kharkhordin concludes, the practice of mutual surveillance had become "thoroughly routinized," and citizens were concerned to maintain only its forms, not its content.[4] Soviet citizens did not define themselves in accordance with the *kollektiv's* goals, but instead, they did so in accordance with their own sense of individual morality. This morality was defined by their selection of heroes and by the judgment passed upon them by their own, self-selected community, be that a sports club, a professional group, or simply their own circle of family and carefully chosen friends. Often, this individualism was expressed through the accumulation of certain possessions or the adherence to a certain style of fashion or action.[5] "Individualism," for purposes of this study, therefore is defined as the desire to select one's own relevant *kollektiv*—an informal grouping of friends, associates, or others with common, self-defined interests—and to conduct oneself according to the norms of that informal *kollektiv*.

For the young specialists, a defining element of their individual morality was an emphasis on treating people as *humans*. That is, it was their moral principle that persons should have the ability to pursue their own interests. That ability was to be generated by a combination of material wealth, personal security, and freedom from arbitrary treatment. Those interests might be academic, professional, recreational, and so on but in all cases would be considered as 'moral' only if, in their pursuit, the citizens conducted themselves responsibly and treated others with respect, generosity, and compassion. This study refers to this element of young specialists' morality as "humanism."

The same censorship, which the regime believed would strengthen the short-term stability of the country, also generated pressures and frustrations that isolated the specialists from one another and shaped their focus on human values as a moral principle. Thus, individualism and humanism became part of the ethos of the young specialists.

This chapter explores the specific development of that individualism and humanism. It seeks to answer those basic research questions that focused on the personal beliefs of the young specialists and their relationship, as individuals, to authority, that is, to answer questions about their beliefs as young, well-educated Soviet citizens and to explore those beliefs that were not directly related to their membership in any formal group, be it school, profession, or work. Group and professional or vocational beliefs and values are discussed in the next chapter. The issues addressed here attempt to answer the following questions: What kind of relationship did the young professionals have with the Communist Party of the Soviet Union and the official ideology of the regime? Did they hold common aspirations, frustrations, and fears? What were their attitudes toward family life and friendship? How did they spend their free time and discretionary income? What did they believe in?

The public transcripts recorded in the Soviet press provide flashes of insight into the answers to these questions. Deeper, more thorough insight is gained into the young specialists and their beliefs by analyzing their unpublished letters as well. A third, particularly valuable view of young specialists' beliefs is available in the records of the discussions, meetings, and strategy sessions of Party propagandists who were responsible for instructing young specialists. The questions, complaints, and suggestions posed by young specialists to these official advocates of the regime represent a key point of interaction between the public and hidden "transcripts" of Soviet society. Formerly classified KGB documents also illuminate those transcripts and are included here as well.

The published letters, petitions, and articles from, or dealing with, young specialists frequently focused upon statements of "moral principle." Unpublished letters and petitions, on the other hand, tended to levy specific criticisms about the functioning (or lack thereof) of the Soviet economic system. The archival records of propagandists' meetings indicated that the young specialists desperately sought factual information about the performance of Soviet economic enterprises and their Western counterparts for comparison purposes. The KGB reports help explain the regime's shaping of the public transcripts.

In keeping with the rules of engagement for petitions, published material discussed ideals and principles and was often directed primarily at incompetent or corrupt individuals. Systemic flaws, usually implied in published sources, were more openly raised in unpublished material. The criticism and commentary of the specialists revealed a self-confidence and optimism about their abilities to confront and solve problems, born of their advanced education as well as some extremely interesting insights into their value system. As will be shown, that value system stood in stark contrast to the public values held by their parents and is highlighted by a number of linguistic markers that set the young specialists apart. The accuracy of that public image and hence of the regime's role is called into question by unpublished documents.

The chapter opens with a discussion of young professionals' attitudes toward family, friends, and free time. It then explores the young specialists' formative experiences at work. The relationship to the hierarchy through work is followed by a discussion of the specialists' relationship to the official ideology and the Communist Party of the Soviet Union (CPSU). This is followed by their expressed aspirations for their own children and their philosophical outlook. Finally, the chapter turns to issues of dignity and autonomy, which lead into the analysis of their professional beliefs and the role of groups in the next chapter.

FAMILY, FRIENDS, AND FREE TIME

In writing of the "middle class" of Soviet society in the Stalin years, Vera Dunham noted that those educated, upwardly mobile Soviet citizens sought "careers backed by material incentive" to include housing, consumer goods, and free time. She termed this trait "*meshchantsvo*" and said that it was embodied in material acquisition and the focus on private concerns.[6] Perhaps then, the young professionals shared more with their grandparents than the stand on principles and conscience discussed later. This section seeks answers to questions about the young specialists' attitudes and beliefs on such "private concerns" as raising a family, how they spent their leisure time, and whom they chose for close friends. [7]

Nearly every Western observer of Soviet society has remarked upon the unique intensity of the Russian *kruzhok*, or "circle" of friendships. Very selective, Russians choose their closest friends carefully and share their innermost thoughts and warmth only with those in this circle.[8]

The vast majority of young professionals held colleagues from work or old schoolmates among their closest friends.[9] Mutual interests, especially professional—and, to a lesser degree, recreational—interests, were the foundations of most friendships for this group, not accidents of geography (neighbors, etc). This may have been due to the types of activities that the young professionals enjoyed in their free time. The vast majority of specialists interviewed indicated that their favorite pastimes in the Brezhnev era were primarily sedentary, intellectual types of activity, activities well suited to a quiet family and friends environment, such as reading and visiting the theater or cinema. Very few listed sports, traveling, or more "active" types of activity.[10]

This may have been due, in part, to practicality rather than desire. Young professionals took part in two press discussions on the lack of recreational equipment in the later 1970s. In January 1977, *Literaturnaia gazeta* published an article called "I'm Looking for a Sail," in which a journalist decried the noise, pollution, and generally unpleasant conditions created by massive numbers of motorboats on the Volga River near the city of Saratov.[11] R. Reikkenen, a young professional who designed sail and oar boats as a hobby, was interviewed by the newspaper in July 1978.[12] Reikkenen described the obstacles that he had encountered in seeking commercial production of a recreational sail and oar boat that he had designed. Red tape and bureaucratic obstruction prevented production of his design, despite the fact that large numbers of readers asserted the genuine desire for such craft.[13]

Tennis players, on the other hand, were so frustrated with the same type of bureaucratic obstacles that they began the first steps to take matters into their own hands. V. Kuibyshev, a candidate of architecture, complained to *Literaturnaia gazeta* that participation in tennis was not growing due to lack of equipment and courts, despite the fact that shortcomings were pointed out "several years ago" in *Literaturnaia gazeta*.[14] "Clothing for tennis players is a bad problem that the USSR Ministry of Light Industry should have taken care of by now." Kuibyshev knew, as an architect, that each microborough was supposed to have a certain number of courts based on number of residents. "But," he noted, "urban planners break this rule all the time." He went on to say that players were beginning to organize and construct their own private tennis clubs with their own money, including holding tournaments. Kuibyshev closed by noting that this practice was not yet "recognize and accepted" and was therefore limited to a very small number of clubs.[15]

As a result, at least in part, of a lack of recreational sporting equipment, young professionals spent their free time in quiet leisure with their family and friends. The friends, as discussed, were usually connected in some way with work. "Family," on the other hand, normally meant a spouse, one child, and possibly parents and in-laws.

The majority of young professionals were married. Most married during or shortly after graduation from the *vuz*.[16] The vast majority also lived with the parents of one spouse or the other for at least some time after the wedding.[17] While many complained about crowding or lack of privacy, most were nevertheless satisfied with their initial living conditions.[18] This indicates that the young, newly married professionals had expected to live temporarily with family and accepted this condition. Most eventually found their own apartments and settled in to focus upon their own nuclear family.

Like parents everywhere, the young professionals had dreams for their children. These dreams normally reflected the aspirations and beliefs of the parents and, as such, can provide effective insight into those beliefs. Before discussion of the young specialists' dreams, however, this study turns to the reality of their lives in dealing with the social and economic hierarchy of work, which naturally raised questions about their relationship with the system and the Party.

IDEOLOGY, THE SYSTEM, AND THE CPSU

In a 1995 retrospective interview, Professor Nikita Pokrovsky, a young and energetic scholar of English literature, philosophy, and, ultimately, sociology, summarized his outlook on life in the Brezhnev era as one in which: "Everyone, including me, thought that the Soviet system was not very efficient. Not very human or humane, if you wish. Not very efficient in terms of giving advancement to talented people, rather blocking them than supporting them. But I should be honest with you; no one thought that this particular system would collapse so fast. Everyone thought of the system as being eternal."[19]

Professor Pokrovsky was not alone in these beliefs. Svetlana (interviewed earlier) and many other young specialists addressed the themes of the system's inefficiency and its failure to deal with individuals as thinking, feeling, and talented human beings. They expressed these feelings in two types of critiques. Critiques of the first type were in keeping with the traditional Leninist doctrine of "criticize, don't generalize." These criticisms were generally directed against incompetent or corrupt individuals and, at first glance, complied with officially accepted parameters. But frequently, criticisms of the social or economic system were implied as well.

Obviously, the gradual trend toward public systemic criticism, even implied criticism, could not have occurred without the acquiescence of the regime. As seen later, archival documents reveal that young specialists had, in fact, been levying direct, often blunt criticism toward the system for some time. The fact that the Brezhnev regime allowed even a watered-down version of this criticism in the open press represented a major change in the "public transcript" of Soviet society. To understand the significance of this trend, both the young specialists and the regime must be examined once again within the domination-resistance paradigm.

Normally, groups occupying a subordinate position in a society submit "protests and challenges—even quite violent ones—in the realistic expectation that the central features of the form of domination will remain intact."[20] Professor Pokrovsky's assertion that he and his peers regarded the Soviet system as "eternal" is therefore quite in keeping with their subordinate status within Soviet society.

Equally consistent with this subordinate status were the traditional criticisms directed against individuals. Barrington Moore believed it to be a "main cultural task" for an oppressed group to "undermine or explode the justification of the dominant stratum. Such criticisms may take the form of attempts to demonstrate that the dominant stratum does not perform the tasks that it claims to perform and therefore violates the social contract. Much more frequently, they take the form that specified individuals in the dominant stratum fail to live up to the social contract."[21] In their frustration, young specialists moved beyond criticism of "specified individuals" and began to question whether the Soviet elite was, in fact, performing "the tasks it claim[ed] to perform." [22]

In 1972, chemical engineer I. Mironovich wrote to *Sotsialisticheskaia industriia* to complain about the fact that a new flame retardant that he and his section had developed was not being put into mass production, despite the apparent need for it in several industries.[23] Mironovich suggested that the reasons for the nondevelopment of his product were not objective but rather subjective. "The Ministry of Shipbuilding and the cellulose-paper industry could long ago have begun to use [it] to satisfy basic needs. Either they don't want trouble, or for other reasons, but a valuable product which the national economy needs is not on the market." Even the title of the article ("They Found Themselves a Concern") focuses attention on individual actors as opposed to systemic problems. In this way, Mironovich's complaint avoids the folly of generalization and conforms to the parameters for a petition.

Nevertheless, Mironovich's straightforward criticism of "they" who make the production decisions is not the norm for young specialists. More frequently, young professionals' published complaints began to lay blame, at least implicitly, on aspects of the system. Consider, for example, the case of Olga Ivanova Golubenko, a 1971 graduate of the Chernovitskii State University, a young teacher who failed to complete her first teaching assignment after graduation. Her case is an excellent example of a "mixed" critique, as well as providing some significant answers to the question of what the young specialists did believe. She openly criticized the conduct of the principal at her assigned rural school and the way that the other teachers acted.[24] But she also made implicit criticisms of the systemic practice of using schoolchildren for farmwork, the values held by other teachers, and the system by which teaching assignments were handed out to *vuz* graduates:"I'll begin with the job assignment. When I wrote 'accepted,' my hand shook . . . . Of course, I had heard stories about how difficult it was for young specialists in rural areas. But I wasn't afraid, I was confident: ready and willing to work, and competent. I considered myself prepared for the inevitable difficulties. I had worked in construction detachments."

Her initial obstacles included a dilapidated schoolroom and days in the fall when only half her students were present (the rest were in the fields). But "these were difficulties I had expected." So she got down to work. When she issued poor marks to those students who did not attend class because of fieldwork, she came into conflict with the school director, Ivan Vasilievich Zhovmir. A veteran principal with 20 years in his post, Zhovmir had little patience and less sympathy for his young charge. When she complained about the holes in her classroom walls and its broken stove, Ivan Vasilievich only laughed and asked, "Are you really some poor widow that I must come and see?"

But it was the attitude of her fellow teachers (all older than she) that most aggravated Golubenko, and her criticism of them provides insight into a that value she held especially dear. Olga Ivanova despaired at the "pattern of behavior" that her teaching colleagues accepted. Within that pattern, the students who were "barely getting by were nevertheless good machine operators." Golubenko classified this justification as the cause of "everything; the weak discipline and poor progress, the forced grades of '3' [acceptable], and the mediocre level of instruction." But the ultimate sin of her school for Golubenko was that "for the past several years, not one graduate of our school had managed to get into an institute."

Clearly, Golubenko believed in the value of higher education. She was incredulous that her older colleagues did not share that belief strongly enough to be distressed by this failure of any of their students to progress. Of course, their age was certainly not the only factor in this difference of perspective. Their own rural environment and personal life experiences contributed to their outlook. Nevertheless, as indicated by Svetlana earlier, the belief in the value of higher education as both a means and an end was common among the young specialists.[25] They recognized the changes in their own lives made possible by their education and believed that the more Soviet citizens who completed higher education, the higher the overall cultural level of Soviet society would be.

In this case, this belief of the young specialists coincided with the values of their parents and the ideology of the Communist Party of the Soviet Union.[26] The draft program of the 24th Party Congress called for a dramatic rise in the number of engineers and other specialists produced in the USSR. In a 1971 *Literaturnaia gazeta* discussion, a journalist criticized a basic tenet of this draft program as being a good idea in theory but not in the actual conditions of the time: "The rise in the portion of engineers and technicians among the overall number of production sphere workers in other, different circumstances is in and of itself good, insofar as it enables the liquidation of the difference between mental and physical labor, serving as one of the basic indicators of the people's cultural level."[27] The fact of Soviet demographics in the 1970s was that the USSR had too many engineers with higher education and insufficient technicians and scientific workers with specialized secondary education. That Belkin did not openly mention this fact may have been a result of censorship. His meaning, however, would have been very clear to *Literaturnaia gazeta*'s readership. Unpublished letters from specialists to *Pravda* and other newspapers several years later revealed that specialists were indeed aware of the true circumstances. For example, two young specialists wrote to *Pravda* in 1976 to complain that the draft 25th Party Congress program once again failed to specify the precise number of specialists and technicians to be trained, noting that, in the lack of such specifics, the system produced too many engineers and specialists and not enough technicians.[28]

Golubenko's comments indicated that her beliefs coincided with the Party's position on the value of higher education, but her actual experience led her to implicitly question the manner in which young specialists were assigned employment. When her dispute with Ivan Vasilievich reached the district level, the principal was fired "for poor work with young specialists." Olga Ivanova's colleagues began to find fault with many of her actions, and she soon "understood with bitterness that they do not need me at this school." She left the school as well, officially to care for her sick mother.

At first glance, this episode would seem to be merely a direct case of individual criticism, Golubenko versus Ivan Vasilievich. But Olga Ivanova, when discussing the aftermath of her return home, noted, "Some of my classmates did not take assignments in accordance with the general distribution. They look on me now as if they are the victors . . . not without reason." While again a seemingly personal criticism, this passage implicitly damns the "distribution" system—the assignment of jobs to newly graduated specialists.[29] If this sanctioned job distribution was the vital tool and serious obligation that the official ideology made it out to be, how could some of her classmates escape such assignment? That they commonly did was universally known.[30] Why was it that Golubenko said that her "hands shook" when she accepted the assignment? The proximity of the description of "stories" about young specialists in rural areas to that of her feelings at her assignment acceptance was not accidental.

In this discussion, *Komsomolskaia pravda* highlighted the personal aspects of the criticism. Even the title "*They* Didn't Get Along" may have represented a conscious effort to keep the criticism at the individual level. But Golubenko managed to insert implicit systemic criticism, which was clearly apparent to the readers of the story.

Explicit criticism of the job distribution system, which specialists' evaded, was forthcoming from young specialists but did not appear in the press in a direct or open form. This irked at least some young specialists. For example, in 1978 the newspaper *Sotsiologicheskaia industriia* (SI) held a series of feedback meetings with readers. At one of them, a young engineer, L. Dorovskii, challenged the editorial staff: "SI sometimes sharply discussed the degradation of engineering work based upon concrete examples [of poor performance]. Now, during the Scientific-Technological Revolution, specialists are not being used as assigned. But there's little on this in the paper. You should sharply publicize this phenomenon so action can be taken at the state level."[31]

In other cases, the editing of the newspaper itself would create a mixed criticism by openly juxtaposing examples of individual and systemic criticism. For example, *Literaturnaia gazeta* repeatedly placed such criticisms under the rubric "The Letters Argue" in a 1972 discussion of the rights of scientific inventors.[32] One such juxtaposition featured a letter from candidate of technological sciences E. Kulaga, which placed blame for the dispute about who should receive credit for inventions on the principal antagonists in the discussion, both of whom Kulaga referred to as "individualists."[33] Candidate of techonological sciences A. Tsvetov's countering argument insisted that the root of the problem lay in the quantitative system of calculating and rewarding scientific prestige.[34] The young specialist (born in 1942) at the heart of the dispute, Viktor Andreevich Belov, also classified the problem as critical because of the fact that the practice of including administrators as coauthors of scientific work had "already gone into the system."[35]

In much the same manner as Golubenko, Belov directed most of his wrath against one person, the director of his laboratory, yet worked systemic criticism into his arguments as well. Belov, however, gained a great deal more support for his criticism of the scientific administration system than Golubenko earned for her job distribution question. In follow-up letters and commentary on the Belov discussion, the overwhelming majority of readers, journalists, and senior scientists who took part joined Belov in blasting aspects of the system. Particular criticism was levied at the manner in which persons making marginal contributions to scientific work or inventions were given equal credit as coauthors or coinventors.[36] Also subject to heavy criticism was the academic training system, which caused a lack of administrative and technical assistants and which therefore forced young specialists to engage in menial tasks.[37]

By the end of the Brezhnev era, young professionals were heavily engaged in open criticism of the systems underpinning Soviet society. In a letter appearing in *Pravda* on 11 November 1982 (ironically, the day Brezhnev's death was announced), L. Nevodchikova, a candidate of geologic and mineral sciences assigned to a geological institute with a petroleum exploration mission, described how her institute sent 15 people per day, six days each week , to work in a vegetable depot. The institute has done so for "not just one year." After describing the specifics of her grievance (essentially the use of skilled researchers for manual labor to compensate for poor productivity at the depot—a long-standing and widespread Soviet technique), Nevodchikova noted that when the depot was preparing for its annual review, it included in the display a point about increasing labor productivity by 3% in 1982. This achievement was prominently highlighted in an exhibit staged for regional Party leaders. Nevodchikova pondered what those leaders must have thought: "It is impossible that they didn't fall to thinking: what kind of production increase are they talking about when the collective from year to year cannot cope with the plan by means of its own resources, and it digs itself out with the help of ever more people from other organizations? Why has this become the system?"[38]

It is possible that she referred only to the system of relations between her institute and the depot. However, she followed this question with a general declaration of her understanding of the importance of the harvest and of the necessity for all citizens to struggle for its safety. Having thus paid tribute to the official ideology and established her place as a loyal citizen within the Soviet hierarchy, she fulfilled the traditional parameter of petitioning. However, she closed by invoking that same ideology to elevate her specific complaint to the universal level. She declared that the "means which we choose for its [the safety of the harvest] resolution must be well thought out, economical, and without reproach from the viewpoint of socialist legality."[39] Given the proximity of her question about the "system" and this final generalization, as well as the otherwise typical construction of her petition, Nevodchikova's questioning of the system marks a significant step toward the generalization of complaints, that is, a breaking of one of the "cardinal rules" of petitioning.

A final example from 1982 reinforces how far young specialists had come from the traditional paradigm of petitioning. N. Ivanova, a 34-year-old teacher from Moscow, complained of the incongruity between the official ideology toward children (the state had promoted studies that pronounced three children as the ideal size for the Soviet family) and the reality of conditions in the workplace when work schedules opposed organized day care or family schedules.[40] Ivanova concluded her letter with an appeal for mass support: "After all, life isn't possible without children. Not for men or for the state. Please print my letter. You will see how many women support me."

Ivanova's letter removes any doubt that the "gap between words and deeds" was a matter of everyday concern to young specialists by the end of the Brezhnev era. An awareness of the inefficiencies of the system and its failure to address issues of human concern, as highlighted by Professor Pokrovsky at the start of this chapter, overrode instances of agreement on philosophical issues between young specialists and the Party. Corrupt or incompetent individuals remained targets of criticism, as they always had within the traditional rules of petitioning, but by 1982, the system itself was targeted in the open press in an increasingly direct manner and with greater frequency.

Ivanova's appeal for mass support was directed toward getting the elite of Soviet society to live up to the norms specified by Soviet ideology. Questioning the actions of some members of the elite (in Ivanova's case, those individuals directly responsible for day-care policy) is not such a dramatic act, despite her paradigm-breaking appeal for mass support. But Nevodchikova stepped beyond such individually targeted action and questioned why a phenomenon that, in her view, violated those norms had "become the system." In so doing, she greatly expanded the target of her criticism. At least implicitly, Nevodchikova called into question the functioning of a much larger portion of the elite. That a frustrated young specialist would make such a comment is not surprising. That the comment appeared in *Pravda* itself is critical.

As the following archival documents demonstrate, young specialists had levied direct (and unpublished) criticisms concerning the country's economic performance, the medical system, and the regime's restriction of various types of information for years. Unpublished sources emphasized their desire for improvements to the system itself. They sought technical details and data to improve the system and emphasized the way the that system dealt with people as human beings.

Although such criticism was censored, it nevertheless was noted. Its volume and specificity generated pressure to which the regime eventually responded by allowing some limited public expression. Occasionally, in unpublished sources, systemic criticism was supported by facts and figures generated by the regime itself. In the discussion of the Draft Program of the 24th Party Congress in early 1971, *Komsomolskaia pravda* received letters from "many" readers who "not[ed] the high tempo of economic development and request[ed] to comment on reasons as to why a number of industrial branches are lagging behind." I. Sabolev wrote a very specific criticism that raised critical questions about the system, instead of about individual officials. He compared the directives of the 23rd Congress of 1966, which were to be completed by 1970, with GOSPLAN's report for 1971. He provided the statistics in Table 3.1.

Table 3.1
Comparison of Output Goals, 23rd Congress versus GOSPLAN Revisions

Type of Production	1966 Goal	1971 Plan
Coal (millions of tons)	665	633
Gas (billions of cubic meters)	225	211
Electric energy (billions of kwh)	830	790
Steel (millions of tons)	124	120
Trucks (thousands)	600	334

Sabolev simply stated, "I'd like to know the reasons for this lack of fulfillment of the XXIIIrd Congress' directives. Were the directives unbalanced or were the five critical branches working poorly?"[41]

Sabolev, like most letter writers, probably hoped that his letter would be published. Therefore, it is likely that he practiced self-censorship. This could explain why he limited himself to his straightforward question, and left other, equally obvious questions unstated: Why was GOSPLAN lowering the target outputs? Was this the first time? What action was being taken to prevent recurrence? But even without such questions, the data that Sabolev gleaned from Soviet sources would likely have "riled" people to an unacceptable level, prompting questions that the regime did not want to answer in public and therefore could not be published.

Some elements of the Soviet public were already "riled" as the nation prepared for the 24th Congress, and they were much less circumspect about their anger and frustration than was Sabolev. The editor of *Komsomolskaia Pravda* introduced a review of letters to the newspaper during the same pre-Congress period with the following comments to the Central Committee: "With their criticisms and proposals, our readers point out not only this or that perpetrator of evil, but also signal their stance in opposition to some tendencies in the staging of political-ideological work in collectives or on the pages of the press."[42]

In addition, readers sharply posed questions about the increase of Party and administrative responsibility of communists—or leaders—for their assigned site in work and proposed more strict punishment for violations of Party and government discipline. One youngster wrote of misuse of state property for private use—such use was especially prevalent among the working class—where local workers had failed to meet norms for eight years and asked why no leader was accountable.[43]

Given this type of feedback about readers' feelings based on information from Soviet sources, it's not surprising that the regime sought to control foreign sources of information. But young citizens, and especially young specialists, often sought data from or about foreign countries. Their requests for such information often caused great consternation among those faced with the requests. Frequently, those confronted with the requests were the regime's propagandists, those who conducted the political briefings and meetings that were the bane of every Soviet workplace. An especially fascinating set of archival sources records the reactions and questions that such requests generated among the propagandists themselves.

The journal *Agitator*, published by the Central Committee's propaganda department, was designed to provide material to the regime's most ardent advocates for use in preparing their presentations. As recorded in a remarkably insightful collection of documents, activists met with representatives of the editorial staff of the journal *Agitator* in a series of feedback sessions between February 1973 and April 1975. The journal sought feedback from its most avid readers about the effectiveness of the journal and suggestions concerning its content. A team of journal staff members traveled throughout the USSR to meet with activists. Despite the geographical and demographic diversity of the cities visited, demands for statistical analysis were uniform. Just as common and most critical for this study was the demand by the activists for increased information about "educating the young" and "making socialist competition more relevant to contemporary conditions."[44] The records of those meetings provide a glimpse at the "hidden transcript" of Soviet ideology.[45]

In political meetings and sessions with propagandists, Soviet citizens, by the mid-1970s, increasingly sought an objective appraisal of their country's economic performance compared to that of the West. More precisely, they demanded "facts and figures comparing their industries with parallel industrial branches in developed capitalist states" and "figures to unmask the vices of capitalist society which underlie the apparent face of the so-called free world."[46] Such was the request of 38 *Agitator* subscribers at a meeting with the editorial staff at the Krasnoiarsk Hydroelectric Station in October 1973. Those same subscribers based their request on their perception that the journal was not providing sufficient "examples, facts and expositions of the intrigues of bourgeois ideology" for use in the education of employees *"especially among the young, who demand such concrete information."*[47]

At other such feedback meetings, propagandists requested "supporting facts and figures" because, without such material, the journal "insufficiently addresses problems of working with youth." Repeatedly, that same group of subscribers requested "special materials to help them conduct work with the young . . . including publication of methodological elaboration to help teachers" deal with young workers and young specialists.[48] A third such meeting specifically sought information on "how to inject the young with love for their chosen profession" and "statistics that enlighten relative to the US-USSR economic competition."[49] In addition, that same group demanded that Soviet journals "regularly publish statistics on problems of Soviet wage structures by branch—compared to other socialist countries."[50]

Repeatedly, the propagandists insisted that they had to have access to such material in order to answer questions posed by young workers and specialists. But the young weren't just interested in information about foreign countries. They also sought increased information about Soviet domestic policies and productivity. For example, in 1976, a group of activists in Tiumen oblast' asked the journal's representatives to provide "more on internal CPSU policy, including figures and statistics on the Soviet way of life."[51] Other aspects of the Soviet "way of life" that were especially prevalent in discussions about dealing with young people were demands for more material on "moral-ethical issues" and issues of "atheist" education.[52]

Facts and figures about economic issues were not the only types of comparative information sought by Soviet citizens. Grigorii Syrkov, a propagandist from Karelia, wrote to *Agitator* in 1977 with a request for access to information about the Constitution of France. Syrkov had been asked by personnel at his workplace to compare the draft of the new Soviet Constitution to that of France. To him, the request seemed reasonable, given that the Soviet Union had "more or less normal relations" with France. This, therefore, made the French Constitution more appropriate for comparison than that of the United States, which, Syrkov said, "everyone looks at," thereby "giving help to those who are the implacable enemy of our country." Syrkov was frustrated and surprised when he could find only the constitution of socialist countries in his local library, but "nowhere [could he] find anything about the French constitution, or what kind of articles it has." Therefore, he turned to *Agitator* for the information and told his comrades at the editorial staff that "we'd be grateful for articles and help which you direct toward us agitators and propagandists." [53]

Agitator's reply reflected the extreme reluctance of Soviet authorities to release this seemingly innocuous information. "We will try, with time, to fulfill your request about a comparison of the Soviet constitution with those of some bourgeois states."[54] So Syrkov was deprived of the materials needed to make his own comparison, despite his status as a propagandist for the regime. The activists, for their part, in turn demanded of the journal (the Party) facts and figures to support their own beliefs in the strengths of the system. They noted that the "formation of communist morality" was a basic Party task but that *Agitator* rarely provided material to support such formation. Within this transcript, the young used the regime's own claims against it, demanding proof and demonstrating that they were aware of disparities between the world of ideology and the real world.

Taken together, this material provides fascinating insight into the interaction between the regime's most ardent supporters (the activists who read *Agitator)* and the Children of Victory.[55] In essence, the young specialists (and youth in general) were questioning the basic precepts of the official ideology, challenging the gap between words and deeds, and demanding that the activists provide more than just "artistic formulations" to support the regime's claims of the superiority of developed socialism.

"Artistic formulations" was the term used by the director of the political information section at the Krasnoiarsk Hydroelectric Station during the October 1973 feedback meeting with *Agitator* mentioned earlier. He specifically criticized the journal's column "Seminar on Active Agitation" as providing little more than words—"artistic formulations"—when the young specialists whom he faced on a daily basis demanded "examples, facts and concrete information."[56]

LINGUISTIC MARKERS AND VOICELESS EXPRESSION

The language used by young professionals in their letters to the press was often just as important as the targets of their criticism and commentary. Often, the level of specificity determined whether a letter would be published or not. Within the realm of published letters, as many of the following examples will demonstrate, the phrases that specialists used set them apart, as did their incorporation of official rhetoric and phrases into their messages.

In the letter from L. Nevodchikova, for example, several linguistic features make her letter remarkable and may help to explain why her letter was published in *Pravda* itself, while other young specialists' criticisms were relegated to the archives of unpublished letters. By projecting her own fundamental question, "Why has this become the system?" into the thoughts that the regional Party officials must have had when viewing the display, Nevodchikova employed a time-tested tactic of subordinate groups. She cloaked her question in the official discourse of the social contract by which the Party ruled. Within the context of that discourse, Party officials were entrusted with the objective, efficient, and scientific administration of Soviet society. Therefore, any reasonably responsible official would have to see the illogic and inefficiency of the vegetable depot's system of operation. By making an appeal that remained within the official discourse, Nevodchikova achieved several ends as a member of a subordinate element. She provided herself a route of ready retreat if any retribution for her letter proved forthcoming. After all, she could always say that she merely "guessed" what must have been in the regional leadership's thoughts on seeing the display. She managed to criticize an entire stratum of the elite leadership, not just a few individuals at the depot or institute. But she did so without openly challenging the principles by which the Party ruled the society.[57] Therefore, *Pravda*, organ of the Party, could logically assume the mantle of reliable overseer, using Nevodchikova's criticism to focus the attention or correct actions by Party officials.[58]

In their efforts to get the Soviet system to be more "humane" and more efficient, young professionals had to employ such indirect methods if they wanted their petitions to appear publicly. Because they expected the system to last a long time, it made sense to act within its parameters. Most young specialists believed that they had no direct voice in the shaping of the system of their society or the state,[59] so they frequently had to resort to the same type of indirect or "voiceless" expression that Nevodchikova employed. Projecting their thoughts onto "reasonable" officials represented one method of voiceless expression. Another was the incorporation of official rhetoric or slogans into their messages to serve their own cause.

A. Artisbashev, the young delicatessen manager encountered earlier, called his predicament into sharp relief by noting that a current recruiting slogan used by the Young Communist League to encourage enrollment in business management programs was "Youth—go into the services sphere." He noted this in the same context in which he described that "sometimes employees quit and go to work in the factory, to obtain housing, day care and other amenities which are not available in the services sphere."[60]

In a similar fashion, R. Metelnitsky, a young architect, called for increased creative freedom in designing structures, arguing that architects should be allowed to compete in designing new living quarters, and should be treated and paid like writers and other creative workers.[61]   He believed that chief architects should be able to select the architects working under them on their projects based upon professional evaluation of their ability. He summed up his argument with the Marxist dictum, "From each according to his ability, to each according to his work," thereby adopting a sacrosanct bit of rhetoric to advance his criticism of the extant system of employing architects.

Finally, V. Iudintseva, a young stenographer, wrote to *Pravda* in 1981 to protest bonuses and sliding wage scales, which were part of the same preferential treatment accorded to workers in the "production" sphere that Artsibashev decried earlier. Iudintseva insisted that wages be paid to "each according to his work."[62] While Iudintseva most likely held a specialized secondary education rather than a *vuz* diploma, her technique, age, and work in the "nonproduction" sphere put her in similar circumstances as those of most young specialists.

Several unpublished examples of young specialists' adoption of official slogans help demonstrate how letters and stories were selected for publication. Artsibashev could incorporate "Youth—Go into the Services Sphere" and appear in print because that slogan clearly embodied a legitimate, current goal of the regime. (That the slogan was very much in favor was emphasized by *Komsomolskaia pravda*'s series of investigative articles, of which Artsibashev's story was a part.) On the other hand, when a frustrated rural youth complained in 1971 to the journal *Sel'skaia zhizn'* about the lack of opportunity in rural areas and the exodus of young people to the cities, he concluded: "I'm trying to fulfill the slogan, 'Soviet youth must take initiative into its own hands.'" [63] That slogan, which appeared in *Sel'dkaia zhizn'*, was directed toward just such rural youth. It did not often appear in urban media.

An even more pointed (and therefore unpublished) example of a young specialist's asking the regime to live by its own rules and laws comes from a 1971 review of letters to *Komsomolskaia pravda* in the period before the 24th Congress: "We often read in the press how this or that person was severely punished, reprimanded, or warned ... but in Party and Komsomol charters, this kind of punishment does not exist. It follows therefore that they are illegal... but practically no one knows what is a crime, or how it is defined. Society is bearing an enormous moral hurt: the reality and stability of laws are being violated."[64]

This particular example offers another insight into the young specialists' ethos. Official political slogans and Party regulations were not the only aspects of the official discourse adopted by young specialists into their critiques. Just as common and more insightful in terms of personal beliefs were confident assertions of "principle" or "moral" concerns that distinguished the personal ethos of the young professionals from that of their parents.

PRINCIPLES, PRACTICALITY, AND GENERATIONS

The most striking points of the young specialists' personal ethos available in the *public* press transcript are their repeated emphasis upon "moral choice," "conscience," and "principle" in making decisions and their emphasis on "human" factors. This emphasis is particularly striking when contrasted with the emphasis on issues of personal security and collective interests that marked the public transcript of the specialists' parents. *Unpublished* archival sources indicate a different, though not contradictory, view. Letters from young specialists themselves and comments about young specialists by propagandists and others who worked with the young emphasize the overriding concern of young specialists for practicality and rationality. The young specialists were optimistic about their futures and confident in their abilities. They believed that they could, if given the opportunity and data to do so, solve society's problems and create a working, equitable social and economic system in the USSR. They wanted to build a system that worked and that did not neglect citizens as human beings. The public transcript often cites situations in which young specialists apparently stood upon moral and ethical issues. When they did so, it was frequently a position that they took to protest against some arbitrary or irrational aspect of the Soviet system, often an aspect that violated their sense of human dignity. The primary public emphasis was on moral principle, while the unpublished emphasis was on practical achievement. Why, then, did the regime, through instruments such as the "Moral Choice" column in *Literaturnaia gazeta* and that paper's definition of "realism" discussed earlier, insist on portraying young specialists as fixated on moral principles and their parents as obsessed with practical concerns and individual security? Why were the public images of the two generations almost diametrically opposed to the images revealed by the archival sources? Was either image accurate, or was the truth somewhere in between? Formerly classified KGB documents may provide some answers to these questions.

Formerly classified KGB reports about young people and their viewpoints provide important potential insight into this distinction and shed some light on one possible relationship between the published and unpublished sources. Those same reports also provide insight into the regime's perspective on the young specialists and the role that the Party and state played in the selection of issues and petitions for public airing.

Just as interesting are the unpublished commentaries of the specialists' parents. The available archival documents indicate that at least some of the parents' generation recognized that the patriotism and optimism of the young were being neglected or even abused, with both moral and practical implications. Published accounts, on the other hand, tended to criticize the stands that young specialists took against elements of the system, particularly when the specialists' positions compromised their parents' view of realism or personal security.

Literaturnaia gazeta itself injected the notion of "moral choice" into the public discourse by adapting this phrase as a rubric for a number of discussions that appeared throughout the 1970s. This, no doubt, contributed to its popularity among young specialists.   Obviously, the existence and durability of this column also indicate the level of acceptability (perhaps even some sort of sponsorship) that selected issues of "moral choice" held for the regime.

In his criticism of Soviet business practices, A. Artsibashev declared himself to be disgusted with the "connections" necessary to "insure the life and activity of his trade enterprise."[65]   Business practices were so contrary to Artsibashev's perception of what was right and proper that he declared, "You even have to consider: if you want to act according to your conscience (*postupat' po sovesti*), you have to close the store." Such clear and pronounced emphasis on the importance of conscience is common among many criticisms rendered by the young specialists, as additional examples demonstrate later.

But before moving on, another aspect of Artsibashev's critique must be examined.   Artsibashev, like Nevodchikova, found a way to hedge his condemnation of the system. He recognized that some readers would want to know, "Who demands sweets? Who asks for fur coats and crystal?" Artsibashev asserts, "I could name names, but sometimes it's hard to decide what comes within legal norms and what borders on the criminal code." Here, Artsibashev provides himself an avenue of escape in case of retribution, and at the same time he avoids naming only certain elite individuals. But this partial dissemblance does not indicate that Artsibashev is trying to back off from his criticism. His very next statement is, "I don't want to keep silent. The atmosphere in some organizations of trade in our city is intolerable. It gives rise to nepotism and lends itself to abuse."

In these few sentences, Artsibashev reveals some key characteristics of the personal ethos of the specialists. He asserts that he wants to act in accordance with his academic training and his personal beliefs in what is right. He condemns not just individuals but the system itself. He used terms that emphasize his dignity as a human being (such as "disgust" and "conscience"), and he is self-confident enough to come forward and propose change.[66]

Or, possibly, that is how the regime wanted Artsibashev to appear. He was, after all, selected as the subject of *Komsomolskaia pravda* because he had been fired from his job. These may, in fact, have been his genuine feelings on the subject. A look at other published and unpublished sources on similar issues reveals more perspective on this potential relationship.

Acting according to conscience cost another young specialist his job. Even so, it was not he but his mother who wrote to *Literaturnaia gazeta* to tell the story. This fascinating discussion demonstrates the striking differences in perspective of this young engineer and his mother, between his generation and hers.

B. Mukhina, a librarian from Novosibirsk, wrote to *Literaturnaia gazeta* in March 1982 to explain why her 28-year-old son had lost his job as a senior engineer.   She wrote not to seek her son's reinstatement but to criticize the newspaper itself for encouraging him to make "moral" choices instead of practical ones.[67] Her opening sentence betrayed her stance. When describing her son's dismissal, she noted that "formally, they did it because of three absences. But in reality it was because he, the little fool, believes too much in order and nobility."

Mukhina's son, a 1979 *vuz* graduate, was working as a senior engineer. One of his responsibilities was to nominate workers for a special bonus "for assistance with an invention." The established practice at the factory, prior to his promotion to senior engineer, was that the factory administration "prompted" his predecessor as to who should be nominated, even if they had nothing to do with any inventions. Normally, the factory administration used the invention bonus fund to reward good workers, for whom bonuses would not otherwise be available.

When Mukhina's son (his name was never given) approached his supervisor, the chief engineer of the factory, and told him that in the future he would nominate only those workers "who earned" consideration as opposed to "those required" by the administration, his boss was sympathetic. But the chief engineer warned him to "stop asking for trouble, we are with you in other important areas." Nevertheless, Mukhin did not nominate workers who had not contributed to inventions. Shortly thereafter, he was fired for unexcused absences from work. His mother portrayed these absences as not unusual or unexcused in the normal sense and said that the administration took note of them only because it wanted to fire her son.

B. Mukhina then describes how "all my son's friends are shocked at this injustice of the factory administration and are trying to persuade the lad to take it to court." Given that most young specialists socialized with friends who worked with them,[68] it is likely that some or most of Mukhin's shocked friends were also young specialists. B. Mukhina said that her son's comrades regarded him warmly, as one who "acts responsibly toward his work. They say that he acts 'not for fear, but for conscience' (*ne za strakh, a za sovest*) and that all of this must be very pleasing to me, his mother." She added: "It really is pleasing to me that my boy is an honest man." But then she betrayed her perspective when she added: "But why does to live 'for conscience' necessarily mean to live 'not for fear?' I never taught him anything like this idea to live without fear. I didn't want to, and could not have [taught him this way]. Not for fear? What foolishness!"

B. Mukhina went on to place the blame for her son's foolishness squarely on *Literaturnaia gazeta*:

Newspapers, and in particular your *"LG"* demand of their readers to ask for trouble at any time, not protecting their own life, to struggle for "the interests of the cause," to come forward "irrespective of persons." Do you know that such articles appear as an "egging on" to inexperienced young people like my son? What advantage comes from these "heroic individuals" like my son?. . . Is it so moral to urge them on to these conflicts?

Early on in her letter, B. Mukhina had declared that her main concern in the entire situation was not wondering whether or not her son would be rehired but wondering "how will my son go on living now?" His actions were completely foreign to her, even if she did admire some of his ideas. The contrast in the values of mother and son are vivid and instructional in terms of comparing their respective generations. Several phrases highlight their strikingly different perspectives.

For B. Mukhina, the most damaging idea that her son and his friends learned from *Literaturnaia gazeta* was the notion "to ask for trouble at any time, not protecting their own life" (*Lezt na rozhon, ne shchadia zhivota svoego*). Directly related to the concept of "asking for trouble" was that of acting "not for fear, but for conscience." It was this notion that Mukhina classified as "foolishness."

Indeed, the very concept of considering the organization of one's life for an ideal, that is, for "principle" or "conscience," marked a definitive distinction between the ethos of the young specialists and that of their parents by the 1970s. The Children of Victory had never known the deprivation of war or famine, the uncertainty and terror of collectivization, purges, or Stalinist terror. But their parents had, either as children or young adults, and the different experiences shaped the gradual evolution of different value systems in the two generations.

"My parents' generation, they're the real lost generation. They gave in to everything," said one young man to Georgie Anne Geyer in 1971.[69]   When Geyer concluded five years of research on Soviet young people in 1975, she summarized her observations with, "To the older generation, economic security was more important than anything . . . because it had known such misery in impoverishment." But to the younger generation, she noted that man was gradually being seen as " a value in himself," and Russia of the mid-1970s was beginning to see the gradual reassertion of "the values of individualism, of questioning. . . of the ethical personality, of human relations."[70]   B. Mukhina's son certainly seems to fit Geyer's image of the young, well-educated, human-focused Soviet citizen, with the value that he placed on "conscience," "questioning," and "the ethical personality."

It would be an oversimplification to say that B. Mukhina, or the other parents of young specialists, could not fathom or understand the difference in perspective between their respective generations in the 1970s. Geyer was certainly correct in her conclusion that "economic security" was vital to the older generation because of their life experiences. But we know more about those experiences now than Geyer could have known in the early 1970s. B. Mukhina and others of her generation were indeed shaped by the poverty, suffering, and terror of Stalinism and war. But by the 1970s, they had been shaped by life under Khrushchev and Brezhnev as well.

B. Mukhina and her contemporaries grew up in the 1920s and 1930s. In her recent study *Everyday Stalinism*, Sheila Fitzpatrick concluded that Stalin's regime was not without support from its citizens. Further, she noted:

Less inclined than their elders to react to economic hardship, urban youth, or at least an impressive proportion of that group, as well as many young peasants with some schooling, seem to have assimilated Soviet values, associating them with a rejection of all that was boring, corrupt, unprincipled, old, and routine, and identified, often passionately and enthusiastically, with Soviet ideals.   They were ready to go adventuring in the Soviet cause.[71]

In other words, many of B. Mukhina's peers, the parents of the young specialists of the Brezhnev years, had once been true believers, willing to accept economic difficulty in exchange for the bright shining Soviet future. They were no less committed to revolutionary ideals in their youth than the public image of their own children would be to moral or humanistic ideals. But by the time of their maturity in the 1970s, economic security became paramount, and their children's commitment to ideals became anathema. By the 1970s, B. Mukhina could not accept her son's willingness to act for a "cause" itself without regard to the impact of that action on officials or persons. This is what made her son a "heroic individual." Mukhina's strong opposition to her son's course was certainly shaped by the betrayal of her own revolutionary ideals by the cold, hard facts of life under the Little Deal. But her feelings were likely also strengthened by the nature of his actions themselves. Action as an individual was something that B. Mukhina's generation had been taught was wrong. Rather, their emphasis had always been on the *collective* interest.[72] A brief example of such action by another young specialist will show that this kind of action (and her type of response) was not limited to B. Mukhina's son alone.

Ella Kirova was born in 1945 and graduated from a language institute in 1966. In 1982, she had an affair with a married man, became pregnant, and made the conscious choice to bear and raise her child herself. The reactions to her decision by her peers and the reactions of her mother and her mother's generation were dramatically different and were illustrative of the individual versus collective mind-set held by the two generations:[73] "People of my own age are becoming slightly more modern in their outlook. In the office . . . where I worked, the women of my own age when I told them of my intention, without exception were understanding and did not withdraw their friendship. But with some of those who were older, it was not so."

In keeping with the attitudes of her older colleagues from work, Kirova's mother epitomized the reaction of the older generation.

For my mother, it was much more difficult. In our country it is frowned upon that a woman who is not married should have a baby. Why should anyone do such an extraordinary thing, when it is so simple to have an abortion and no one thinks less of you that you should do so? But to be so obstinate and stubborn that you go ahead and have a baby, especially when you are not married—well, this is a very bad thing to do. It is against convention, and you are behaving in such a way it is almost as if you are trying to be insulting to everyone. This is almost entirely the attitude of all people of the older generation like my mother.

B. Mukhina and the mother of Ella Kirova were unanimous in their reaction to the decisions of their children to act as individuals, according to their own definition of human or moral principles. They rejected their child's decision to act contrary to the collective spirit held sacred by the mothers' generation. Ella Kirova is no less a "heroic individual" for her decision than B. Mukhina's son was for his. But perhaps mothers are not the most objective evaluators of their own children. So another example that does not include family ties may be more instructive.

When Viktor Andreevich Belov, the young specialist at the heart of the debate on scientific coauthorship described earlier, declared his refusal to include his lab director, he emphasized, "In general, this is a violation of the elementary norms of scientific ethics. . . . I refuse to do this even out of principle. I refuse, do you hear?"[74]

The lab director, in his turn, fell back upon his generation's cherished ideal of the *collective good*. Comparing scientific research to an assembly line, Vladimir Mikhailovich Kozhin noted that, in modern science, discoveries were truly cooperative efforts, with many individuals making contributions to the final result. "If Belov were to work by himself alone, he would not only disrupt all of our deadlines, but would ruin the institute. I'm not disputing that he could accomplish [the work] by himself, but at what a cost!"[75]

B. Mukhina, Kirova's mother, and lab director Kozhin were all consistent in their adherence to the notion of the collective good, and all were of about the same age. But three examples are not sufficient justification to condemn the parents of the Children of Victory as "the lost generation," in the words of Geyer's young subject. Therefore, this study now returns to the follow-up discussion of Mukhin's choice to seek answers to the following questions: How was this young specialist perceived by his countrymen at the same time? How did his peers and those of his parents look on this young man and his decisions to act "not for fear, but for conscience?" Interestingly, *Literaturnaia gazeta* did not include editorial commentary with B. Mukhina's letter, other than to state, "Reserving the right to comment on this letter later, we turn it over to the judgment of our readers."[76]

Not until December 1982 did *Literaturnaia gazeta* publish the second installment in this discussion. In that follow-up discussion, *Literaturnaia gazeta* noted that reader mail had held widely divergent views on the issue. Some had supported the mother; some, the son.[77] Those letters who supported the son generally came from authors who were cynical about the motives of the factory administration in awarding the bonuses. Those who supported B. Mukhina tended to focus on what constituted "realistic" behavior for both the administration and the engineer himself. [78]

At this point the editorial staff (and hence the censor/regime) took an active role in shaping the discussion and focused on the issue of what behavior was "realistic" in this situation. *Literaturnaia gazeta*'s editorial staff combined a letter from a medical inspector with a case study that *Literaturnaia gazeta* used to define modern "realists." The medical inspector sarcastically noted that everything was possible for a director "with balanced accounts" and that such a director could continue production even if it hurt the public health. His point was that a factory director could choose to use the "invention" fund as an incentive for others, not out of some malice but because of the "imperfection of the awards system." If that director's plant had "balanced accounts," no one would question his decision.

Rather than endorse this de facto policy of "the ends justifies the means," *Literaturnaia gazeta*'s case study instead lauded the joint effort of a creative director and health inspector who maintained production at an obsolete factory while preparing a new, pollution-free production facility. *Literaturnaia gazeta* called "these people, [who] manage to properly evaluate objective circumstances, and when necessary, overcome them," the new realists. *Literaturnaia gazeta* noted that in overcoming such "objective circumstances," they act "not in a cavalier attack, with spears lowered, not carried away in some romantic fashion—this achieves little—but competently and in a qualified way." *Literaturnaia gazeta* concluded this first section with its definition of the "modern realist." It stated that in order to be a genuine realist, one must be a realist "in both thought and action."

Literaturnaia gazeta followed this by contradicting a reader's view that one should act to change things only when sure of winning, via a historical example of one who successfully took action despite long odds (the story of a botanist who successfully struggled to overcome obstacles to his research in the Stalin years, becoming a Lenin Prize laureate and academician). Clearly, *Literaturnaia gazeta* was enthusiastic about its role in spurring people to action. But this commentary was followed by the caveat: "If a newspaper article is read only as a call to official conflict, that means that this article is written incorrectly or in vain . . . . But the paper usually puts before itself quite another task: to think, along with readers, about how, in what way, should we defend and stand up for our principled work positions."

Literaturnaia gazeta in this case sounded as if it wanted to have it both ways—to be free to incite people to action on principle, yet to caution them to take only feasible action. In this way, the paper combined the idealistic, "for conscience" public image of the young specialists with the "defense of one's own life" image of their parents.

Clearly, the regime wanted to encourage young specialists to seek the kind of low-level innovations and improvements implemented by the health inspector and the director. Such individual initiative at the lowest levels would comply with the parameters of the "Little Deal," fostering economic improvements while avoiding "cavalier attack, with spears lowered," which might pose political challenges to the regime. But why did the regime choose to emphasize in public these two particular images, the parents' practicality in contrast to the commitment to moral principle on the part of the young specialists? Generational conflict certainly existed, but contemporary interviews and archival documents indicate that it did so at a different level from the one portrayed in public.

Some members of the parents' generation had come to believe, by the middle of the Brezhnev era, that: "Our children want everything right away! . . . It took us years to get our own apartments. Why should they be in such a hurry?"[79] Others felt: "The older generation thinks it fought the war and rebuilt the country, the younger ones want everything and then don't appreciate it when they're given things."[80] G. I. Ulianovskaia, a propagandist from Odessa, did not see the young specialists whom she lectured as preoccupied with moral principles. As she complained to *Agitator,* quite the opposite was true: "A very acute problem arises whenever an older person works with the young. Whenever we begin a conversation, they want facts, figures and examples. . . . That means that the politinformator [propagandist] must gather such materials! But where can you get this information?" Ulianovskaia's letter also made it clear that she was uncomfortable with the notion of having to gather such information. In her view, "it seems we need to impart to the younger generation a deeper sense of love for their motherland."[81] If this was done, she implies, the young would be less demanding of specific facts and examples. E.S. Iakhonin, a propagandist from Tashkent echoed her concerns, and her image of the young specialists as preoccupied with statistics, not principles. He lamented that he found himself faced by "a new kind of young people [for whom], new material is needed each and every day."[82]

Other archival documents reveal that some members of the parents' generation recognized that the young specialists' fixation on facts and figures grew from shortcomings in the fulfillment of precisely the kind of moral principles that the regime so desperately wanted Soviet youth to follow. "Comrade Karpov" in Fergana, a "Communist since 1953" and therefore likely a member of the parents' generation, wrote to *Komsomolskaia pravda* on the eve of the 24th Congress:

The question of our young must be discussed, first and foremost the question of their upbringing. We have never taken much notice of this question, but today it must stand in first place. Our enemies are undertaking efforts to turn the ears of Soviet youth, using our slightest mistakes and blunders—to which we ourselves have not attached much significance or have not wanted to note. But oh, how these mistakes inflict harm on the hearts of our young people.[83]

In describing such "mistakes and blunders," Karpov noted the growing annual dissatisfaction of groups of young students over harvesting cotton in Uzbek fields. He emphasized that this annual rite "negatively affects both their academic progress and their mood." He noted that in the past year (1970) the groups in the fields decided not to celebrate the October Revolution during the harvest. He then criticized the Komsomol as too passive, used by the young only as a tool to get ahead, and proposed a review of the practice of sending youth to the fields "when farmers themselves are not inclined to such work." Karpov closed his letter by insisting that the 24th Congress address the problems of youth and their moods. His letter was followed by a note from the editor to the Central Committee: "It seems to me that many simply cannot believe that our Soviet leaders remain indifferent to this problem, that our youth have never really been recognized for going to the fields to help out in difficulties. We must not abuse their patriotism; they will not forgive us for this."[84]

The editor then summarized the content of the remaining letters. "Many of the letters speculate about the roles of youth in the economy and the efforts to improve or correct the poor living and working conditions of young people. Many letters complain about Komsomol activity, either complaining about the lack of genuine activity or raising issues of conflict—these letters contain thoughts, and sometimes the pain, of defeat."[85]

The archival documents clearly show the type of feedback that the regime was receiving from its citizens. Young specialists were preoccupied with data, facts, and statistics about economic performance. Many in their parents' generation, including officials such as the newspaper editor, recognized that the young were being disillusioned and demoralized by the daily facts of life. Police reports represent a unique form of historical source, the background of which must be briefly considered.   In her 1994 work on the peasants of the 1930s Sheila Fitzpatrick discussed police reports as "wonderful" sources but cautioned that they have their own "built-in bias." Secret policemen, after all, especially in the Stalin years, were paid to "dig up dirt." Therefore, they tend to emphasize problems and the reasons for those problems.[86] Likewise, reports to secret police agencies from informers tend to emphasize problems and their causes. Taken together, these types of police documents represent an especially valuable source of insight into the difference between the public and unpublished images of the young specialists and their parents.

In November 1968, KGB chairman Iurii Andropov presented a "secret" document to the Central Committee that came from a young informer in Odessa. Andropov informed the CC that the document "deserves attention inasmuch as many of its positions correspond with opinions in other sources of ours."[87] The informer was a *vuz* student who associated with young members of the creative intelligentsia (artists, poets, painters, etc.). His report is a very detailed analysis of the evolution of the worldview of *vuz* students, with significant commentary on young specialists as well.

In brief, the informer describes the evolution of the new *vuz* student from a compliance with the institution's rules in the first year, through disillusionment and frustration as a fourth-year student and initially as a young specialist. He says that first-year students "develop a sense of themselves as a social group" when they make their first trip to the villages to help out with the harvest. For most, he said, this group awareness coalesces around the question, "Why should we help them?"[88] The other major discovery that first-year students make is that the study of Marxism-Leninism, which all first-year students must take, "is not really a subject." He considers all students as "very susceptible to Western propaganda, because the 'free world' seems to them a place of general prosperity." In his view, all students try to join the Komsomol if not already members, so that they can advance their own career potential, and many consider joining the Party in order to conform.[89]

Most importantly, from the perspective of this study, is the transition to the social category of young specialist upon graduation. Here, the informant reported, is when "further psychological development occurs."

"A genuine collision with the production sphere undermines in a great many the belief in the working class as the vanguard of the construction of communism. The disorganization of labor and poor planning lead to the opinion that everything in our industry is chaos." Engineers therefore want to work in science where there is more order. "The widespread opinion of the factory is that it is a place where you get disqualified as a specialist."[90]

In summary, this informer saw the young specialists of the late 1960s as disillusioned about the regime's ideology because of what they saw in the everyday working of the system. Such an assessment is consistent with their fixation on data, facts, and figures in trying to develop improvements to that system, as described earlier. The attention that they paid to the West was because of its apparent prosperity, not necessarily for its ideology. Most importantly, they saw the system's treatment of the human element as a critical systemic flaw, as did Professor Pokrovsky. Two of the other specialists interviewed in Moscow in 1995 told stories that were remarkably consistent with this assessment.

Born in 1946, Sergei Tumanov was not a stereotypical young professional. Initially, he did not obtain higher education but finished instead a machine-building technicum and took a job in a factory. He soon came to question his vocational choice: "When I began work in the factory, things did not work out well. At first I thought this was because the workers were bad people, who did not know how to work. Therefore, in order to find out a method for understanding why they did not work well, it was necessary to understand their psychology."[91]

This was in 1967, and the young Tumanov decided to enroll in the philosophy faculty at Moscow State University. However, he was unable to successfully complete the rigorous entry exam and returned to work in the factory. The same situation occurred in 1968, and Tumanov continued working. Finally, in 1969, Sergei passed the entrance exams and entered the philosophy faculty at Moscow State, from which he graduated in 1974. "By then (1969) I understood that the problem wasn't with the people, it was the conditions in which they worked. It was with this sense that I began to study sociology. At that time, sociology was a specialty within the philosophy faculty."[92]

Tumanov was not alone in making a dramatic change of focus within his own life. Alexander Nikolaevich Kurin also began his career with a technical orientation. However, he worked in the technical world for an extended period before changing his emphasis.

Born in 1945, Kurin graduated from the Moscow Energy Institute in 1969 as a radio-physicist. He was immediately called to serve two years as a lieutenant in the Soviet army. When his service ended, he began work in a factory that manufactured electronic equipment, where he worked until 1978. "I had great optimism at the time I left the army. Once I went to work in the factory and saw how terribly the system worked I lost some of my optimism. . . . The directors were just as much drunkards as the senior officers in the army. The conditions in the factory helped inspire my interest in psychology. . . . I became pessimistic about the system of the Party and the administration."[93] Kurin returned to school and earned his candidate's degree in psychology.

By the mid-1970s, the official KGB assessment of students and young specialists recognized that they had become even more alienated from the system than portrayed by the Odessa informer at the end of the 1960s. In contrast to his report that the young specialists were dissatisfied due to the system's shortcomings and its failure to satisfy the human element, the KGB officers who prepared the report found dramatically different causes for that alienation.

Entitled "Analysis of the Characteristics and Reasons for Negative Phenomena among Pupils and Student Youth," the December 1976 KGB report immediately staked its position. Its opening sentence noted, "Soviet youth is considered by the enemy as one of the most important objects of ideological diversion."[94] To prove its point, the study listed the numbers of Western radio programs available to students and "young intelligentsia" each day. This exposure to Western propaganda undermined the young people's sense of commitment to Soviet values. This lack of commitment was manifested in the fact that students viewed Komosomol activity as nothing more than "careerism" and therefore refused to participate.[95] In short, students and young specialists were disillusioned not because of the internal failures of the Soviet system but due to Western subversion and their own lack of dedication to Soviet moral principles.

These KGB documents help illuminate the complicated relationship between the public and private images or transcripts of the young specialists. As noted earlier, the public image of the young specialists emphasized their fixation on moral principles, often protection of themselves or others from corrupt individuals within the system (e.g., Golubenko's insensitive school director, the factory administrators who fired Mukhina's son). The image put forth by unpublished sources emphasized their desire for improvements to the system itself. They sought technical details and data to improve the system and emphasized the way that the system dealt with people as human beings.

The public image of their parents, on the other hand, emphasized self-protection and the collective good. The parents' public image condemned commitment to "principles" as impractical and to individualism as counterproductive (Belov's factory director and those who agreed with him). The unpublished material available on the parents' view, however, indicates that some of the parents recognized the system's abuse of the young specialists' patriotism and optimism as the repetition of their own experience.

The official KGB position, that external factors were the problem, explains some aspects of the differences in public and private images. The regime recognized that the young were alienated but could not admit the systemic problems. In keeping with the Little Deal, it encouraged young specialists to fight corruption and pursue local initiative, consistent with Soviet principles. Those same Soviet principles had to be emphasized to counter Western subversion. By using the public "voice" of the parents, the regime could reiterate the importance that it placed on the potential rewards to those who focused on the microlevel, rather than any systemic or political challenges.

It is also possible that, by emphasizing in public cases where young specialists acted on moral principles, the regime may have sought to soften the harsh perception that their parents' generation had of the young as materialistic and impatient. As discussed, in their youth, the parents of the Children of Victory had responded to the ideological siren song of the revolution. Perhaps, by portraying their children as heroic moral actors, the regime sought to generate sympathy for the children and foster cooperation and understanding between the generations.

Another "voice" appeared in the public transcripts to reinforce the regime's efforts to influence the focus of young specialists. When their reliance upon principle, conscience, and individual action was the subject of press commentary, quite frequently the young professionals gained support from an unexpected quarter: successful members of their grandparents' generation.

In the initial installment of discussion of Belov's complaint about his laboratory director's demands for coauthor status, the senior director of the institute that controlled the laboratory (his name was not given) and a member of the Soviet Academy of Sciences, A. Ianshchin, each sided with Belov, taking stances in opposition to the laboratory director. Academician Ianshchin termed the situation "intolerable," even using an identical expression as did young Belov, declaring, "Science must be done with clean hands." Like Belov, Ianshchin condemned the coauthorship practice as "having nothing in common with the traditions of Soviet science."[96]

The director of the institute likewise agreed with Belov's position—to a degree. When asked specifically if he would have insisted upon coauthorship if he had been in Kozhin's (the lab director) position, this elderly director stated: "I would not have insisted upon co-authorship, as Kozhin did. But maybe my outlook is outdated."[97]

Academician Ianshchin had no such qualms about his outlook. He strongly criticized the institute director for "closing his eyes to the fact that Kozhin is unprincipled. I am amazed at the stance taken by the director."

Other senior scholars also sided with Belov. In two detailed letters and six excerpts published in the initial installment, seven of the authors agreed with Belov, with varying levels of emphasis on scientific ethics and tradition. Surprisingly, many of these senior scholars blamed the system of calculating scientific prestige as a key factor in inspiring research administrators and directors to insist on coauthorship rights. The most junior of the seven was a candidate of science, but the majority were doctors of science, professors, or academicians.[98] Only one respondent, E. Kulaga, supported Kozhin. Like Kozhin, Kulaga was a laboratory director. Like Kozhin, Kulaga emphasized the "collective" nature of modern science.

In the remaining discussion of the coauthorship issue, the published responses overwhelmingly supported Belov's position. Nearly all the articles and letters published were from senior scholars who emphasized scientific ethics and tradition as paramount. In addition, the more senior the rank of the respondent, the more likely he (no women's responses were printed) was to criticize aspects of the academic or scientific systems as well. Some criticized the training of specialists in the *vuz*, some the process by which administrative personnel were selected, and others, like Ianshchin, the system of rewarding scientific achievement.[99]

Well-trained young specialists, confident in themselves and optimistic about their future, found common ground in the public transcript with successful members of their grandparents' generation. Emphasis on principles and ethics, action by "heroic individuals" "for conscience" and "out of principle" distinguished the young professionals from their parents, who were more likely to act for the "good of the collective" or "in defense of one's own life." In contrast to the unpublished emphasis on systemic failures, the public transcript sought to reemphasize principles consistent with official Soviet positions (e.g. "science must be done with clean hands") and to reinforce the microlevel focus of the Little Deal. Each of the preceeding examples centered upon issues that developed in the working lives of the young professionals yet provided insight into their beliefs as private persons as well. This study now turns to focus upon their aspirations, leisure time, and family lives, in the hope that additional insight into those private beliefs will develop.

ASPIRATIONS

In early 1978, *Literaturnaia gazeta* published a survey asking readers to speculate on the type of person the man of the future would be.[100] *Literaturnaia gazeta* asked five questions that were specifically directed to the parents or prospective parents of young children. Those questions were as follows: How would you like to see your child? (What kind of mannerisms would you like him to have, what kind of activity would you like him to engage in, what kind of moral qualities would you like him to have?) Do you think he will have one profession or several? How do you think he or she will spend free time? What do you want most of all for him? (From the viewpoint of material wealth, living conditions, spiritual necessities?) What do you not want most of all for your child? (Character traits, moral qualities, life situations). What, and via what means, do you think he should achieve in life?

Young specialists' answers to these questions provide direct insight into many aspects of their ethos. One specialist, historian N. Ashmarin (born 1947), stated his own realization of this potential insight: "My answers to the survey are not his [my son's] mirror, not his horoscope or his choice, but this [the survey] is our mirror. A child, after all, almost always is the chance for parents to realize things they did not achieve on their own."[101] Equally valuable for this study is the fact that the young professionals' responses were published side by side with those of specialists from other generations, providing a unique opportunity for comparison.

The questionnaire itself was inspired by a letter from A. Popov, who described himself as "not only an old reader of *Literaturnaia gazeta*, but also, simply, an old man."[102] Popov included in his letter his reminiscences of conversations that he had in the 1920s, when, as a young man, he and his peers celebrated Russia's "new, harmonious society, in which there would be no oppression of one individual by another . . . no humiliation of human dignity." In those conversations, he and his friends had argued about the nature of the man of the future, the "man of communist society." Popov noted that "of course, [in hindsight] some of this, as it appeared then, may today seem naive." Whereas in the 1920s people had speculated that the man of the future would have multiple careers, interests, and talents, "now, when the professionalization and specialization of activity are becoming more profound, the dream of a person freely changing professions at a stretch in his life is clearly utopian."

Popov's concept of a person's having multiple careers and talents may have seemed "utopian" to him by the 1970s, but at least some of the young specialists who participated revealed a similar reverence for the idea of a multitalented "Renaissance" man. Historian N. Ashmarin declared, "I would like my son educated in such a way that he, according to his wishes and enthusiasms, could peacefully change his line of work."[103] Ashmarin envisioned a mixture of work and leisure time that also had a Renaissance cast:

I'd like to see him become an architect. For some reason I believe that the sad standardization in architecture will end in his time, and each building will be unique . . . . To the point, architecture, in my opinion, reunites both the humanities and the exact sciences. . . I would very much like for my son to be able to do much with his own hands. For his leisure, very likely some kind of physical work—an invention and the embodiment of the invention in some sort of material, such as work with wood, with a chisel.

Ashmarin rounded out his vision of his son as a Renaissance man by hoping that his son's education would include "more humanities—a knowledge of languages would be good. If he could master either Latin or Chinese or Japanese; then he could read and select good books. I will try to teach him this." But, for Ashmarin, intellectual strength and versatility alone would not be enough. He hoped that his son would develop physical strength and agility as well as his intellect. To this end, Ashmarin sought to involve his son in gymnastics, swimming (or preferably, diving), or slalom skiing, not figure skating (which, Ashmarin declared "annoys me") or hockey ("too rough and dangerous"). "Perhaps tennis will be good for him—it will give him an understanding of the beauty of sport and greater workouts."[104]

Both the old Popov and young professional Ashmarin shared certain beliefs on the image of the man of the future, demonstrating again that the young specialists shared values with their grandparents' generation. That consistency of interest and the contrast between the ethos of the young specialists and that of their parents were especially well demonstrated in the survey responses that *Literaturnaia Gazeta* published on 1 February and 12 April 1978.

Alexei Matiushkin, a 70-year-old cinematographer (born 1908), hoped that the man of the future would "pursue a life goal by studying, studying, studying" and yet would still have "free time for language and exercise."[105] Matiushkin also believed that the child should be raised "entirely by society," which placed him in contrast to Ashmarin, who envisioned teaching his son many things by himself. But Matiushkin's reliance upon society (which in itself may be a marker of his and Popov's generation) was inspired by his belief that many modern families raised spoiled, "lily-fingered children with the psychology of individualists, consumers, bribe-takers, thieves, drunkards and libertines." While much less extreme, a similar reaction against the notion of future persons as individualists and consumers was expressed by a married couple, both young professionals.

Iurii Mumrikov and his wife, Galina Mumrikova, noted that many parents went to great lengths and considerable expense "so that their children have it as good as (or better than) others," thereby contributing to the mind-set that so repelled Matiushkin. But the Mumrikov's believed that "what is most important is that they [the Mumrikovs' children] are growing up in a family where they learn mutual respect, concern, affection and responsibility."[106]   Like Ashmarin, the Mumrikovs believed that they, as parents, must play a direct and personal role in the education of their children.

Interestingly, the only reply that even mentioned the ideologues of Soviet socialism came from P. Simonov, a doctor of medicine who was a member of the "parents'" generation, the same generation as the laboratory director Kozhin in the coauthorship example. Simonov's primary aspiration for his children was that they "serve people, and not live in vain."[107] In his opening paragraph, Simonov declared that he based his answers to the survey "upon the ideals of Lenin, Marx, Tolstoy, Dostoevski, Dzerzhinski and the educator Sukhomlinski."[108]

In fairness, it must be noted that Simonov did allude to "conscience" in his reply. He hoped that his children would not "encounter situations which would force them to act against conscience and their own convictions." Without additional evidence, it is risky to read too much into this phraseology, but it nevertheless is interesting. Did Simonov believe that such "situations" existed in which one should act against his or her own beliefs? Was there significance in the fact that Simonov included conscience in a "negative" sense (i.e., hoping his children would not act "against" conscience as opposed to hoping they would act "for conscience" or "out of principle," in the phrases used by young specialists mentioned earlier)? Nevertheless, he remains the only respondent to allude to the heroes of the dominant official ideology of the Soviet Union in describing his aspirations for his children. But this difference in outlook was not the only one expressed in the replies.   Not only did differences exist among respondents from different generations, but in one case, a young, professional father had dramatically different aspirations for his own son and daughter.

Ia. Pavlov, a 40-year-old engineer, believed that "every person, regardless of his specialty, should be trained in history and master historical thinking, which is the basis for social awareness and a genuinely cultured outlook." In this he was consistent with the emphasis on the humanities specified by other young specialists. He wanted his two children to both grow up to be "independent thinking, honest, tolerant and kind people with the ability and intrinsic need to work."[109] Again, in this sense, his aspirations are much like those of his peers. But then comes the most interesting portion of his response:

But beyond that, my desires for my two children differ: Whereas I want my son to be strong, I want my daughter to be gentle and feminine. I believe that my son should possess boldness of thought and the ability to follow all his ideas through to their logical conclusion, even if he does not like where they lead. But I do not care if my daughter's thinking consists entirely of non-sequiturs, so long as it is sincere and she has a pure, intuitive knowledge of the difference between right and wrong. I think that a man's career is a much more important and definitive area of his life than a woman's is for her. I believe that a woman's private life is what is most important for her, and that her work is important only insofar as it enriches her private life. One of the main reasons I would like my daughter to find an interesting occupation is so that she might be self sufficient in the event that she and her future husband are divorced.

Pavlov's ideals and aspirations, especially for his daughter, have been tempered by some of the harsh realities of Soviet life. In this case, his thinking was shaped by the fact that more than half of Soviet marriages ended in divorce by the mid-1970s and that his daughter should have her own education and career to fall back upon in case of divorce.

Another response from a young engineer similarly revealed the impact of demographic reality upon the Children of Victory. V. Prokhorov, a 34-year-old (born 1944) engineer, cited demographic reports and then asked: "Just what will prompt potential parents to have children at all?"[110]

Each of these responses, tempered by the harshness of reality, is consistent with the basic philosophical emphasis of young professionals upon the human condition. That emphasis is clear, whether viewed in terms of the system's "efficiency in rewarding the best people"[111] or as the basis of the group's optimism, described as "a certainty, a belief that sooner or later, as that period [in which the country's conditions were not the best] ended, we would have a normal, humane life."[112] Were such emphases strong enough to classify the basic philosophy of the young professionals as a type of humanism? Or were the injections of Soviet reality enough to lead one to characterize their basic philosophy as a type of realism? These are the questions to which the final section of this chapter now turns.

PHILOSOPHY

The primary sources currently available are insufficient to assert that one, single, overall philosophy was shared among the young specialists. But the sources available do indicate some basic philosophical tenets that the young professionals generally did hold dear. Likewise, the sources do indicate some philosophical or spiritual vacuums that they sought to fill.

The common basic tenets held by the young specialists consistently focus on a realistic knowledge of people, their nature, and their capabilities, both positive and negative. Possible reasons for this emphasis involve aspects of young specialists' attitudes toward the Soviet system, some of which have been discussed. The stories of Sergei V. Tumanov, Alexander Tengizovich Gasparishvili, and Alexander Nikolaevich Kurin illustrate practical examples of the development of the "human" emphasis in specific young professionals and may exemplify the turn toward humanism taken by the Children of Victory. Tumanov and Kurin were introduced earlier. Gasparishvili's experience was different, but reveals a similar philosophical orientation.

Alexander Tengizovich Gasparishvili graduated from Moscow State University's philosophy department in 1977. A brilliant young student, he had originally intended to major in physics. When asked how he chose his final speciality, he stated: "That's very difficult to say because I don't know. It was an accident. I finished a physics-mathematics school, and I wanted to enroll in the Moscow Physics-Mathematics Institute. But at the last minute before I enrolled, I changed my mind. I thought that I would prefer a humanities field. The most human department of the humanities seemed to me to be the philosophy faculty."[113]

Taken together, these three men eptiomize the philosophical shift between the Children of Victory and their parents. Originally trained as a builder of machines, Tumanov became a student of people, of human nature. Gasparishvili represented one of the best and brightest young minds of his generation. As such, he was encouraged to pursue the prestigious study of physics and mathematics, which left him unfulfilled. Likewise, Kurin devoted his youth to radio physics, only to become disillusioned with the system that he saw at work and turn to search for answers in the study of the human factor.

In an interview in the early 1970s, Vladimir Ivanov, an elderly member of the presidium of the Society for the Preservation of National Monuments of Culture and History, spoke about the reasons for the growth of the society's membership: "People living in the big cities want to learn the sort of life of other times . . . they have found that physics is not enough to satisfy man—they need something to excite the mind and soul."[114] While Ivanov spoke of those seeking intellectual satisfaction during their recreational time, clearly the three preceding examples indicate that science and physics had problems satisfying the young specialists at work as well. On a generational scale, the parents of the young professionals focused on the output of the collective (as in the examples of Kozhin and Kulaga in the coauthor discussion). Their children, on the other hand, came to believe that people should be the critical emphasis, as they became increasingly aware of the inefficiency of the output-oriented system. As they focused on people, they did so with open eyes. They were not naive about the fact that human nature has both its positive and negative side. For example, N. Ashmarin, the historian who envisioned his son as a future "Renaissance man," did not want his son shielded from the less positive aspects of human nature: "My son must grow to be good, a lover of mankind. He must be able to understand another's heart and the causes which inspire people. . . . I'd like him to be aware of himself and different manifestations of nasty human qualities—that is, he should suffer in some measure because of people . . . suffer enough that he becomes aware of it. If only he himself thereby learns not to bring suffering to others."[115]

In desiring that his son "be aware of himself," Ashmarin is consistent with another basic tenet of the philosophy of the Children of Victory. To be aware of oneself is to know one's conscience, and Ashmarin concluded his description of his aspirations for his boy with, "I will try to inspire in him that good and worthy goals should be achieved only by good means, that good actions cannot stand at the cost of slanders, servility or concessions to conscience."

As Ashmarin himself noted, the responses to the *Literaturnaia gazeta* questionnaire about the person of the future were, in reality, a mirror not of the children but of the respondents themselves. In this way, Ashmarin realized that the responses represented a transcript of the beliefs and experiences of those who wrote them. Having asserted that the basic philosophy of the young specialists rested upon a human focus and emphasized the importance and essence of one's conscience, this study now briefly reviews these responses as a transcript.

The words used by the young specialists in their responses sometimes convey meaning by what they do *not* say, which may be as significant as what they *do* say. For example, Ashmarin wished his son could be an architect, because "I believe that the sad standardization in architecture will end in his time and each building will be unique. . . . Architecture *reunites* both the humanities and the exact sciences."

Why "*re*unites" instead of "unites"? It may be that Ashmarin viewed the "sad standardization" in architecture as a part of the Soviet system that he disliked. Or could it be a broader, implicit criticism? In light of his and other specialists' emphasis on the humanities and their general human focus, perhaps Ashmarin's comments represent a reaction against the heavy Soviet emphasis on science and engineering and the restrictions placed upon research in the humanities. Likewise, Ashmarin hoped that his son could "peacefully change his line of work." Is this something that Ashmarin, his father could *not* do? Without additional evidence, such speculation is of limited value, but it does provide fertile ground for potential future exploration.

SUMMARY

Individualism and humanism became critical parts of the personal ethos of the young Children of Victory. They expected the Soviet system to last a very long time. Most of them did not believe that they had a direct voice in shaping the system. Nevertheless, they remained self-confident and optimistic about their future. They demanded that the regime provide them access to statistics and data necessary to justify its claims of success and to provide them the opportunity to solve their society's problems. In their quest to build a humane, efficient system, they adapted official rhetoric and expression to serve their own purposes in an effort to overcome the "voiceless" status that they held in Soviet society. Their confidence was reflected in their increasing willingness to criticize the Soviet social and economic systems for both philosophical and practical reasons, instead of merely criticizing corrupt or incompetent officials. Their confidence was also reflected in the value systems that they chose as their frame of reference. Linguistic markers in the public transcript portray the young specialists as having a different perspective from that of their immediate predecessors. They were more likely to act "for conscience" and "according to principle" than were their parents, as well as to question fundamental practices of the regime for reasons of efficiency.

Again, in the public transcript, they often found themselves more in harmony with members of their grandparents' generation (those born in the 1890s and 1900s) than with their parents. This was true despite tremendous efforts of the regime to educate them to the sacrifices of the past that earned them the benefits of victory, such as free education and health care. Unpublished documents demonstrate that the perspectives of the young specialists and their parents may not have been quite so dramatically opposed. The regime may have manipulated the public transcript to enforce the young specialists' focus upon the "microlevel" specified by the extant social contract, the Little Deal. The fact that humanism and individualism were publicly expressed in their aspirations for their children lends credibility to the notion that these were genuinely important aspects of the specialists' personal ethos. They devoted their leisure hours to quiet pursuits, normally in the company of their family and close friends.

Much of the material presented in this chapter has focused upon the shortcomings of the Soviet system, perceived by the young professionals, in Professor Pokrovsky's words, as "not very human or humane." That focus on people as talented, individual human beings was also reflected in their professional lives, in which they sought recognition of, and increases in, the level of dignity and autonomy as well-trained, capable professionals. The search for increased dignity and autonomy inspired in the Children of Victory a corresponding search for horizontal connections with their professional peers, as addressed in the next chapter.

NOTES

1. Professor Elena Iurevna Zubkova, interviews by the author, transcribed tape recording, Moscow, Russia, June and July 1999. In addition to her specialization in contemporary history, Zubkova is a member of the generation of young specialists at the heart of this study.

2. Svetlana was born in 1949 and graduated from the Moscow Energetics Institute in 1974. She requested, as did many of my interview subjects, that I not reveal her family name. Interview by the author, transcribed tape recording, Moscow, July 1999.

3 . This is a greatly oversimplified version of the thesis of Oleg Kharkhordin, *The Collective and the Individual in Russia: A Study of Practices* (Berkeley: University of California Press, 1999).

4. Ibid., 301.

5. Ibid., 355-357.

6. Vera S. Dunham, *In Stalin's Time: Middle Class Values in Soviet Fiction*, (New York: Columbia University Press, 1990), 17-21.

7. Because any disposition toward "material acquisition" is closely tied to income levels, that subject is addressed as one of the "professional" concerns in Chapter 4.

8. One of the best descriptions of the warm, intimate nature of the *kruzhki* by a non-Russian is Hedrick Smith's in *The Russians* (New York: Ballantine Books, 1976), 141-148. Anyone who has spent long, wonderful hours clustered about a tiny Russian kitchen table discussing anything and everything can appreciate the warmth and intimacy of Russians' friendship and its stark contrast to their public behavior.

9. Only 3 of the 53 specialists surveyed in 1995 and 1999 listed "neighbors" as among their close friends. All included colleagues from work and old schoolmates, as well as family members, among those with whom they preferred to spend their free time.

10. Twenty-nine of the 53 professionals surveyed listed reading and theater. Only 7 listed more "active" pursuits such as sports.

11. G. Borovikov, "I'm Looking for a Sail," *Literaturnaia gazeta*, 12 January 1977, as translated and presented in *Current Digest of the Soviet Press* (CDSP) 29, no. 3 (1977), 14-15.

12. Also published under the rubric "I'm Looking for a Sail," *Literaturnaia gazeta*, 6 July 1977, as translated and presented in *Current Digest of the Soviet Press* 29, no. 32 (1977), 12-13.

13. Readers' comments were published by *Literaturnaia gazeta* in March 1977 (*CDSP* 29, no. 3, 14-15) and in the discussion's final installment in *Literaturnaia gazeta*, 10 May 1978 (*CDSP* 30, no. 20, 15-16).

14. V. Kuibyshev, "Once Again about Tennis," *Literaturnaia gazeta*, 31 January 1979, 13, as translated and presented in *Current Digest of the Soviet Press* 31, no. 6 (1979), 19.

15. Clearly, these tennis players were not limited to young specialists, but it must be noted that several indicators of tennis players as a subordinate element are apparent in Kuibyshev's letter. From the tennis player context, the Ministry of Light Industry and the "urban planners" are clearly the dominant element. This recognition of one's opponent and the construction of one's own social space (private tennis club) demonstrate the awareness of "negation" and "cohesion" on the part of the tennis players. A subsequent article in *Literaturnaia gazeta*, 1 September 1982, 13 lamented the sad state of Soviet tennis, no longer competitive at world-class levels. In wondering why, the author hammered the USSR sporting goods industry for producing minimal amounts of shoddy equipment and for the lack of courts. He then used the absence of tennis from Olympic competition to explain the country's lack of emphasis and criticized shortcomings in the training and selection of talented children players.

16. Forty-two of the 53 specialists surveyed were married, and 41 of them had

children. A KGB "informer" from Odessa characterized engagement or marriage as a normal part of the fourth-year student's life. That KGB report is found in TsKhSD F5 O60 D48 L120-153 and is addressed in detail.

17. Thirty of the 42 married specialists lived with parents and in-laws for some time.

18. Eighteen of the 30 declared such conditions as "satisfactory," though they often added caveats such as "difficult."

19. Professor Nikita Pokrovsky, interview by the author, tape recording, Moscow, Russia, 16 March 1995.

20. James C. Scott, *Domination and the Arts of Resistance: Hidden Transcripts* (New Haven, CT: Yale University Press, 1990), 92. It should be noted that I use the methods of Scott's domination-resistance paradigm here as tools to gain insight into the relationship between the young specialists, the regime, and Soviet society as a whole, not to argue that the young specialists formed a subordinate or subaltern group in Soviet society in the same sense as traditional subaltern groups, such as peasants or slaves. This distinction is addressed in more detail in the next chapter.

21. Barrington Moore Jr., *Injustice: The Social Bases of Obedience and Revolt* (White Plains, NY: M.E. Sharpe, 1987), 84. Scott cites and discusses this passage in *Domination*, 90-95. While Moore was writing about "oppressed groups" that were dramatically different from the relatively privileged young specialists, the specialists dealt with their sense of frustrations in the restricted environment of Soviet society in some similar ways to those traditionally "oppressed" groups such as peasants or slaves in other societies.

22. Elite conformance to its own publicly professed standard of conduct is a vital aspect of Scott's "public transcript" and isdiscussed in greater detail later.

23. "Nashli sebe zabotu," *Sotsialisticheskaia industriia*, 8 October 1972, 1.

24. "Ne srabotalis', ili pochemu ushla iz sel'skoi shkoly molodaia uchitel'nitsa," *Komsomolskaia Pravda*, 16 July 1977, 2. Many of her comments regarding the principal and the other teachers reflect issues of professional dignity, autonomy, and pride. As such they are addressed in the next chapter.

25. Additional examples of this belief will appear later.

26. That many young specialists were the children of intellectuals was discussed earlier in Chapter 1.

27. V. Belkin, "Skol'ko 'stoit' inzhener?," *Literaturnaia gazeta*, 10 March 1971, 10-11 (emphasis added). Belkin was trying to illustrate a gap between the Party's official philosophy and stance on the training of engineers and the objective conditions of the day, which included a shortage of workers and massive problems in proper utilization of specialists with higher education. As noted earlier, this problem continued as the Party prepared for the 25th Congress five years later. This study returns to discussion of Belkin's positions later.

28. TsKhSD, Fond 5, Opis 69, Delo 495, Listok 1-15, especially L7-10.

29. While their education was free, *vuz* graduates were expected to pay for their education by accepting an assigned job for two or three years following graduation.

30. In fact, the majority (31) of the specialists surveyed in 1995 and 1999 had found their first jobs after graduation on their own, with the minority (22) accepting posts according to the "distribution."

31. RTsKhIDNI F638 O1 D23 L32-33.

32. Several installments of the overall discussion "Otkrytie sdelano: A kto zhe avtor?" appeared under the rubric "Pis'ma sporiat." See *Literaturnaia gazeta*, 1 March 1972, 12; 15 March 1972, 12-13; 19 April 1972, 12. The root issue of this discussion was one of scientific prestige and professional reward. Therefore, it is explored in depth in the

next chapter.

33. E. Kulaga, "Konflikt bez podopleki," *Literaturnaia gazeta*, 1 March 1972, 12. Kulaga stated that he'd been the head of a small collective for nearly 10 years. This most likely placed him well out of the age group of "young specialists."

34. A. Tsvetov, "Podopleka--nauchnyi prestige," *Literaturnaia gazeta*, 1 March 1972, 12. Unfortunately, no overt indicators of Tsvetov's age were provided with the letter.

35. "Otkrytie sdelano: A kto zhe avtor?" *Literaturnaia gazeta*, 26 January 1972, 11.

36. "Iz redaktsionnoi pochti," *Literaturnaia gazeta*, 1 March 1972, 12. This section listed excerpts from readers' letters in response to the initial discussion of Belov's complaint. Six of those letters were from senior scientists, ranging in rank from candidate of philosophy to corresponding member of the Soviet Academy of Sciences. Five of the six supported young Belov's contention that administrators should not be listed as coauthors. Only one supported Belov's lab director.

37. V. Perevedentsev, "Kollektivism istinnyi i lozhnyi," *Literaturnaia gazeta*, 19 April 1972, 12. The shortage of technicians and administrative assistants was a major issue in the 1970-1971 survey "Kak vam rabotaetsia?" first published by *Literaturnaia gazeta*, 15 July 1970, 11. V. Belkin also addressed this problem and proposed solutions in "Besplatno--dorozhe," *Literaturnaia gazeta*, 23 February 1971, 10.

38. "Privykli: pis'mo c ovoshchnoi bazy" *Pravda*, 11 November 1982, 3.

39. "Socialist legality" was a phrase that intentionally highlighted the responsibility of officials to act in accordance with the laws and procedures of the Soviet Union and the CPSU. It stood in direct response to, and contradiction of, arbitrary and capricious action (or inaction) by members of the elite.

40. "Ili rabota, ili deti?" *Literaturnaia gazeta*, 14 April 1982, 12.

41. Sabolev's letter was part of a summary, "About Basic Tendencies in Mail Received by *Komsomolskaia pravda* in the Pre-Congress Period," sent from the *Komsomolskaia pravda* editorial staff to the Central Committee. The summary was dated 18 January 1971 and classified as "secret." The editor of the summary, V. Chikin, described Sabolev's letter as "typical." TskHSD F5 O63 D90 L5. Declassified May 1995.

42. TsKhSD F5 O63 D90 L11.

43. TsKhSD F5 O63 D90 L13-14.

44. RTsKhIDNI, F614 O2 D39 L5.

45. The records of *Agitator*, including letters, reviews of letters, and the records of feedback meetings for the years 1956-1975, are contained in RTsKhIDNI Fond 614.

46. RTsKhIDNI F614 O2 D39, L7.

47. Ibid., L6 (emphasis added).

48. This material is from a meeting of *Agitator*'s editorial staff with subscribers in the city of Perm, December 1974, RTsKhIDNI F614 O2 D39 L11-12.

49. This meeting was held in April 1974 in the Ural city of Nizhni Tagil. Ibid., L29.

50. Ibid.

51. Ibid., L37-38.

52. Ibid, L12, 13, 27, 28.

53. RTsKhIDNI F614, O2, D27, L99-100

54. Ibid.

55. While the focus of this study is on those young specialists who did not work primarily for the state or Party, it is important to note that some did so. I encountered several letters in the *Agitator* archives whose activist authors identified themselves as young specialists. For example, RTsKhIDNI F614 O2 D27 L23-24.

56. RTsKhIDNI, F614 O2 D39 L6.

57. This "gradient of radicalism" in subordinate criticism was developed by Barrington Moore. The first step is to criticize some members of the elite; the second is to criticize all or part of the entire elite stratum; and the third, most radical criticism would be to repudiate the very principles of the 'contract' that the elite ostensibly uphold. See Moore, *Injustice*, 84. Scott describes this gradient in an example of Japanese peasant petitioning in *Domination*, 94-96.

58. Of course, it is possible that Nevodchikova's letter was ghostwritten or edited by Pravda to enable the paper to assume just such a role. However, such criticism did appear in archival sources as well.

59. The vast majority of specialists surveyed in 1995 and 1999 (39/53) believed that they had no such direct voice.

60. "Po tu storonu prilavka," *Komsomolskaia pravda*, 14 March 1975, 2.

61. R. Metelnitsky, "Who Are We?" *Literaturnaia gazeta*, 11 October 1972, 11 as translated and presented in *Current Digest of the Soviet Press* 25, no. 11 (1973), 22. The issue of architects' creativity is addressed using this and other sources as a professional concern in the next chapter.

62. V. Iudintseva, "Po trudu," *Pravda*, 1 February 1981, 3.

63. TsKhSD F5 O63 D90 L104.

64. TsKhSD F5 O63 D90 L13.

65. A. Artsibashev, "Po tu storonu prilavka," *Komsomolskaia pravda*, 14 March 1975, 2.

66. Obviously, the self-selecting group of young specialists who chose to write letters to the press all must have possessed such confidence. But the overwhelming majority (39 /53) of specialists surveyed between 1995 and 1999, none of whom ever wrote a letter to the press, also classified themselves as optimistic and self-confident in the Brezhnev years. They firmly believed in their knowledge and skill and wanted to put them to use. Only 5 of the 53 declared their outlook as "pessimistic," while the others avoided such categorization (5/53) or counted themselves as "neutral" (4/53).

67. B. Mukhina, "Za chto uvolili moego syna," *Literaturnaia gazeta*, 17 March 1982, 12. This discussion appeared under the rubric "Moral Choice" (Nravstvenny vybor) discussed earlier.

68. Twenty-four of 53 specialists surveyed listed colleagues from work or former schoolmates as their closest friends. Fifteen listed "friends" and did not specify the origin of those relationships. But only 3 listed neighbors or others as among their closest friends. It may therefore be assumed that at least some of these friends who were "shocked" were also young specialists.

69. Georgie Anne Geyer, *The Young Russians* (Homewood, IL: ETC, 1975), 148.

70. Ibid., 283-284.

71. Sheila Fitzpatrick, *Everyday Stalinism, Ordinary Life in Extraordinary Times: Soviet Russia in the 1930s* (New York: Oxford University Press), 1999, 224. Fitzpatrick devotes a chapter to the Soviet "myth" of "Palaces on Monday," in which she describes all of Soviet society in the 1930s as utopian, focused on improvement of themselves and society, *especially* the younger generation (the parents of this study), 67-88 (emphasis added).

72. This was not a new generational dilemma in Russian history. The young "rational egoists" who championed social activity by individuals in Chernyshevskii's *What Is to Be Done?* stood in stark contrast to the professional revolutionaries who favored collective political action in Lenin's work of the same name.

73. Ella Kirova, interview by British journalist Tony Parker, in *Voices of Russia* (New York: Henry Holt, 1991), 283.

74. "Otkrytie sdelano--a kto zhe avtor?" *Literaturnaia gazeta,* 26 January 1972, 11.

75. Ibid.

76. *Literaturnaia gazeta,* 17 March 1982, 12. At this point, I am deliberately withholding consideration of the third logical entity involved in this discussion and the question "What was the role of the regime in this process?" That question and an answer to it based on archival sources are offered later.

77. "My i obstoiatel'stva," *Literaturnaia gazeta,* 15 December 1982, 12. This article appeared under the same "Nravstvennyi vybor" rubric as Mukhina's original letter.

78. Unfortunately, no age indications are provided for authors of the letters, and the excerpts are very brief, with no obvious generational markers in the wording.

79. Hedrick Smith recorded this conversation between a CPSU member and her American friend in *The Russians,* 246.

80. Geyer, Research Notebook II, 18.

81. RTsKhIDNI F614 O2 D27 L166-168.

82. RTsKhIDNI F614 O2 D18 L80.

83. TsKhSD F5 O63 D90 L5-7. Originally classified "Secret." Declassified May 1995.

84. The summary of letters was submitted by V. Chikin, the deputy main editor of *KP.* Ibid., L7.

85. Ibid., L8.

86. Sheila Fitzpatrick, *Stalin's Peasants: Resistance & Survival in the Russian Village after Collectivization* (New York: Oxford University Press), 1994, 327. See also her comments on police reports as sources in *Everyday Stalinism,* 164-168.

87. TsKhSD F5 O60 D48 L120. Declassified January 1994.

88. The actual report is found in TsKhSD F5 O60 D48 L120-153. The document was printed in its entirety in Russian as "Otchuzhdennoe ot partii sostoianie," *Istoricheskii arxiv,* no. 1 (1994), 176-193. All subsequent references to the document are as it was published in the journal.

89. Ibid., 178-179.

90. Ibid., 180.

91. Dr. Sergei V. Tumanov, interview by the author, tape recording, Moscow, April 1995.

92. Ibid.

93. Alexander Nikolaevich Kurin, interview by the author, tape recording, Moscow, Russia, April 1995.

94. "Otchuzhdennoe ot partii sostoianie," *Istoricheskii arxiv,* no. 1 (1994), 195. The original document is located in TsKhSD F4 O25 D36 L1-47. My translations here are based on the journal.

95. Ibid., 205.

96. A. Ianshchin, "Eto nedopustimo!" *Literaturnaia gazeta,* 26 January 1972, 11. Ianshchin made his "clean hands" assertion in the 13th paragraph of his article. Belov made his assertion, "One must do science with clean hands," in the 31st paragraph of his interview with the journalist, "Otkrytie sdelano--a kto zhe avtor?," *Literaturnaia gazeta,* 26 January 1972, 11. It must be noted that while both Belov and Ianshchin emphasized the ethics and traditions of science, Ianshchin consistently included the "Soviet" modifier while Belov did not (possibly a marker of Ianshchin's generation?).

97. The institute director's age was not given. I make the inference that he is nearly the same age as academician Ianshchin because the reporter noted, "As a student, I had studied his [the director's] chemistry text."

98. I consider it surprising because, by the very nature of their academic

credentials, they have been most successful in precisely that system that they criticize. These eight responses appeared under the same title as the original article "Otkrytie sdelano--a kto zhe avtor?" Two of the letters were juxtaposed in a "Pis'ma sporiat" configuration and the six excerpts grouped as excerpts, "Iz redaktsionnoi pochty," *Literaturnaia gazeta,* 1 March 1972, 12.

99. *Literaturnaia gazeta* printed three follow-up installments, each of which carried the title "Otkrytie sdelano-- a kto zhe avtor?" at or near the top of the page. Those installments appeared in *Literaturnaia gazeta,* 1 March 1972, 11; 15 March 1972, 12-13; 19 April 1972, 12.

100. The original survey questions appeared in "Chelovek budushchego, kakov on? Vash syn, vasha doch' v 2000 godu," *Literaturnaia gazeta,* 1 January 1978, 10.

101. Ashmarin's comments were published as one selection "from the first 500 responses" to the questionnaire. N. Ashmarin, ". . . Neutolimoi zhazhdy dykhovnoi!" *Literaturnaia gazeta,* 1 February 1978, 11.

102. A. Popov, "Priglashenie k mechte," *Literaturnaia gazeta,* 1 January 1978, 10.

103. Ashmarin, *Literaturnaia gazeta,* 1 February 1978, 11.

104. If the USSR could only overcome the difficulties with equipment production, training, and court availability, discussed earlier.

105. Alexei Matiushkin, "Pust' rebenok tselikom budet na vospitanii obshchestva," *Literaturnaia gazeta,* 1 February 1978, 10.

106. G. Mumrikova and Iu. Mumrikov, "You Can't Buy Dreams," *Literaturnaia gazeta,* 12 April 1978, 11, as translated and presented in *Current Digest of the Soviet Press* (*CDSP*) 30 no. 16 (1978), 16. Note: I was unable to locate a complete copy of this issue, in print or in microfilm. I found only copies that included the first eight pages of this issue; therefore, I had to rely on the excerpt of this letter presented in *CDSP*.

107. P. Simonov, "Chtoby byl polezen liudiam, chtoby zhil ne zria," *Literaturnaia gazeta,* 1 February 1978, 10.

108. Unfortunately, Doctor Simonov did not elaborate upon *which* ideas of these men he based his answers. His inclusion of Dzerzhinski (founder of the Cheka [later OGPU, NKVD, KGB]) is intriguing.

109. Ia. Pavlov, "All Thinking People Should be Historians," *Literaturnaia gazeta,* 12 April 1978, 12, as translated and presented in *Current Digest of the Soviet Press* 30, no. 16 (1978), 16.

110. V. Prokhorov, "Letter to the Editor," *Literaturnaia gazeta,* 12 April 1978, 11, as translated and presented in *CDSP* 30 no. 16 (1978), 15.

111. Professor Nikita Pokrovsky, interview by the author, tape recording, Moscow, March 1995.

112. Dr. Sergei V. Tumanov, interview by the author, tape recording, Moscow, April 1995.

113. Alexander Tengizovich Gasparishvili, interview by the author, tape recording, Moscow, Russia, April 1995. Gasparishvili's exceptional academic potential enabled him to make such a last-minute change of mind. When he graduated from MGU, he was only 20 years old. By the age of 24, he had completed his candidate's degree as well. He did stick to his humanities focus. When I interviewed him, he was the director of the Laboratory for the Study of Public Opinion at MGU's Center for Sociological Research.

114. Geyer, *The Young Russians,* 34.

115. N. Ashmarin, *Literaturnaia gazeta,* 1 February 1978, 11.

4

Children of Victory: Groups, Professional Values, and Beliefs

Professionally, those graduating from *vuzy* between 1964 and 1982 should have faced a future filled with bright potential. As beneficiaries of the economic and political stability of the Brezhnev years, the most stable in Soviet history, the young specialists often entered the workforce with high expectations for both creative opportunity and material rewards. In many cases, those expectations were met. However, by the late 1970s, many members of the generation began to sense that their academic diplomas were not a golden ticket to the future and that both their future prospects and their material situation could have been substantially better.

Complaints about professional prestige, autonomy and dignity, daily working conditions, and even their higher education itself were set forth in a "generalized portrait" of the generation created by one of its own. In his article "Mnogovariantnyi Posudnikov," described in the introduction to this study, young doctor of chemistry Alexander Rusov created a composite symbol of his generation in the form of a young scientific researcher turned taxi driver.[1]

I remember how he said that at the *vuz* they taught him nothing that he had come across at the scientific research institute. He was right about that in part, but only in part.
Even more, remember, Posudnikov said something disapproving about written work and that he, he said, craves life's action. It seems that he also complained that they forced him to carry nitrogen cylinders, to wash the lab glassware and to work in a vegetable depot. It is quite possible that it wasn't Posudnikov who said all this to me, that it was someone else. A dissatisfied, critical intellectual.
And still he, Posudnikov, said something about parents, under whose influence he had enrolled in the institute. Only, why would he have said this to me? What do parents have to do with leaving and driving a taxi? I, for example, also enrolled in the institute under parental influence. But when they say to me now that "You ran off into journalism," I indignantly reply that I have not run off to anywhere.[2] Where I went, I continue to go. So this observation of Posudnikov's has no bearing on reality. But it seems, once again, that these things were said to me, not by Posudnikov, but by someone else.
I could be, for instance, combining in his image all the young, unsatisfied *vuz* graduates who

were assigned to scientific research institutes and who left. Those [for example] who complained about the insufficient knowledge of *vuz* graduates, and those who consider such things superfluous in the circumstances of "swamp life" at scientific research institutes. With the help of this composite Posudnikov, I would try to tell about those who cite the presence of wives and children, who complain about insufficient time for work on the side or who cannot earn enough via translations and synopses. I could if you wish, write that all of this is truthful, although for me, for example, in my own time, the extra earnings for translations and synopses were sufficient.

Within this generalized self-portrait of the young specialist, Rusov raised a number of issues that lie at the heart of this study. How did common educational experiences or career patterns influence the young specialists' development? Did they find satisfaction in their work? What were their professional goals or aspirations, and how well did they succeed in attaining them? In addition, this chapter seeks answers to the following basic research question: Did they establish unofficial or horizontal professional connections or unofficial groups? If so, what influence, if any, did those connections or groups have on Soviet society as a whole?

CIRCLES, COLLECTIVES, "VIRTUAL" GROUPS, INTEREST GROUPS, AND FORMAL ASSOCIATIONS

As discussed earlier, an important part of the ethos of young specialists (and other Soviet citizens) was their tendency to choose a specific community of associates (their "circle," or *kruzhok*) whose shared values would be the standard by which the individual specialist's morality would be judged. Because the Little Deal allowed only microlevel associations, this community of associates remained small and exclusive. In contrast, all Soviet citizens belonged to formal *kollektivy* based upon their school, profession, or occupation. These entities did not exist in isolation from one another. By the end of the Brezhnev era, some convergence or at least tendencies toward convergence among these entities had begun to occur. This chapter demonstrates that Soviet newspapers, as the public forum for petitions, gave limited impetus to the expansion of group consciousness beyond the parameters of the Little Deal, creating some horizontal awareness among specialists as "virtual" groups ("virtual" in that individual petitions took on the appearance of *kollektiv* expression, as shown later). A few isolated cases of genuine interest groups' forming despite the strictures of the Little Deal also shaped the ethos of the young specialists and are described here. Finally, the chapter further shows that Soviet citizens in general and young specialists in particular began efforts to incorporate the same kind of choice or selectivity into formal groups as they had to their circles.

The letter of six elementary school teachers formed the basis of an article in the teachers' newspaper *Uchitelskaia gazeta* that appeared 17 April 1982.[3] In keeping with the rules of engagement for Soviet letter writers, each of the authors wrote only as an individual teacher or, at most, as a member of a school collective, claiming no other group affiliation. The reporter and editorial staff noted the correlation of the letters' themes from diverse regions of the country and attributed these common themes to the teaching profession in general. By doing so, the newspaper contributed to the awareness of teachers everywhere of their "horizontal connection" with other members of their profession.

This elevation of individual opinion to the level of group consciousness was a widespread and frequent practice of Soviet newspapers and exemplifies the unique role that the press played in the expression of "group" opinions. The voices of individuals, which were muted by the rules of engagement, were incorporated into the voice of the reporter or the newspaper staff. Clearly, participation in such letter writing was not universal, as the majority of Soviet citizens did not write letters to the press.[4] But the society-wide process of collating individual opinions into "mosaics" representing "virtual" group or professional interests served as a gradual expansion of public opinion beyond the basic strictures of the Little Deal. From the regime's perspective, these collated opinions were acceptable as the voice of the common *kollektiv* of the members (the teaching profession, in this example).

Every mosaic needs individual components, and the Brezhnev regime actively encouraged Soviet citizens to submit their opinions and criticisms and issued grave warnings to those who would impede such submissions. *Pravda* itself was the forum, and the head prosecutor of the Russian Republic was the author who cited Brezhnev's comment that the suppression of criticism "is a violation of the norms of communist morality and the Basic Law [Constitution] of the USSR. It is an evil that must not remain unpunished. We highly value popular initiative, and no one will be allowed to undermine this source of our strength!"[5] This same article admits that some administrators react to criticism "as if someone were treading on their own pet corns" and judge all critics from the perspective of their own hurt pride. It cited several instances in which critics were first punished, then reinstated. To prevent further such abuses, the article suggested that those who suppress criticism should compensate the victims from their own pockets. *Pravda* continued this discussion the next year, noting that the USSR Supreme Court met and discussed the necessity of punishing those who exact vengeance for criticism and the means by which courts should exact such punishment.[6]

Official encouragement and the Russian tradition of "petitioning" guaranteed a ready supply of individual opinions for the press to collate into mosaics of group opinions. Among the earliest mosaics to take on the appearance of genuine group opinion in the USSR was an alliance of ecological concerns, which evolved gradually in the USSR throughout the Brezhnev years.

When the Soviet Ministry of Timber, Paper, and Woodworking announced plans in 1958 to construct two cellulose mills in the Lake Baikal basin, those plans generated opposition almost immediately. Localized at first, the voices raised in protest against the pollution of Baikal grew to include a nationwide coalition of scientists, writers, academicians, and reporters. Between 1960 and 1976, "non-institutionalized, ad hoc environmental lobbies" developed and worked through the Soviet press and with state environmental protection agencies to secure more stringent environmental protection of Lake Baikal than otherwise would have been possible.[7]

At the forefront of development of this movement was *Literaturnaia gazeta*. Between 1965 and 1975, *Literaturnaia gazeta* published dozens of letters, articles, official responses, proclamations, and commentaries on the subject of

Baikal, usually under the heading "Priroda i My" [Nature and Us]. Upon publication of new, stricter environmental regulations for the industries of the Baikal region, *Literaturnaia gazeta* engaged in a bit of self-congratulations. The editorial staff introduced the new regulations with a brief commentary, which noted, "The Baikal problem has been discussed in a vast readers' audience. . . . Sometimes the most extreme, polemically sharp points of view have been expressed. Public opinion has crystallized. The discussion played a well-known role in deciding the fate of Baikal."[8]

Literaturnaia gazeta's role in the Baikal discussion set a precedent for the manner of expression of additional concerns, environmental and otherwise. Letters from readers and specialists were published in *Literaturnaia gazeta*, while governmental decrees and regulations were normally published in *Pravda* and *Izvestia*. *Literaturnaia gazeta*'s readers would discuss these regulations on its pages, as would Party and government officials. While the pronouncements of decrees or regulations adopted in *Pravda* or *Izvestia* were usually sterile reproductions of legislation, the give-and-take in *Literaturnaia gazeta* was always lively and occasionally controversial. Several examples, each taken from other environmental discussions, will serve to illustrate the candid nature of the exchanges and the role of specialists in them.

In December 1974 (on the same page that trumpeted the success of the Baikal campaign), *Literaturnaia gazeta* published an open letter from writer Oleg Volkov to the minister of timber and woodworking industry, N.V. Timofeev. Volkov pointed out a series of shortcomings in the ministry's activities in regions surrounding the Baikal-Amur [railroad] Mainline (BAM) and directly asked Minister Timofeev if the ministry was "ready to organize its enterprises in the BAM region on a strictly scientific basis."[9] The minister responded with a letter of his own, published in March 1975, which commended Volkov and other "literary types" for their concern for Soviet forests and cited statistics and plans intended to demonstrate the scientific basis on which the "forest-industry complex" in the BAM area was based.[10]

The two letters, directly and personally addressed, seemed to successfully stalemate one another. That is, they offset each other's arguments until F. Shtilmark, a candidate of biological science with extensive experience on the ground in the BAM region, wrote a detailed letter to *Literaturnaia gazeta*. Noting that the minister had classified logging operations along the BAM as "especially reasonable," Shtilmark countered with his own description of environmentally disastrous clear-cutting operations and his overall assessment that "unfortunately, the Minister's clear formula is not always firmly embodied in reality."[11]

Ministers, writers, and professional specialists often engaged in such discussions (though the direct "open letters" of this one were somewhat unique) of environmental issues, with the lines of agreement or disagreement taking on many various forms. Sometimes the three sides represented here (ministers, writers, specialists) joined forces against another, often in the form of local officials. For example, in 1973 and 1974, *Literaturnaia gazeta* ran a series called "Conflict on the River Bank," in which the pollution of the Ural River and Caspian Sea was highlighted in comparison to industrial development in the area. The authors exposed the failure of local industrial managers to adhere to ecological directives and policies.[12] In an "official reply" the head of the "Zhuka" hydroelectric institute, D. Iurinov, agreed that the "criticism of the primitive and unacceptable means of protection of the water from pollution is absolutely justified" and that, if directives had been properly implemented, the problem "should have been settled long ago."[13]

One final example illustrates the extensive influence of the "environmental lobby." Once again, local officials were the targets, and again, Oleg Volkov was the reporter providing the "expose." But this time the discussion occurred in *Komsomolskaia pravda* and was initiated by a letter from nine scientists and conservationists that protested a proposed highway across the Caucasian State Preserve. Both the letter and article protested the destruction of the preserve's natural beauty and the danger to wildlife, including some rare species, posed by the highway.[14] *Komsomolskaia pravda*'s editorial staff wrote to the Russian Ministry of Highway Construction and Maintenance. The official reply was deemed unsatisfactory and not entirely accurate, leading the editorial staff to ask, "Does the Ministry think the damage that will be done to the Caucasian State Preserve [by this plan] is an objective necessity?"[15] Just over one month later, the USSR Ministry of Agriculture's Chief Administration for Nature Conservation investigated the complaint and directed that highway construction be halted and that an alternative route be found. In addition, the directors of the preserve itself were reprimanded for not maintaining the sanctity of the preserve and for allowing cabins, souvenir stands, and so on to be built.[16]

Environmental groups represented an exceptional example of the public interaction among alternative and official opinions. The widespread appeal of environmental issues is clear from the genuinely enormous number of participants, the fact that a reporter such as Oleg Volkov could gain a national reputation as a leading environmental crusader, the longevity of the issue and its popularity in multiple newspapers, and the unabashed zeal with which *Literaturnaia gazeta* and *Komsomolskaia pravda* trumpeted their respective roles in discussing the issues.[17] Nevertheless, as an ad hoc group, the environmental "lobby" remained an exception. It was not an official, recognized group. Nor was it a group with consistent or readily identifiable membership.[18] The fledgling environmental movement in Brezhnev's USSR was more a cause célèbre than an actual group. Nevertheless, it set precedents upon which other, more formalized groups would build.[19]

One such group was the Old Russia Society for the Preservation and Protection of Monuments of History. Writing during the Soviet period, some Western analysts described this group as focused upon the restoration of historical structures and documents but placed that description within the context of a resurgence of Russian nationalism during the Brezhnev era. Georgie Anne Geyer, for example, noted that the society had 6 million members by 1972 and described it as working "with the government on projects, but operating mostly on a private basis."[20] Just over a decade later, Gail Lapidus logged its membership at 12 million and labeled it the "first grass-roots organization to emerge in the USSR."[21] Both Geyer and Lapidus linked the widespread appeal of the society to a "crisis of belief" among Soviet citizens and posited that the society helped fill a philosophical vacuum that the regime's ideology could not.

Founded shortly after the ouster of Khrushchev, the "aim of the group is to correct the harm that has been done to our true heritage in the past, and to involve people to take practical steps to save what is left. We want once more to instill into people a sense of pride in their heritage, and to express their patriotism in this way."[22] By 1991 the society had established a record of opposition to Western influence and rock music, but its most visible manifestation, the work in which most of its members were involved, was support for the physical restoration of historical monuments.

While an analysis of the society's political views and impact is beyond the scope of this study, the popularity of monument restoration among specialists provides valuable insight into the evolution of Soviet society. In May 1971, *Literaturnaia gazeta* published a letter from several eminent scholars in Leningrad under the title "Stop the Bulldozer!—In the Defense of Historical and Cultural Monuments."[23] Introductory comments by the editorial staff noted *Literaturnaia gazeta*'s long association with the subject of architectural restoration, including the newspaper's sponsorship of design competitions and conferences on the subject. But it is the letter itself that is most revealing. It provides a fascinating juxtaposition in which a group asserts itself in a document framed by Lenin's legacy.

The very first sentence of the letter demonstrated the lasting influence of Lenin's admonition to "criticize, not generalize." The prominent scholars who signed the letter spoke volumes about their experiences by opening this critical letter with the statement: "We have no wish to generalize. Our letter will speak of only one city." Such adherence to the "rules of engagement" is expected from a group of authors that included two academicians and a number of professors and doctors of science, one of whom proudly included "Member of the Communist Party of the Soviet Union since 1918" with his signature. But the tone and language of the letter itself contrasted greatly to this traditional framework. The authors criticize the fact that "serious mistakes and omissions were permitted by Leningrad architects" in the destruction of several historical structures. The authors stated that this was done "in spite of *objections from the community's side*" (emphasis added).

Throughout the letter, this emphasis on the interests of "the community" or "society" was repeated. But these are not just general phrases. The authors specified exactly who they believed constituted this "community." They condemned the "impunity of responsible officials" and noted that "they are planning new destruction of buildings in the city's historical center." The scholars declared that the pending destruction of the historic Ismailovskii barracks "was not discussed by the city's society. The creative unions, the Committee of Veterans of the Great Patriotic War, the military-historical sections and the museum workers only learned about it from the newspaper." Clearly, these unions, committees, sections, and workers were considered key elements of the city's "society." According to the scholars, the central cause of poorly planned destruction of historical monuments was "the fact that the builders . . . and architects and designers don't want to consider the community's opinion, [they] develop their own projects in closed architectural surroundings, and then, ignorant of the community's opinions, try to establish [those projects] at higher levels of authority," thereby presenting the community with a fait accompli.

While this article provides insight into some groups that may have pressed the boundaries of the Little Deal, it also highlights the limitations of such interest groups in the Soviet society of the 1970s. These authors were citing some officially sanctioned groups that were *not* consulted and that were therefore impotent in the decision-making process. Quite often, such groups were cited as endorsing one policy or another to bolster an argument. But, to date, one rarely finds archival records of any actual discussions of such groups, rendering their utility as a means of further exploring public opinion or social expression quite limited. Nevertheless, the assertion by the prominent scholars that these groups could and should have an active role in the development of state construction plans remains an important piece of evidence that civil participation in official decision making was expected as a right by at least some elements of Soviet society.

Officially sanctioned interest groups, such as the creative unions and veterans' committees discussed above, represented social manifestations of "horizontal connections," that is, people united by some common interest or experience. Unlike the broad "cause" espoused by the coalition of environmental interests, the common interest or experience of officially sanctioned groups was usually defined much more narrowly. In general, however, genuine participation of such groups in official decision making of the type desired by the letter writers above was minimal. Officially recognized groups and associations were often stigmatized by their very official status. To demonstrate such stigmatization, this study now turns to the one type of official group to which nearly every young professional belonged.

Of the 53 specialists surveyed, 52 were members of some professional association (*profsoiuz*). Most specialists, in fact, were automatically enrolled in *profsoiuzy* upon completion of their education. Despite nearly universal enrollment of specialists in *profsoiuzy*, these organizations did not develop into components of civil society. Within the very public context of the organization, most specialists pursued private goals.[24]

Olga Nadimova, a writer born in 1941, described her membership in the Writers' Union in this way: "It is something you may think is cynical. Yes, it is cynical: I joined it for the advantages. . . .[The Writers' Union] is a trades union, which gives benefit to its members [such as] pension, financial support, medical care and holiday houses. . . .So there are many benefits, and it is for these that I am a member. Only for these, and nothing else."[25]

Even those specialists who classified their membership in *profsoiuzy* as "pro forma" or automatic stressed the utility, even the necessity of such membership. Boris Vidimskii, a radio-physicist born in 1947, described his membership in the Union of Scientific Workers as "a formal membership. It meant nothing. But if you were sick, you could get money, stay in the hospital, etc."[26] The overriding classification of *profsoiuzy* membership by the specialists was that membership was a pro forma requirement of life in the USSR and nothing more.[27]

The marginal role of "group" opinions made the role of the newspaper in collating individual opinions ever more critical. The process by which newspaper reporters compiled "mosaics" of opinion into "virtual" groups was described earlier.

The regime, as noted, accepted these "mosaics" as expressions of the officially recognized *kollektivy*. As the following section indicates, the elevation of opinion by the newspaper from the individual to the group level had some real impact on the coalescence of individual opinions as well.

As with the individual ethos of the young professionals, a combination of published and unpublished sources must be used to validate elements of the young specialists' public image as a group. Professionally oriented discussions were more common in the press than the personal ones addressed in the previous chapter. Unpublished materials about professional and group issues are much more consistent with the public portrayal of the specialists than was the case with personal or individual issues. Therefore, the sources surveyed here provide greater quantitative and qualitative insight into the professional and group ethos of the Children of Victory and into the position of the Soviet regime relative to that professional/group ethos than was possible in personal terms.

HORIZONTAL CONNECTIONS: "NEGATION," "MUTUALITY," AND COHESION

When the factory sociologists discussed earlier recognized and challenged bureaucratic obstacles to the growth of independent ties with their peers or their access to reference materials, they demonstrated an awareness of the system that imposed those obstacles as an opponent. Such awareness often comes prior to or as a first glimmer of oneself and one's peers as a class (i.e., as a sense of "us versus them" or, in this case, "us versus the system"). Scott termed this "mutuality" to be a logical consequence of "negation." "Mutuality" is the development of a sense of association or cohesion among identifiable members of a subordinate group, receiving its initial impetus from the subordinates' desire to protect themselves from the efforts of the elite to isolate them from each other.[28] "Negation" is an action by another group, usually an opponent, that inspires a group's sense of cohesion. (The negation here is the denial or prevention of horizontal ties.)

Young specialists' letters about horizontal connections often focused upon issues of dignity or more precisely, issues of indignity that the petitioner perceived *not as an individual but as a member of a profession.* Here it must be kept in mind that the Little Deal did not prevent personal association but did restrict group action to officially sanctioned groups. On one hand, such a portrayal seems to be in keeping with the "collective" spirit of official Soviet ideology. Yet, at the same time, the manner in which petitioners described or defined their "collective" frequently raised issues of professional dignity, prestige, and status that highlighted the importance of such issues for nonworkers in the workers' state.

This redefinition of the "collective" to which they considered themselves attached represented another major factor in the young specialists' ethos. Having redefined and identified themselves, in contrast to Soviet tradition, as distinct individuals by their emphasis on personal principles, individual standards of "compensation," and professional recognition, the young specialists likewise began to collectively identify themselves in nontraditional fashion. A. Bakuta, principal of a secondary school in the Kirgiz Republic, lodged a complaint with *Pravda* in

December 1981 about the frequent and extended delays to the start of the school year while the students harvested potatoes and cotton.[29]   After describing the annual mobilization of students and conceding the importance of the harvest, Bakuta questioned whether or not this annual mobilization might not "cover for the disorganization, lack of administrative capability or irresponsibility of other workers." She noted that "workers of the state and collective farms don't rush to gather cotton by hand—it's wearisome, low-paying work; they must call for the help of the schoolchildren, must mobilize the pedagogical collectives and even evaluate the teachers' work in terms of the quantity of cotton gathered or potatoes dug." Clearly, Bakuta's indignation goes beyond concern for the students alone; it also causes her to lash out against "them" (other workers and administrators) while speaking out to both protect and praise "pedagogical collectives." Thus, in this one brief passage she clearly displays both negation and the mutuality characteristic of a member of a subaltern or subordinate group. Whether or not young specialists were a genuine subaltern group is not the key issue here. What is critical is that Bakuta clearly demonstrated her awareness of her professional peers as a unique, specific group. The fact that she does so in the Party daily *Pravda* should be noted as a significant insertion of that group's perspective into the most public of the Soviet Union's public transcripts.

The petitions of teachers in *Uchitel'skaia gazeta*, the journal of the teachers' union, consistently demonstrated these same elements of negation and mutuality and often did so much more directly and forcefully. In April 1982, seven teachers wrote to the journal to complain about being forced to collect money from elementary school students to pay for membership dues and stamps.[30] They described themselves as "embarrassed before the students and their parents for these requisitions."

In another collection of petitions to *Uchitel'skaia gazeta*, teachers complained stridently about the classification of street cleaning as a "professional obligation," for which school directors were fined by a district executive committee if the cleaning was deemed substandard.[31] In describing the executive committee's street-cleaning orders, the teachers protested, "They began to abuse our conscientiousness."[32] Further, the teachers noted that the executive committee repeatedly "forgot" about the holiday set aside to honor teachers, on one occasion directing a teachers' collective to assist in leveling truckloads of dirt at a construction site on Teachers' Day. Most irritating to the teachers was the impersonal and condescending manner in which the executive committee communicated these orders—with an impersonal telephone message (telefonogramma) to the school office at the start of the school day. They summarized their feeling thus: "It's not [a question of] labor insulting a *person's* dignity. It is the relationship [with the executive committee] which is insulting the dignity of the *profession*" (emphasis added).

That the teachers described themselves as "embarrassed" and that they consistently mentioned the dignity of themselves and their vocation raise an important consideration. In his discussion of domination and resistance in societies, James Scott paid particular attention to issues of "dignity and autonomy" as forming a major part of the insertions of the subordinate into the public transcript. As Scott noted, such issues "have typically been seen as secondary to material exploitation" in the traditional discussion of elite-subordinate systems (such as slavery, colonialism, etc.), yet his studies indicated that "slights to one's dignity . . . figure as prominently in accounts of exploitation as do narrower concerns of work and compensation."[33] It is in the realm of dignity and autonomy, rather than in the sphere of economic compensation, that the young specialists of the Brezhnev years most commonly expressed their feelings of subordination.[34]

When Olga Ivanovna Golubenko, the young urban teacher assigned to a rural school, complained about her working conditions, she listed her schoolroom's broken door, collapsed stove, and blocked chimney as "difficulties which I had expected."[35] It was not poor physical working conditions or her pay that most roused her indignation but rather the fact that the school director and others casually discussed and accepted the fact that no recent graduates of her secondary school had been admitted to institutes. She was incensed that such conversations were allowed, given that "they would undermine all the teachers' work and make their very existence senseless." Thus, it was Golubenko's professional dignity as a teacher and her expectation that professional teachers should share and treasure that dignity that formed the crux of her complaint.

In a similar situation, *Uchitel'skaia gazeta* listed a serious and growing problem for rural teachers: the inability to obtain firewood or fuel for schools in cold northern areas.[36] Noting that "most schoolteachers are women, who under the law are not supposed to do loading work," the newspaper cited examples of teachers who were told, "Get your own fuel" by local officials. The correspondent closed the article with an affirmation of the professional dignity that teachers deserved: "The local soviets and principals seem to have forgotten that the Law on Public Education mandates greater concern for teachers."

The teachers' complaints in the public transcript of *Uchitel'skaia gazeta* in the late 1970s and early 1980s were preceded by similar comments that were kept hidden. In September 1975, a young teacher from Ordzhanikadze responded to a series of *Komsomolskaia pravda* articles on parent-teacher relations. Closely following the traditional petitioning format, she complained that school directors (and she used specific names) forced teachers to collect money from students' parents "for repair of classes and corridors: they even force [us] to equip classes with textbooks and to buy curtains to spread in the windows—all of this at parents' expense."[37] She then noted that money was released to the factory director responsible for supporting the school in sufficient quantity and concluded: "It's likely that this money gets 'spread out' on its way to the school, having organized for all the teachers and their families a banquet at a restaurant that corresponded to the completion of repairs. I'd like to know if someone could check up on all of this and limit this shameful levy from parents. Believe me, I don't write for any ulterior motive."[38]

Teachers were, of course, not the only specialists to develop a sense of negation, that is, a sense of themselves as a group opposed to another in a "we versus they" mind-set. In his letter to *Sotsiologicheskaia industriia* in 1972, chemical engineer I. Mironovich protested the failure of the responsible ministry to bring a new product developed in his factory into full production. In so doing, he displayed a clear sense of negation, placing his factory section into opposition to "them"—the government officials. He wrote: "Some are saying that 'They have found themselves a concern, so your work is in vain.' The ministry of shipbuilding and the cellulose paper industry could long ago have begun to use [the product] to satisfy basic needs. Either they don't want trouble, or for some other reason, but a valuable product which the national economy needs is not on the market."[39]

Mironovich's awareness was centered upon his local professional peers, that is, those in his own factory section. His perception of the oppositional status of his group versus the officials in question is another example of negation.

The young specialists of the Brezhnev era had developed horizontal connections that went beyond mere negation. On several occasions, they promoted or discussed the creation of a different type of professional association from that of the normal soviet "*soiuz*."

Typically, a young professional automatically had dues deducted from his or her paycheck for membership in a professional association.[40] As discussed earlier, such membership was important in the arrangement of vacations and housing, but not in the sense of developing professional associations or mutual support that such organizations normally emphasize in the West.

In some sources, late in the Brezhnev era, specialists either discussed the merits of a "closed" professional association or openly called for the establishment of such an association in order to protect the interests of their profession. The first such discussion comes from a senior accountant, not one of the Children of Victory but one who advanced arguments that some young specialists would later repeat.

In a letter to *Pravda*, V. Golubov, a senior accountant, called for the formation of an all-union accountants' association in order to "raise prestige and facilitate bonds among colleagues."[41] Golubov's letter made it clear that he saw such an association primarily as a means of escape for the accounting profession from its woefully subordinate status. Golubov noted the nationwide shortage of accountants with higher education, which he blamed on the "unjustified drop in the prestige of the profession." Golubov then proposed an all-union accountants association in order to raise the prestige of the profession, facilitate bonds among colleagues, and formulate guidelines for professional conduct.

Golubov was not alone in making such a proposal to raise accountants to a more prestigious level. Three years after his proposal, A. Kolesnichenko, another accountant who did hold a higher education, called the ongoing government efforts to raise the number of accountants with higher education "insufficient."[42] Kolesnichenko put forth a number of proposed "requirements" that every professional accountant should have and chastised the Ministry of Higher and Specialized Secondary Education for not developing a more thoroughly professional accounting curriculum for *vuz*-level students. Finally, Kolesnichenko told the story of one of the best and brightest students in a local school who said that when he announced his intention to become a professional accountant because both his father and grandfather before him had done so, "even his teachers complained openly about the young man's choice."

While accountants sought a closed, professional association to raise their prestige, other young specialists sought such association to create a channel for developing and enhancing the professional respect of colleagues, described as highly valued.

A 1981 *Komsomolskaia pravda* article discussed the problems of recruiting talented young people into the engineering profession. Noting, as many others had done, that Soviet *vuzy* seemed to be producing large numbers of mediocre engineers, the authors proposed the creation of a "selective" engineers' union. Such an association, whose membership would be based upon "qualification and colleagues' approval," would serve to "separate the real engineer from the de facto technician produced by the engineering college." The wording of the proposal was particularly interesting and merits extensive quotation here:

The creative professions emphasize their special rights by admitting the most talented people to their creative unions. Joining a union is a matter of prestige, and what's more, provides considerable benefits, which the members of a profession value highly. Engineers have their own union, and so do inventors. But the fact that membership in them is easily gained, and is in fact open to almost everyone, robs the idea of its meaning. An exacting, highly selective union that is concerned about the quality of its members can create a field of attraction strong enough to influence even the attitude of outsiders toward professional engineering mastery. Today, however, the only way an engineer can raise his rank is to transfer to the research community and defend a dissertation, that is, to betray his true calling.[43]

The similarity of this proposal and the previously mentioned architects' calls for increased professional autonomy in directing projects and selecting subordinates is striking. In each of these proposals, the emphasis is on the selectivity of professional associations based upon merit and talent. A firm belief that promotions should be rewarded based upon merit and talent formed a critical element of the ethos of the Children of Victory and sometimes placed them in direct opposition to the "stability of cadres" philosophy that anchored bureaucratic decision making in the Brezhnev era.

In addition to their desire to selectively admit members to formal professional associations, specialists desired to establish practical working relationships with other professionals in order to solve daily problems. This desire was especially prevalent in readers' letters and comments to the newspaper *Sotsialisticheskaia industriia (SI)*. It became a popular forum for specialists and engineers, as evidenced by its letter receipts. In its first full year of publication (1970), *Sotsialisticheskaia industriia* received 12,838 letters from readers. By 1981, it was receiving more than 180,000 per year, with nearly 190,000 received in the first eight months of 1982.[44]

A consistent request in these letters (and in the readers' conferences held by the paper) was the desire for "extensive examination of economic problems"[45] and "more complex evaluations [of problems], including not just the opinions of the author and reporter, but also those of interested specialists, designers, economists, et cetera."[46]   This notion of broadening dialogue among professionals, with *Sotsialisticheskaia industriia* as the forum, indicates the specialists' frustrations with the lack of open reference material and difficulty of cooperation/consultation with peers outside one's own enterprise. Such frustrations and desire for cross-communication were clear in a variety of Soviet industries and geographic locations.

V.N. Derevianko, chief engineer in a Dnepropetrovsk factory, asked at a readers' conference in October 1978 if *Sotsialisticheskaia industriia* could "include more discussions in which readers of various backgrounds would participate." His goal was that the paper should become more than just "an informer" and that it should "more often and more deeply conduct thorough analysis of various economic branches."[47]

In similar fashion, V. Khokhlov, chief engineer in an Ivanovsk cotton *kombinat* lauded *SI*'s rubric entitled "Our Dialogues" and requested that the paper "publish more conversations under this rubric," which he and his coworkers found extremely useful. In particular, Khokhlov awaited "material about the refitting of his enterprise and information about similar enterprises in the USSR."[48] *Sotsialisticheskaia industriia* seemed to provide a forum where such cross communication could take place between specialists in different enterprises as well as between specialists in the academic and the production realms.

Such was the request of P.O. Korostik, deputy director of technical administration in the Ukraine Heavy Metallurgy Ministry. "We have institutes" that study the mechanization of metallurgical work, "but their base [of experience] is weak. They can't solve our serious problems. Perhaps the paper could publish others' experiences" in a section on new innovations in technology.[49]

Even at the end of the Brezhnev era, in August 1982, specialists continued to agitate for more information. At a meeting with *SI* readers, chief engineer V.A. Stopin took the *SI* representatives to task. The newspaper had published a pictorial history of Soviet industry entitled "Steps of Industry, a Photo-Yearbook." Stopin called this an "excellent topic" but criticized *SI*'s presentation as "too superficial and scanty. We, your readers, want to know more."[50] At the same meeting, lab chief Iu. Ia. Britchenko commended *SI* as being very popular and having "great authority" with its readers, but echoed Stopin's concerns about detail. "We want to see more detailed articles, correspondence and notes about people in the [electrical] industry."[51]

Soviet specialists sought international professional communication as well. At the same readers' meeting in Dnepropetrovsk in October 1978, R.M. Kosulnikov, deputy director of a pipe industry research institute, called on the newspaper to "more actively focus on the interdependence of institutes and production enterprises to facilitate new ideas and developments." Kosulnikov focused specifically on the issue of corrosion prevention in pipelines. His letter to *SI* mentioned various corrosion prevention techniques used abroad and suggested that *SI* address and evaluate these foreign procedures in its readers' forum.[52]

That is not to say that Soviet specialists were ignorant of world standards of technical achievement. On the contrary, they were often exposed, albeit indirectly, to the latest in world technical advances. Soviet specialists selected to attend international conferences on topics related to their specialty filed trip reports on their return.[53] While those specialists who were selected to attend the conferences were universally senior specialists, there is no doubt that the information that they gained and brought home was circulated to younger specialists as well. For example, in 1970, a delegation of Soviet specialists attended a conference in Budapest on the use of natural gas in Hungary. Specialists from throughout the Soviet bloc and several Western European states attended the conference. A key issue for the Soviet delegation was the protection of underground pipelines from corrosion. They submitted a report to the conference on Soviet methods of corrosion control and brought back copies of similar reports submitted by other delegations. One of the senior Soviet delegates noted: " The material set forth in this report has great scientific and technical interest for Soviet specialists. . . . It would be expedient to publish material from this report in the Soviet press." But he was critical of many other offerings of the conference. Many aspects "did not present or arouse great interest, as analogous work has already been done in the USSR."[54]

While questions of international cooperation might seem best suited for the highest levels of Soviet industry, *SI* received repeated requests to focus on practical, day-to-day concerns of young specialists and middle-level leaders as well. *SI*'s editorial staff conducted a basic review of readers' letters at the end of 1978 and summarized the "wishes and criticisms" expressed in those letters as follows: "The paper must become closer to the workers, young engineers and economic directors of middle management. Write about them and what worries them. Many general questions are of interest only at the highest levels. [We should] analyze basic problems of raising production effectiveness 'from below' to its basic, living practice."[55]

The same summary indicated that the desire for foreign information was expressed by many more than Kosulnikov: "[We received] many proposals to broaden and improve scientific-technical information, in particular, wishes were expressed to acquaint readers with the experience of foreign enterprises and firms regarding questions of machinery, technology and the organization of production."[56] Clearly, Soviet specialists, both young and more experienced, understood that the problems that they faced were not unique and demanded information that could enable them to learn from, and attempt to improve upon, world standards.

From the outset, the Brezhnev regime defined itself via contrasts with those of Stalin and Khrushchev that had come before. The political elite sought refuge from the arbitrary tyranny of Stalin, while both the populace at large and the elite sought to leave the chaotic pace of Khrushchev's "harebrained" reform schemes behind. The resultant "social contract" was one in which the political elite provided stability in economics and politics in exchange for a certain level of quiescence on the part of the population. That is, the people could be assured of stability if they forsook political activism and focused on the "microlevel" relationships of the Little Deal. The leadership could, in its turn, expect a "stability of cadres," long tenure in office.

While questions about autonomy in professional associations or on project decision making helped specialists begin to define themselves as professionals, the negation and mutuality that arose from the "stability of cadres" contributed to the horizontal awareness of the Children of Victory as *young* specialists. Once again, the Soviet press provided a ready source of inspiration for such awareness by discussing the problems that the "stability of cadres" presented.

Late in 1981, *Pravda* proposed to intensify the progress of scientific research and to address the problems of high turnover rates at research institutes and the dearth of young people seeking higher technical education. To do this, the USSR must "restore the influx of fresh manpower" into the field.[57] The article proposed a twofold approach to achieve this end: restore the primacy of wages and prestige that scientific research previously held in the country and take the following steps toward "freeing jobs for the novices": "Existing personnel must be stringently reviewed. Labor legislation has to permit institutes' management to discharge employees with the wording 'released due to termination of research project,' . . . Reducing the number of employees in research and research services would permit wages to rise.   At the same time, research would be freed of unproductive employees, whose departure would be no loss to science."

Literaturnaia gazeta voiced similar proposals in 1982, when it proposed a "weeding out" process to reduce the number of scientists (especially those engaged in "pure science") to raise the effectiveness and productivity of scientific institutions.[58] The article proposed that "having reached retirement age, the scholar must show that age for him is not a hindrance, and that he can give many of the young a run for their money. After all, the work ability and value of a scholar is not always linked to his actual age." The article went on to propose alternative activities, such as teaching, literary, or bibliographic work for the "retired" scientist. The title of the article emphasized the principal point from the young specialists' view: "When Will the Openings Come?"

The efforts of the regime to infuse "fresh manpower" into specialized fields may, at first glance, seem to represent a convergence of interests with the young specialists. But major problems of perspective between the regime and specialists as to what issues were most important here (cases of "ambiguity" and "code-shifting") complicated that convergence and ultimately increased the frustration of young specialists.

During the major press discussions of how to most effectively manage research potential and the assignment of specialists that took place at the end of 1981, *Izvestiia* focused on the numbers and duties of administrative personnel. Citing a resolution of the 26th Congress of the CPSU that called for "Limiting Increases in and Reducing Personnel in Administrative Jobs and in Certain Branches of the Non-production Sphere," *Izvestiia* described decrees issued by the Soviet Council of Ministers intended to reduce administrative taskings and enhance productivity.[59] Those decrees established reduction rates in the administrative area for "design agencies, research organizations, institutions and organizations of science and scientific services, material and technical supply organizations and marketing organizations."

Ironically, the same month that *Izvestiia* published this article, *Pravda* received a letter from Dr. S. Bogdan, the head physician of a clinic in Chernigov. Bogdan was upset by a *Pravda* article published in February 1981, that called for improving the public health sector by "raising the standards and cultivating a sense of responsibility for assigned actions" on the part of doctors serving as head physicians.[60] The article criticized "doctors who consider their time in the important post of public health organizer [head physician] as temporary or part-time. We must promote exactness to these administrators, to inculcate in them a sense of responsibility for their assigned work."

Dr. Bogdan entitled his reply "Not a Part-Time Duty."[61] In his letter, he argued just the opposite of what the regime had been calling for in the *Izvestiia* and *Pravda* articles. Instead of reducing the number of administrative personnel, Dr. Bogdan called for an increase in the number of specially trained medical administrators and the transfer of many of the head physician's duties to these and other administrative personnel. According to Bogdan, the head physician is faced with so many additional administrative tasks (procurement of medical supplies, parts for buildings and facilities, repair orders etc.) that he has no time to "really be a physician." In his view, that is the reason that "it's all the more difficult to find people who are willing and able to take on [the head physician post]."[62]

Bogdan's concerns mirror closely those of the young school directors mentioned earlier, as well as the complaints of young teachers, engineers, and research associates. Nearly a dozen years before the latest government initiatives on administrative personnel and Bogdan's letter, young scientists and engineers made it clear that administrative positions appealed to them even less than applied industrial work.

V. Obozenko, a young architect from Novosibirsk, contributed a letter to a *Literaturnaia gazeta* discussion of the prestige of administrative work in 1970. Obozenko cited examples of peers and acquaintances who refused to be "promoted" into administrative positions.[63] In each case, the potential promotees were capable young specialists who were happy working within their academic discipline and who saw the 10-20% pay increase that they could earn as administrators as insignificant compared to the increased workload and loss of prestige that they would suffer in administrative work. Obozenko specifically cited the trivialities with which administrators were forced to deal: arranging child care and home repairs for workers, fighting bureaucratic procedures to acquire and then distribute office supplies, arranging the scheduling of shop personnel for auxiliary agricultural and construction work. Obozenko described the administrator's job as "the role of a nanny—which I know by way of some little experience—would be guaranteed for me the very next day [after assuming such a post]."

Obozenko's letter was followed by a report from a prominent Soviet sociologist that explored the relative prestige levels of various professional positions among engineers, workers, and white-collar employees, and then compared their perceptions to those of second-year and graduating *vuz* students. Each group rated 23 positions in order of prestige. The workers and engineers ranked the engineering position 7th of 23 and the occupation of section head 12th. Second-year students ranked engineers 3rd and section chiefs 10th. Finally, graduating students posted similar responses, listing the engineer in 5th place and the section chief in 9th. Thus, each group held a relatively high view of the post of engineer and section chief, though the view of the engineers themselves was obviously affected by the reality of their working lives, which led them to rank their own posts lower than did the students. Nevertheless, among all three groups, none rated purely administrative positions higher than 17th of 23, despite the fact, or perhaps because of the fact, that "a solid one-half of engineers and technicians occupy leadership posts."[64]

Whereas Obozenko had suggested that specialists disdained administrative work due to a lack of ambition or for not wanting to answer for "anything other than himself," E. Fainburg, the sociologist who authored the subsequent commentary, held a different view of the problem's cause. He classified the administrator as a "human relations engineer." As such, Fainburg held, the administrator had to master tasks having little in common with regular engineering work, tasks for which most engineers were not well prepared. Fainburg also noted that Soviet society was only just beginning to classify "administrative organizational activity" as a specific professional activity for which one must first be trained and then be recognized for managerial success.

Fainburg pointed an accusatory finger at the *vuzy* for not providing students any human relations or administrative training during the course of their engineering studies. He also noted the lack of specific institutes dedicated to the training of administrative personnel. Whether due to lack of administrative training or to their traditionally "heroic" view of science with its emphasis on rational, creative work, young specialists resented being bogged down in administrative tasks and echoed Bogdan's call for the training and assignment of genuine "administrative" specialists.

Unpublished documents from the late 1970s and early 1980s add depth to the discussion on administrative training and duties of specialists. In this instance, the archival documents are quite consistent with those appearing in the press.

During commentary to *Sotsialisticheskaia industriia* at a September 1978 readers' meeting, N. Shamskoi lamented the lack of workforce growth relative to growth of new enterprises and asked *Sotsialisticheskaia industriia* to raise the issue of training and preparation of administrators. He noted that directors come from the ranks of engineers/workers who "worked or studied together, but only one becomes a director. Having become a director, some specialists become embarrassed or shy of their colleagues, and don't exercise the necessary rigor."[65] The persistent disconnection between the viewpoints of the specialists and the regime concerning administrative duties exemplified the gradual, yet persistent, movement of the young specialists in a direction different from, and undetected by, the Soviet elite. That movement was part of the evolution of the young specialists' overall professional ethos, summarized later.

EDUCATIONAL EXPERIENCES AND EXPECTATIONS

Both Rusov and his composite specialist Posudnikov noted that their parents' "influence" led them to enroll in the *vuz*. Children of professional parents were increasingly likely to gain *vuz* admission when compared to the children of workers or peasants as the Brezhnev era progressed. But professional parents were not the only ones who pressured their children into working hard for admission to higher educational institutions.

In August 1975, the journal *Smena* published a series of letters from young people who had tried to gain admission to *vuzy* but had failed to do so. In one, a young factory worker proclaimed himself happy in life without higher education.

Sergei P. described himself as "very happy and satisfied" with the fact that he had failed to get into an energy institute, especially when he watched those who were determined to pass the entry exams studying away their hot summer days.[66] Sergei declared that he had attempted to gain admission in the first place only because of his parents. His mother had completed a technical school, and his father was a craftsman. Sergei's mother had "grieved her whole life" about not getting into an institute, and his father was "embittered by his lack of education." Having spent a year in a factory working since his failure to pass the entry examinations, Sergei declared himself happy as a worker, enrolled in a self-study program of the German language, and encouraged others to follow his example.

Was this letter genuine? Sergei's contentment with the worker's lot was extremely atypical for his generation. The opportunity for a graduate of secondary school to earn admission to a *vuz* steadily declined in the post-Stalin era. According to statistics published by *Komsomolskaia pravda,* 38.4% of secondary school students in 1951 could gain entry into *vuzy.* By 1961, that figure had fallen to 22.8%, and by 1970, only 11.8% of secondary school students could find a first-year opening in a higher educational institution.[67] In his classified 1968 report to the KGB, the Odessa informer described how, by the ninth or tenth grade, secondary school students were absolutely convinced that they would gain entry into a *vuz.* They did not realize the exclusivity of this opportunity. In his words,

This is one of the most important shortfalls in the first stage of the formation of the young person's world-view—school. The absence of the realism factor in the school upbringing, the predominance of false pathos and romances in the illumination/elucidation of complicated historical circumstances, the inability to combat the exaggeration of the significance of one's own personality that is inescapable in youth leads to the fact that the new school graduate finds himself in psychological "scissors" between the opportunities he was taught that he had and the opportunities with which reality presents him.[68]

If Sergei's letter was genuine, he clearly adapted to the "psychological scissors" better than most members of his generation. Sociological studies highlighted the enormous prestige of higher education. Archival sources and published documents dramatize the acute shortages of technicians and workers that plagued Brezhnev's USSR, so happy young workers such as Sergei were certainly rare.

Sergei's letter to *Smena* also differed from most published and archival documents reviewed here in that he neither petitioned for, nor complained about, anything. He simply chose to respond to *Smena's* ongoing discussion of education in order to express his opinion. Without access to archival material, it's impossible to confirm the validity of Sergei's letter. Nevertheless, it is useful here for the contrast that it provides to the other documents available.

As the available slots in *vuzy* decreased, the prestige of higher education continued to rise, and competition became more and more intense. By the later Brezhnev years, young Soviets sought *any* opportunity for higher education, regardless of specialty. Higher education had become popular as a ticket to better status and to a better life. This hunger for higher education became the object of scrutiny by both Western and Soviet observers and brought with it unforeseen circumstances.[69]

One such circumstance, discussed in another context earlier, was *Literaturnaia gazeta's* discussion of young foresters who would not go to work in the forests. In the course of that discussion, an official of the Russian Republic's Ministry of Forests noted that young people who knew nothing more about the forest than what they learned on weekend mushroom hunts kept applying (and being admitted) to Russia's forestry *vuzy*. His explanation for this fact was that the young were "burning with the desire to obtain a higher education."[70] Because these urban students were better prepared to pass the intense entrance exams than their rural counterparts, they were admitted, despite the fact that they were less likely than their rural peers to actually work as foresters upon graduation.

If any specialty within higher education was viewed as an avenue of prestige, the same was not true of any institution or method of obtaining one's degree. Full-time study in daytime courses at a *vuz* was held in much higher esteem by the young than was part-time study, night school, or correspondence course study. Oleg Ianson, a factory worker who attended night courses while studying to retake his *vuz* entry examinations, which he had already failed twice, best expressed this disparity in a letter to *Smena*. "It's not that I am unhappy with my work. I do quite well for a newcomer. But why should I stand at the workbench while others study in *vuzy*?"[71] Oleg went on to describe how his girlfriend of three years broke up with him for the sole reason that she had successfully entered an institute, and he had not. "So long as she believed I'd try again, she stayed with me and helped me. She's now in her second year. But gradually I noticed changes. She seemed happier with her daytime classmates, and my night school just didn't stand up. I tried the exams a second time with a crash effort, and fell one point short of admission. But I must get into the institute. They can laugh at me, but for me, at the institute there are more fish in the sea."[72]

While Oleg's desire for *vuz* admission may have been inextricably linked to his pursuit of love, the prestige of graduating from a famous institute or university and pursuing a research career was considered the ideal career path by huge numbers of young Soviet citizens in the Brezhnev era. In a 1971 interview, Alla Beliakova, then the editor of *Smena*, told Georgie Anne Geyer: "Graduates today dream of individual creative work as an independent worker or research worker. They think that is more romantic than being a shop steward. Another problem now is that everyone wants higher education. . . . It's not a question of money, for workers get the same pay. It's not a question of social equality. It is just a question of the diploma. Of prestige."[73]

Beliakova's comments are consistent with archival and interview evidence presented earlier. The Odessa KGB informer related that students widely believed that there was "more order" in scientific research in contrast to the "chaos" of Soviet industrial workplaces. The personal sagas of Sergei Tumanov and Aleksandr Kurin also substantiate the informer's perception.

Additional consideration of prestige among the young professionals in the context of their working lives is discussed later. In the current context of their educational experience, suffice it to say that the initial delineation between the young specialists as a select group and the rest of Soviet society was their successful completion of entrance examinations. The critical motivation to succeed in passing those examinations came in part from their parents but was primarily the prestige that they expected to hold as *vuz* graduates, that is, as young specialists.

Once they breeched the barrier presented by the entrance examination, would-be specialists faced a number of decisions that would shape their long-term outlook on life and work. One such decision, debated by the students themselves and in Soviet society as a whole, was the question of whether a professional should be a narrow specialist or a broadly educated person.

This question was widely debated in the Brezhnev era, including at the top levels of the political hierarchy. Party ideologist Mikhail Suslov's warnings to Soviet social scientists condemning the "still-persistent inclination toward scholastic theorizing" as "one of the major obstacles in the development of the social sciences" were discussed earlier, as was his call for social scientists to devote themselves to training specialists capable of assisting the Party and government in resolving specific "concrete" problems of social and economic development.[74]

Given Suslov's position as the Party's leading ideologist and his seniority in the Politburo by 1981, it is not surprising that his view was the one that appeared in *Pravda*. That does not, however, mean that all other high-level officials accepted his view.

The debate as to whether Soviet specialists should be broadly educated or should maintain their narrow field of expertise was both prominent and ongoing. In the mid-1970s, the Central Committee of the Communist Party of the Soviet Union (CC CPSU) directed that higher educational institutions should increase the amount of "humanitarian" preparation of young specialists in their *vuz* years. In response to this direction, Professor Zhdanov, the rector of Rostov State University,[75] developed a test curriculum. He submitted that curriculum to the CC for consideration in April 1976. In a petition that embodied all of the "classical" elements of the petitioning process, he cited the following reasons for broadening the engineering curriculum.

"As Marx predicted, today there exists a contemporary convergence of social, natural and technical sciences."[76] He used pollution as an example to support his position and the accuracy of Marx's vision. Caused by the machines of the technical sciences, pollution must be analyzed by natural scientists and studied by social scientists for its effect on society. The rector supported this example with detailed quotations from Marx. He then asserted that "the broader an engineer's education, the better the engineer. Because they're going to be directors or leaders, they have to learn how to work with and lead people."[77] Following a series of quotations from Lenin, the rector concluded his arguments by noting, "Our opponents in the ideological struggle ridicule our specialists' lack of breadth."[78] He then proposed an experimental curriculum that included courses on the "legal development of culture," "society and nature," "science as a form of culture," "ethics as a study in social-individual cooperation," "aesthetics as a science of the formation of beauty," and "ideology and the system of social values."[79]   The rector's curriculum proposal was approved by the CC in June 1976 for implementation on a trial basis.

The positions set forth by Suslov in his comments to the social scientists and in Rector Zhdanov's proposed curriculum framed the general parameters of the debate. The government's public (Suslov's) emphasis on solving "concrete" problems via narrow specialization was asserted in specialties outside social studies as well. Four months before Suslov's speech, *Pravda* published a feature entitled "A Place for an Engineer," which called for "the precise and statutory division of our technical education into different institutions: on one hand, engineering schools that provide . . . specific-purpose narrowly specialized training and, on the other hand, technical universities that provide basic general education and specialized training."[80] The author, Professor A. Grigoriev, head of the Kalinin Polytechnical Institute, noted that engineers with broad general training were valuable for their contribution to the acceleration of scientific and technical progress but that the narrowly specialized engineers sorely needed in industrial activities were lacking due to the lack of prestige and pay that such positions held.[81] He noted this lower pay and prestige as the reasons that "the number of engineers not actually working in industrial shops has become excessive." The issue of theoretical research versus applied work in factories and industrial shops was of keen importance to both the specialists and the state, and their viewpoints, like those of the social scientists and Suslov in the preceding discussion, were diametrically opposed.

While Suslov criticized "scholastic theorizing" and stressed the regime's position on the need to solve specific, "concrete" problems via applied science, a professor of physical-mathematical sciences, Dr. Aleksandr Kitaigorodskii, went a step further. Writing in *Literaturnaia gazeta* in 1982, Kitaigorodskii proposed that the best way to inspire young persons to pursue work in the application of scientific knowledge was to stop paying for work in theoretical research, which he termed "pure science."[82] Those engaged in "pure science" could, in Kitaigorodskii's plan, earn their living by teaching and conduct scientific research in their free time. That way, "if he really is captivated by science, don't worry, he'll find free time for scientific work." While Kitaigorodskii's extreme position could hardly have been termed realistic, it did serve to highlight the issue from the regime's position: the Soviet economy desperately needed engineers in industrial work, that is, in "applied" science.

Among the young specialists themselves, work in applied science simply did not hold the appeal of theoretical research. They held a view of science as a "heroic" discipline and emphasized their vision of the successful scientist as one who advances scientific and technical progress through such research. Their letters and responses to surveys indicate that this perception of science was part of their upbringing and was reinforced during their student years. Applied science within a limited industrial context simply did not appeal to them, especially given their perception of the "chaos" and disorganization of Soviet industrial workplaces.

This viewpoint marked a major divergence of the young specialists from one of the most basic "myths" of Soviet tradition. From the outset, Lenin himself had called upon the young Soviet citizens of his age to become "conscious builders" of the future communist society by working to improve their own educational and cultural skills.[83] Stalin had continued this emphasis in the late 1930s, proclaiming that one of the missions of Soviet socialism was to raise the cultural and educational level of the Soviet working classes to that previously reserved for members of the technical elite: in essence, a process of upward social mobility via the expansion of the technical intelligentsia.[84]   The resulting expansion of the technical intelligentsia developed into a major source of both upward mobility for Soviet citizens and legitimacy for the regime.[85] By the late 1960s and into the 1970s, however, highly educated technical specialists in industry found themselves often working in the same conditions and for the same wages as less educated technicians and workers.[86]

Many of the following discussions confirm this assessment that applied industrial work had declined in its appeal and that the young specialists of the Brezhnev era viewed theoretical research work with much greater regard. The conflict inspired by this change in viewpoint became apparent in discussions concerning the appropriateness of material included in the *vuz* curriculum. That curriculum glorified theoretical work at the expense of the practical. It therefore left those destined for applied or engineering work doubly cursed: they viewed their practical work assignments as second-class when compared to classmates who landed research or "theoretical" positions and were unprepared for them at the same time. Meanwhile, those who did earn coveted posts in research or theoretical institutes were often disappointed by their far from glorious work as well.

When Alexandr Rusov sketched his generalized portrait of the young Soviet specialist, his Posudnikov expressed both of these viewpoints, as one "who complained about the insufficient knowledge of *vuz* graduates" and one who "considered such things superfluous in the circumstances of the 'swamp life' at scientific research institutes."[87]

While complaints about the sufficiency or superfluous nature of the knowledge that they gained in the *vuz* were certainly frequent among young specialists, they were not alone in such negative assessments. Throughout the Brezhnev era, perceptions of problems in the way that higher educational institutions prepared graduates for employment were voiced by academicians, government planners, and industrial leaders as well as by young specialists themselves.

In one such case, a group of young mining engineers, interviewed in 1981, were unanimous in their position that the *vuz* had inadequately prepared them for their jobs. They felt that the process through which they had to mature as specialists and develop "vocational independence" on the job could have been accelerated and improved via changes in the *vuz* curriculum.[88] These young miners were focused exclusively upon "production technology." That is, the young mining engineers considered themselves insufficiently familiar with the production equipment and techniques that they encountered upon arriving at work after graduation.

In part, this may have been due to the obsolescence of training equipment used in *vuzy*, in part due to the training level of *vuz* teachers, and in part due to the nature of material included or excluded from the *vuz* curriculum. Viktor Belkin, a doctor of economics, led a discussion in 1971-1972 in *Literaturnaia gazeta* that explored the costs, both direct and indirect, of training an engineer.[89] During the course of his arguments, Belkin acknowledged, "It's no secret that the technical equipment of many *vuz* laboratories lags behind modern demands."[90] An equipment shortfall similar to this may have been one root cause of the mining engineers' feelings of inadequacy in terms of their educational preparation.

At this point, it is important to note that the young miners' specific emphasis on their perceived shortcomings in preparing to operate comfortably with "production technology" fitted well with Suslov's (the regime's) public emphasis on the value of narrowly educated specialists. As such, it is not surprising that their story was told in *Pravda*. The proposed changes to the education system that accompanied their story came from a Union Republic minister and emphasized the close connection between industrial enterprises and the *vuzy* that trained their specialists. Therefore, one must be cautious in accepting the miner's account as representative. In contrast, *Literaturnaia gazeta* adopted, in many cases, discussions that support arguments for "broadly educated" specialists.

But reasons other than equipment problems were offered for the widely perceived notion that *vuz* graduates were poorly prepared. Unlike secondary school teachers with higher education, who studied both pedagogy and psychology as part of their training, less than 20% of *vuz* instructors had ever studied either discipline.[91] Large numbers of young specialists criticized the poor pedagogical preparation of *vuz* teachers during a 1976 discussion in *Literaturnaia gazeta* that focused on "Titles and Knowledge."[92] Far too often, young graduate students or researchers who had demonstrated excellence in research or production taught *vuz* courses without any consideration being given to their ability to actually teach.[93]

Finally, in addition to obsolete equipment and poorly trained instructors, *vuzy* were roundly criticized for the content of their curricula. Again, this criticism came from both young specialists and those who evaluated their preparation.

A. Artsibashev, the young deli manager chronicled in *Komsomolskaia pravda*, lamented that "at school, I learned all the details of how goods are produced and sold."[94] Nevertheless, he found himself unprepared for the actual "rules" of the business world. "Gradually, it dawned on me that personal relations and acquaintances play a large role" in one's business success. Artsibashev's story, in this aspect, tends to support the argument for more broadly educating young specialists espoused by Rector Zhdanov of Rostov State University and those discussions highlighted in *Literaturnaia gazeta*, in contrast to Suslov's positions in *Pravda*.[95] Business specialists were not the only ones who suffered from an overemphasis on the technical aspects of their training at the expense of training in interpersonal relationships or even an evaluation of the would-be specialists' own psychological makeup. Other specializations were also included in the ongoing debate of "narrow education versus a well-rounded person."

In the 1973 discussion of young forestry specialists, V. Primak, the deputy director of administration of leadership cadres and scholarly institutes of the Russian Forest Ministry, complained, "Unfortunately, much attention is devoted to their knowledge, and little to their dedication or preparedness for work in the woods."[96] Primak also noted that the limited number of field exercises on which forestry students was deployed were delayed until late in the curriculum, when the fledgling specialist already had a vested interest in completing his degree, even if such exercises revealed him to be completely unsuited to forest work.

The lack of evaluation of fledgling specialists' psychological disposition toward their chosen vocation was repeatedly decried in the Soviet press. In the follow-up discussions to A. Rusov's portrait of Posudnikov as the generalization of the young Soviet specialist, a number of observers addressed this subject. Two commentators, Professor V. Lavrov of the Moscow Institute of Electro-technical Communications and candidate of psychology L. Kondrat'eva, argued for creation of a scientific-psychological service as part of the *vuz* curriculum to help young specialists "find themselves" as part of their education and preparation to enter the workforce.[97]

Arguments for increasing the breadth of *vuz* instruction appeared regularly in *Literaturnaia gazeta* and *Komsomolskaia pravda*. While such arguments did not normally appear in *Pravda*, archival materials reveal that that newspaper did receive letters and petitions in favor of the "broadly educated" position. For example, in a letter to *Pravda* that was eventually used as part of the agenda for a conference of ideological workers in 1972, V. Tretiakova noted a specific shortcoming in the availability of literature that could provide essential background knowledge and context for certain young specialists: "Having spoken with many young specialists who dream of going to work in Siberia, I'm convinced that they know the history of this enormous part of our Russia only superficially. To the question, have they read Korolenko, they replied negatively. Not to read Korolenko for people wishing to work in Siberia or for people engaged n propaganda means that much is neglected in the evaluation of our accomplishment in educating our young." [98]

Tretiakova's letter was submitted to *Pravda* as part of an ongoing discussion in that paper about shortages of literature in general, not directly connected to the debate on educational scope. Yet it clearly had implications for that debate.

Both sides in the debate could agree that, in general, the combination of equipment obsolescence, poor instructor training, and curricular shortfalls led to the broad perception at many levels of Soviet society that young specialists in all disciplines were not well prepared for work when they left the *vuz*. The widespread nature of this perception is clear from a few examples in discussions already mentioned. In the 1972 discussion of coauthorship issues, V. Perevedentsev commented, "That our higher schools don't adequately prepare scientific researchers is well known."[99]   Also critical of the level of preparation of young researchers was Professor M. Iaroshevskii, a commentator on Rusov's portrayal of the young specialist in the figure of the cabdriver Posudnikov. Iaroshevskii noted that "the *vuz* does not expressly resolve the problem of the preparation of cadres for research institutes, though it does serve as their main source of personnel." Iarshevskii agreed with young Posudnikov that the root of this problem lay in the poor preparation of the specialists.[100] V. Belkin, in his analysis of the hidden costs of training industrial engineers, criticized enterprises for using specialists in worker or technician positions as a way to make up for the "shortcomings" of *vuzy*.[101]

As these examples demonstrate, some potential employers entertained serious doubts as to the ability of the young specialists to perform on the job. Yet this potential confidence problem from the employers' perspective stands in contrast to the young specialists' sense of personal confidence in themselves as intelligent people, capable of solving complicated problems if given the data and opportunity to do so, as discussed earlier. This conflict between personal assurance and fears about their professional competence contributed to young specialists' criticism of the system in which they lived and worked. One aspect of that system that continuously challenged the confidence of the young specialists and frustrated their aspirations was the first post-*vuz* experience of nearly every young specialist— the "job distribution" (*raspredelenie*).

Put simply, nearly every new graduate of a Soviet *vuz* was theoretically obligated to accept a job assignment in accordance with the official distribution system. Industrial enterprises and research institutes placed "orders" for specialists with the Ministry of Higher and Specialized Secondary Education. On the basis of these orders the number of students admitted to the *vuz* was determined. The job distribution system was, in practice, complicated and inefficient. The assignment system allowed for "exceptional" students (prizewinners, valedictorians, etc.) to seek employment on their own. Other "exceptions" existed as well, depending upon the specifics of one's academic specialty, military service, and so on. As such, it represented a significant challenge (and sometimes trauma) that played a major role in the common experience of the Children of Victory.

An extreme case of the disconnection between *vuz* and industrial planning was presented in *Komsomolskaia pravda* in May 1981. Under a column headed "Why?" G. Shagieva, a graduate of Gorky University, submitted a letter entitled "The Specialists Are Not Needed."[102]   Shagieva described the fate of graduates of Gorky University who earned diplomas in "applied linguistics." These people, whom she termed capable of machine translation and dictionary compilation and skilled in information management systems, could find no jobs. Only two of the 25 most recent graduates were assigned at the request of enterprises. The rest were left to their own devices. Shagieva, incredulous at the difficulty in placing information specialists "in the midst of the information explosion," cited the "scarcity of information about the specialists themselves" as the central problem, that is, the fact that no one in the industries most likely to use these specialists understood what they could do.   When the academic department producing these "linguistic engineers" sent an "advertising listing" to an oil reprocessing plant (whose administration could logically be assumed in need of specialists in information and document management), the university received a reply that said, "Specialists in applied linguistics aren't necessary for us, in view of the absence of medical organizations here."   Despite repeated business trips and personal contacts by university personnel with enterprise directors, heads of research institutes, and so on, these young specialists remained unemployed or at least underemployed.

This extreme example highlights the problems of the job distribution system. In theory, at least, the university should have been training linguistic engineers in keeping with requests from those enterprises or institutes that would eventually employ the graduates. But many other factors had come into play since the early 1960s when the Gorky University had initiated its "linguistic engineering" program, and its graduates had been "hot commodities."[103] Given the often-traumatic impact that the distribution system (or their efforts to avoid it) had upon the young specialists, the system deserves discussion here.

The Gorky State University example was extreme but not unique. In a letter to the Central Committee Section for Science and Scholarly Institutions, the rector of Rostov State Univeristy (RGU), Professor Zhdanov, asserted:

It's again necessary to raise the fact that the graduating class of specialists does not conform to the plan for their assignment. This year, more than two hundred fifty RGU grads did not receive distribution plans. The Ministry plan notes that two hundred fifty graduates are to enter the work force at the discretion of the Director. And so we send them out to arrange whatever they can. But how many worries, tragedies and disappointments have we here: you studied and studied—but no one needs you? In the final analysis, we arrange [something] for all of them. But is this really the thing? Is this really a planned job distribution?[104]

To underscore his position, Zhdanov provided the data in Table 4.1 about the most recent class of graduates from Rostov State University and the number of job openings allotted to the university for placing those graduates.[105]

Table 4.1
Disparity between Numbers of Graduates and Job Availability

SPECIALITY	GRADS	JOBS
PHYSICISTS	94	12
CHEMISTS	84	11
BIOLOGISTS	72	20
MECHANICAL ENG'RS	19	2
PSYCHOLOGISTS	47	2
POL-ECON SPECIALIST	45	2
PHILOSOPHERS	36	1

Zhdanov's data are even more shocking than the Gorky State University example. In the Gorky case, the narrowly defined specialization might be used as an excuse for the difficulty in placing specialists. But Zhdanov's Rostov data include some of the most basic specialties of Soviet science. It is likely for that reason that his statistics remained unpublished. In this case, the published (Gorky) statistics portray the problem as significant but limited in scope, while the unpublished data (Rostov) give light to the full extent of the problem. Most readers of the Gorky case would have at least intuitively understood the implications of that limited portrayal because of their own personal experience.

More than half of the specialists interviewed in 1995 and 1999 noted that they had "chosen" their first job after graduation, as opposed to having their work assigned by the distribution system.[106] Obviously, the theoretically close correspondence between the needs of enterprises and the production of graduates was not true in practice. Of the respondents who declared that they found their work on their own, only five openly admitted that they arranged their employment "through influence" (*po blatu*), with the implication that this arrangement circumvented procedures. One explained that he had done well enough in school to earn a "free" diploma, that is, the right to choose his own employer. The others considered their actions to be the normal way of doing business. Press sources indicate that their consideration was widely held throughout Soviet society.

Pravda addressed the issue of the job distribution and its problems in

1981. In "The Paradoxes of Job Placement: The Higher School and an Order for a Specialist," *Pravda* noted the uneven nature of the job assignment system. In some areas, large numbers of engineers filled technicians' or even workers' posts because of a surplus of available specialists, while in other geographic areas, those same specialists were in desperately short supply.[107]   The author, G. Chumakova, blamed three causes: the poor treatment of newly arrived specialists by enterprises (lack of creative work, no housing, poor wages); arbitrary determinations of numbers of engineer specialists requested by enterprises, determinations that often included "spare" specialists "just in case" or requirements that changed while the specialists training to fill them were still in the *vuz*; and the failure of Republic and Union ministries to develop and present a scientifically based method of requesting specialists (despite the fact the USSR Council of Ministers had ordered them to do so by the end of 1978). The story of Alexei Lobanov, the bright young engineer who earned the right to choose his future work, only to be so frustrated by the treatment he that received at a Union-level research institute that he took a job as a machine-tool adjuster, was included in this article to demonstrate the perils faced by even the best *vuz* graduates.

Archival sources confirm the widespread nature of the problem, its status as common knowledge among large segments of the Soviet population, and the frustration that the problem caused among young specialists. In the period prior to the 24th Party Congress in 1971, *Komsomolskaia pravda* submitted a review of letters on this subject to the Central Committee. In that collection, one young specialist, V. Zarovnii, wrote: "I received my degree as an engineer from the Nikolaevski ship-building institute. In the city of Sosnovok in Krovskii oblast, where I went to work, they thought long and hard in the shipbuilding factory about where to 'put' me . . . then determined [to put me] in the external cooperation section. Everything I studied in the institute, it seems, was unnecessary."[108]

In the commentary accompanying this and other excerpts, *Komsomolskaia pravda* noted:

In the past, the paper has led discussions of the rationalization of job assignment and use of young specialists. But our mail abounds with complaints that young specialists are not used per designation. These letters attest to the tremendous waste of education. . . . These and other letters give cause to speak about the poor quality in distribution/assignment of young specialists. The rights of young specialists and technicians, defined by the "Regulation on the Personal Assignment of Young Specialists" are being violated.[109]

Given the pervasiveness of the problems, it is not surprising that the average graduate was often apprehensive about accepting a job in accordance with the assignment system. Olga Golubenko, the young urban-raised teacher who failed to complete her rural teaching assignment, recalled that her "hand shook" when she wrote "accepted" next to her assignment.[110]

One of the main reasons that graduates like Golubenko were so nervous about accepting assigned posts was housing. The Ukrainian minister of higher and specialized secondary education cited housing as "the most acute problem of job assignment," especially in big cities, where limits on residence permits conflicted with the demand for specialists. The lack of housing complicated placement of specialists in jobs suited to their qualifications and keeping the specialists at the enterprise to which they were assigned when they did in fact report.[111]   Of course, young urban specialists like Golubenko often resisted rural assignments. Golubenko herself revealed their view of provincial life when she declared herself as ready for such rural duty based on the hardships of her experience in working with youth "construction detachments." [112] Other specialists were simply unwilling to work in the provinces. Leonid Romanovich Veintraub, a dedicated archivist and historian, told me in 1999: "I escaped from the mandatory job assignment. Most of us from Moscow or the Moscow region got jobs in the Moscow area. But some were sent to the provinces far away. Anyone who was able to do so escaped the job assignments. That wasn't so hard in the humanities, because they didn't track us the way they did mathematics or physics or other science majors. Specific enterprises or institutes demanded those people, while we were freer."[113]

Conditions at many assigned jobs were so bad that graduates often simply ignored their assignments and found jobs that they wanted in areas that they preferred. The problem existed in all disciplines and in all geographic areas. According to *Uchitelskaia gazeta*, the national fulfillment rate of job requests by pedagogical *vuzy* was only 72%.[114] The same year, *Izvestiia* reported that the report rate for graduates of agricultural *vuzy* was only 58%.[115] The same *Izvestiia* article noted that "the law requiring graduates to report to assigned jobs for three years after graduation is largely ignored by both graduates and by employers who are forbidden to hire graduates within three years of graduation without official paperwork entitling the graduate to seek work on his own."

When the Central Committee received the complaints about job assignments from Rector Zhdanov of Rostov State University, described earlier, the committee asked the Ministry of Education of the Russian Republic to comment. In May 1976, Deputy Minister A.G. Lebedev informed the CC:

For the past five years (1971-1975), the Minvuz of the RSFSR [Russian Soviet Federated Socialist Republic] has sharply decreased the Ministry's requests for young specialists who have received university education. Because of this, many graduates remain without assigned places to work. For example, in 1974-1975, more than 67,000 people graduated from university. Gosplan RSFSR did not guarantee places for 8,417 of these graduates, including 2,560 chemists, 2227 biologists, 1,868 physicists, 439 in philosophy, 405 in mechanical engineering, 292 psychologists and 155 political-economic specialists. In addition, there are local cases where enterprises and organizations have rejected specialists sent to them in accordance with the plan.[116]

Part of the problems with assigning young specialists resulted in the ripples initiated by Minvuz's reducing its requests for specialists over the course of five years. When the ministry changed requirements, it did not "grandfather" to accommodate those already enrolled in *vuzy*. Enterprises and industries changed their quotas the same way. As a result, a student who was projected against a position upon enrollment in school could find that the position no longer existed upon graduation. On a large scale, such shifting requirements created a huge pool of unassigned specialists and unfilled positions.[117]

Proposals for addressing this problem appeared frequently in the Soviet press during the last five years of the Brezhnev era and ranged from recommendations to withhold the diploma until the graduate completed the first assignment to proposals to assign students their future work immediately upon their entry into the *vuz*, so that they would have a better idea of "what to expect" upon graduation.[118] In any event, the problem persisted throughout the Brezhnev era, and the problems associated with fulfilling or escaping their official job assignment formed a common link among young Soviet professionals. It formed a large part of what the Odessa KGB informer referred to as the "collision" with the production world that undermined the newly minted specialists' faith in the system. This study now turns to what happened after specialists came through the trial of the distribution process and actually reported to their first job: what aspirations did the young professionals hold, and what level of satisfaction did they find at work?

WORK SATISFACTION AND ASPIRATIONS

Whether their first job was assigned to them by the distribution system or arranged on their own, the vast majority of the specialists surveyed for this study reported that they were satisfied with their initial work placement. Forty-six of 53 respondents described their first jobs as "appealing" to them. Every respondent considered his or her relations with coworkers as good (though 6 did specify that these "good relations" were limited to time at work and did not signify social interaction). Further, 43 of 53 indicated that they accomplished some sort of professional aspirations in the Brezhnev era. Those achievements included publications (7), promotions (15), the completion of advanced academic degrees (11). In the most general sense, one would therefore conclude that young Soviet specialists normally found some level of satisfaction (at least, in hindsight) with their first jobs. That is not to say, however, that specific problems did not exist. But this general level of satisfaction must be kept in mind as a contrasting perspective while reviewing the press sources, which focused almost entirely on problematic issues.

Of particular importance to the young professionals were issues of their dignity and autonomy as professional specialists. These issues arose as they discovered that the prestige that they believed was their due as diploma-bearing specialists was not always reflected in their daily work environment. In particular, issues of access to reference materials, the performance of manual labor, recognition of their achievements as authors or inventors, and the material conditions of their living standards and wages featured prominently in press discussions. Within the overall context of job satisfaction, these particular issues provide insight into the ethos of the young specialists.

One of the questions that *Literaturnaia gazeta* posed in its 1970-1971 survey of scientific workers was: "Via what channels do you obtain the information which is most vital to your work?"[119] More than 89% of the respondents to the survey cited "specialized literature" as the key source of their professional data.[120] Access to specialized information was clearly the lifeblood of the specialists in all disciplines of research and production. *Literaturnaia gazeta* noted:

Information centers are issuing all possible forms of "condensations."[121] Reference journals, express information, bibliographic reviews, and review handbooks are now being organized either on a branch basis [i.e., the information institutes of various ministries] or are appearing universally. As a whole, they must all be included in one state system of scientific-technical information, the creation of which was stipulated in the Ninth Five Year Plan per directive of the Twenty-Fourth Congress of the CPSU.[122]

The Party's emphasis on the improved dissemination of specialized literature appeared, at least initially, to lead to some specific, positive steps. When an engineer, B. Doktorovich, wrote to *Literaturnaia gazeta* in early 1972 to highlight the need for a specialized journal dedicated to the development and implementation of automated systems of production administration (ASUs), his letter was answered just one month later by a representative of the Soviet Academy of Sciences announcing the pending first issue of just such a journal.[123]

Despite the Party's emphasis on publication of information or perhaps because of the emphasis on "one state system of scientific-technical information," Soviet specialists nevertheless found themselves in the midst of an "information crisis." According to *Literaturnaia gazeta*, the essence of the crisis was the ever-increasing amount of scientific literature available compared to the inability of specialists to ever access all of it.[124] Long lines at the reading rooms of Moscow and Leningrad libraries were the physical manifestations of the fact that material was not available outside the capitals. "Interlibrary subscription is still not ready for the rapid growth of scientific cadres in the country or in the increase in their demands."[125]

Specialists vented their frustration with the limited availability of information in their letters to the press. The industrial sociologists discussed earlier criticized the state for the fact that a study of job categorization, so significant that it represented a "handbook" (*nastol'naia kniga*) of factory sociology, which had been compiled at the laboratory of the "Red Proletarian" machine-tool factory in Moscow, had never been published for wide dissemination, with the result that any sociologist who desired to use it had to travel to Moscow and copy the original.[126] For these sociologists, writing 10 years after the 24th Party Congress and its mandates on the state-run scientific-technical information system, the inaccessibility of specialized information was a decisive obstacle to their professional performance and an infringement upon their ability to function autonomously as professionals.

As with any article from *Pravda*, one must consider the possibility of ulterior motives in the publication of the sociologists' complaints. But this particular piece is consistent with similar complaints in archival sources. For example, in 1974, P. Andreeva, a medical specialist from Novosibirsk, complained that the USSR Ministry of Health repeatedly refused to publish information about alternative methods of treatment. She noted: "World statistics show that allergies, mental, sciatic, and heart-vessel diseases are growing yearly. And it's known not just to medics that many chronic diseases are treated neither by the surgeon's knife nor by medication. Therefore the question of 'new treatment methods' arises. And Minzdrav doesn't have to follow them literally, but should study them, expose doctors to them." [127]

Obstacles to the flow of information worked in two directions, both of which affected the autonomy of young specialists. Boris Vidimskii was a physicist who specialized in laser technology and information recording technology. When he recalled his professional accomplishments as a young specialist in the 1970s, his pride was clearly evident when he discussed the papers that he had published in his field. That pride was tempered, however, by his caveat that, in the 1970s, he had been able to publish his work only inside the USSR. A number of those same papers, he noted, were later published in the United States, Germany, and Japan.[128]

The young specialists were a proud generation of professionals. Their professional achievements inspired them to believe in themselves and in their ability to achieve world-class standards of performance, as Vidimskii did with his articles. Their education, particularly for scientific specialists, had exposed them to at least some knowledge of the world outside the Soviet Union. In the climate of detente that dominated relations with the West in the early-mid 1970s, their appetites were whetted for more such information and for the ability to compete directly with the West.[129] These impulses brought them into conflict with their parents and caused at least some of them to question the state's restrictiveness. Georgie Anne Geyer noted that, in their attitudes toward forbidden authors, the Children of Victory manifested "a real difference" from the perspective of their parents. The parents regarded such authors as "traitors" whose work the children should not even want to read.[130] The children, on the other hand, believed that "we have more in common with intellectuals in other countries than with many workers here, yet we're not supposed to talk to these intellectuals. Can you imagine this—in an age when man is going to the moon?"[131]

This desire for direct contact and competition with the West stemmed from self-assurance. After all, these young professionals had overcome great odds in gaining acceptance to, and completing, higher education. They then overcame shortcomings in that education that left them initially unprepared for day-to-day aspects of their first job assignments. These victories inspired strong faith in their abilities. That same confidence in their own ability caused young specialists to question those who apparently lacked such confidence, including their own political leaders. One young specialist openly asked Geyer: "Why not let people [emigrate] if our society is such a good one? Why are we so lacking in confidence?"[132]

In the aftermath of the 24th Party Congress of March 1971, the USSR began to import Western technology on an unprecedented scale. Naturally, along with the technology came instructions and data on the operation and capabilities of that equipment and technology. Just as important as the data was the impression that the technology made on Soviet specialists as to the relative quality of Western and Soviet equipment. At the same time, the regime began to relax restrictions on some previously forbidden works by prerevolutionary authors and to show an increased number of Western films.[133] These actions may have represented concessions designed to strengthen the microlevel focus of the Little Deal, or they may have been a way of deflecting demands for more solid statistical data about the West. It is also possible that the import of technology may merely have reflected economic desperation. In either case, they contributed to an increase in the exposure of young specialists to non-Soviet ideas and standards. The long-term effects of that exposure will remain the subject of intensive research for many years.[134]

Both public and archival sources reveal that the constraints of the "information crisis" irritated young professionals and gradually undermined their faith in the system. In contrast, the fact that they were often forced to perform manual labor generated outright anger and insult and brought forth immediate challenges to their faith in the system. No other single issue inspired such strong reaction or provides such ample opportunity for insight into the Children of Victory as did their reaction to being forced to perform menial tasks.

The central grievance of many of the sources examined here was the irritation and indignity that many young specialists experienced as the result of being tasked to perform unskilled manual labor that was either only tangentially related or completely unrelated to their professional and academic specialty. The practice of local Party or enterprise officials' assigning specialists to such chores as street cleaning, crop harvesting, ticket sales, and building maintenance generated a great deal of strong reaction. Sometimes the young specialist was individually assigned such labor. At other times, a group of specialists received joint taskings. In both situations, the young professionals' reactions were the same.[135]

Prominent in Aleksandr Rusov's portrait of his generation in the figure of Posudnikov was the latter's lament "about how they forced him to carry nitrogen cylinders, to wash the laboratory glassware and to work in a vegetable depot."[136] A second, more detailed example echoes Posudikov's complaint.

V. Kocheshev, mentioned earlier for avoiding open political commentary in his letter to the press, was a graduate of the prestigious Bauman Higher Technical Institute, a Komosomol secretary, and a member of the Komosomol committee for his city. In 1978, he wrote a letter to *Pravda*, in which he described his career to that point.[137] Because his letter included several salient points, and because it generated a dramatic response, it is cited at length here (emphasis added).

Three years ago, I finished the Bauman Higher Technical Institue and began to work in the Sedin machine-building factory in Krasnodarsk. I came full of hope and plans. . . . From the first day, I turned into an auxiliary housekeeping worker. Among other things, I dug ditches, gathered trash on new construction sites, and painted window sashes. In our section we had an unwritten rule: *messages appeared on the notice board daily*—some people are sent here, some there.
Don't think that I am against participating in the city's health, or cleaning the factory grounds, *if everything is done in moderation*. But every week we have new buildings, new assignments. The legitimate question arises: *What can a young specialist learn from such experience?*
In the factory, [we're] conducting a technical refitting. A new system is being introduced for raising the effectiveness of production, and *the skill of the engineer is needed there no less than, let's say, in the cleaning of the streets.*

Kocheshev's letter highlighted four common traits of young specialists' concerns: the arbitrary and impersonal manner in which the extra assignments were made—in this case, via message board with no explanation; the expressed willingness to engage in such activity at moderate levels, the question of what the specialist is to gain; and finally, the concern that extra assignments detract from the specialists' ability to perform tasks directly involved with their actual position. Some or all of these themes repeatedly appeared in letters from specialists in diverse disciplines often enough to make them one of the most clear-cut aspects of the young specialists' ethos.

Equally as valuable as Kocheshev's letter was the discussion that followed its publication. *Pravda* reporter I. Lukin conducted interviews with Kocheshev's supervisors and others in the factory administration.[138] They were happy to explain the situation, and their explanations provide important insight into the young specialists' dilemma from other perspectives.

Kocheshev's direct supervisor had been Chief Design Engineer V. Semisalov. He lamented Kocheshev's departure even as he affirmed the validity of Kocheshev's complaint. Semisalov noted that he received orders to assign menial tasks "from above" and had no choice but to implement them. Semisalov noted that, of the 58 people working in his section, 38 were women, and he could "not send women to dig a ditch." Of the 20 men in the section, "there are some who are old and sick. So the whole burden is transferred to the young [male] specialists, some of whom are in the section only rarely." Semisalov asserted that the main problem with such use of specialists was that the practice gave "rise to slackness, because an individual is not at his basic job, and it goes without saying that he's not fully occupied on this kind of task."

Lukin asked others, higher in the factory hierarchy, to comment on the situation as well. A senior member of the staff, V. Kopitiuk, explained the rationale for using specialists as menial laborers. "You don't take a worker from his machine—production rises and the plan is fulfilled. After all, the engineer does not directly influence the fulfillment of the program goals." In other words, the short-term impact of lost work time for an engineer did not affect plan fulfillment and was therefore acceptable.

A member of the factory's design bureau, S.P. Velichko, openly stated what Kocheshev had only implied: "It [manual labor by specialists] is understandable when you are talking about harvesting crops and it's a tense situation. There is no discussion—the factory always arrives to help the village workers. But why is it even considered possible to force a design engineer to perform such unskilled work as painting pavilions and benches in the park or to collect trash? After all, there are service personnel there."[139]

His question was answered by a senior member of the design bureau, Iu. Vilkov, who provided another viewpoint: "In our time, when specialists with higher education were not so numerous, they guarded us, looked after us. Now, significantly more have become engineers, but they're often used without regard for [their] designation."

Unspoken in the comments of both young Kocheshev and these senior personnel was the question: Who were "they," the ones who considered such work possible for engineers and who used specialists without regard for designation? *Pravda* correspondent Lukin provided an answer. After noting that even the factory laboratory that was to ensure rational use of all personnel was usually bereft of its specialists due to outside labor tasks, he examined the orders to the Sedin factory from the regional Party executive committee. In four months, 17 such work orders were issued. After describing the tasks involved, Lukin concluded:

For the regional executive committee's directors, it is as if it never occurred that the factory has a program, an obligation [of its own], and that they are diverting engineers, technicians and machine operators from their basic work. No one will argue that the city should not keep parks, squares and projects in good order. But obviously, for such work one must utilize those for whom it is useful. Great responsibility lies on engineers . . . and we must create for them conditions for fruitful creative work. We must free them from shovels and brooms.[140]

That such commentary criticizing regional Party organs appeared in *Pravda*, the Party newspaper, may have signaled that such criticism was acceptable and contributed to the large response that Kocheshev's letter and Lukin's commentary generated. But the content of the response and the fact that much of it came from young specialists indicate that Kocheshev and Lukin had struck chords that resonated among young professionals who chafed at the menial aspects of Posudnikov's "swamp life."

Pravda published an article of response under Lukin's name in December 1978. Lukin cited excerpts from young engineers' letters that asserted that the misuse of young specialists spread far beyond an isolated area of Krasnodarsk region. Specialists argued that "when rakes and shovels often turn out in the hands of a specialist, then they not only take away his enthusiasm, they also lower the prestige of the engineer, they strike at his qualifications."[141] In addition to the negative impact of this practice upon specialists, Lukin raised the problematic issues of the labor discipline of the service and agricultural personnel who should have performed the cleanup and harvesting operations, as well as the responsiveness of local Party and government organs to directives from the center. These points were not lost on young specialists, as demonstrated by L. Nevodchikova, the young candidate of geological-mineral sciences who decried the abuse of specialists from her research institute, who regularly supplemented the work of a vegetable depot, and who was incredulous to learn that the local regional Party committee rewarded the depot with bonuses for plan fulfillment.[142]

Industrial and scientific specialists were not the only ones who resented manual labor not an integral part of their duties. A young docent at a teacher-training institute condemned the need for teacher and student participation in the cleanup of filthy grounds for the start of the school year. "Given that the cleaning staff was not on vacation all summer, they [the teachers] should not have to do someone else's job."[143]

Many other young specialists objected to performing menial or other additional duties. More examples of such objections are studied later. It is important to note, however, that such negative reactions were certainly not unanimous among the Children of Victory. In a response to Rusov's Posudnikov portrait, one older Muscovite wrote to *Literaturnaia gazeta* to describe how her specialist son-in-law was promoted. In two years of work, almost all of which was spent on vegetable farms, Pioneer camps, or shoveling snow and ice on the factory grounds, he never complained. His superiors were so grateful that they promoted him to senior engineer.[144]   Ironically, a culture that traditionally rewarded those who exceeded their work quota in this case promoted a specialist who had never even been asked to perform in his specialty.[145]

Additional duties were not the only way in which young specialists were misused. Vast numbers of diploma bearing specialists filled technicians' and even workers' positions, in both routine and emergency situations. "Lack of auxiliary technical and service personnel" was the most important cause of the decreased productivity of scientific personnel, according to the scientific specialists surveyed by *Literaturnaia gazeta* in 1970-1971.[146] The practice by factories and research institutes of using new specialists to compensate for this lack of technicians on a regular basis was harshly criticized in 1973 in *Komsomolskaia pravda*, as was the widespread tendency to "send engineers to the assembly line when the plant is in trouble."[147]

Distraction caused by menial labor and underemployment in a technician's billet meant extremely limited opportunity for the creative activity required for advancement and professional fulfillment for many young specialists. Posudnikov refused to "stick to the duties of a junior scientific research assistant (which he described as menial labor and the 'swamp life') for one hundred five rubles per month with no chance of defending his candidate's dissertation" and fled to his cab.[148] But many more young specialists stayed within the system and found ways to advance. As V. Perevedentsev noted in his commentary on the coauthorship issue discussed earlier, "every scientific worker must produce scientific results before all else."[149] Thus, many young specialists, forced into technician's duties, sought to make a "name" for themselves as coauthors of scientific work, even if the only concrete work that they performed was as a technician.

Perevedentsev's comment highlighted a professional reality faced by young specialists that stood in stark contrast to the emphasis on "principle" and "conscience" espoused by the protagonist of the coauthorship discussion, 30-year-old graduate student and researcher Viktor Andreevich Belov. Belov's stance and its relationship to the personal ethos of the Children of Victory were discussed earlier. But Perevedentsev's comment on the practical reality of coauthorship as a method for professional advancement by young specialists casts a different light on the coauthorship issue, which this study now explores.

Personally, Belov found the insistence of his laboratory director, Vladimir Mikhailovich Kozhin, that Kozhin be listed as a coauthor of a discovery that Belov had made as an offensive violation of principle and ethics. But what do Belov's position and the subsequent wide-ranging commentary from readers and specialists reveal about the *professional* ethos of young specialists, especially in light of Perevedentsev's practical assertion?

None of the participants in the discussion disputed the fact that the practice of including numerous coauthors in publications had become commonplace throughout the USSR. Whether they agreed with the practice or not, respondents widely acknowledged that coauthorship was the norm. Even as he condemned the practice as having "nothing in common with the traditions of Soviet science" and agreed with Belov's principled stand, academician A. Ianshchin, for example, stated, "I well understand the familiar methods—to include oneself in the number of coauthors."[150]   Professor of law M. Boguslavskii, who otherwise supported many of Kozhin's points, condemned the fact that "many institutes and bureaus have adopted the custom to automatically list the director among the coauthors. This is abnormal, not only from the viewpoint of scientific ethics, but also from the viewpoint of Soviet law."[151]   Likewise, three specialists characterized this practice as the "norm" in the Soviet period when I raised this issue during interviews. One engineer-physicist summarized the young author's dilemmas as follows: "If you want your paper to be published, pick a good coauthor."[152]   Another physicist went into great detail to describe how he had considered the coauthorship trend a normal and natural part of his business. After all, he said, a place as coauthor was legitimate as a quid pro quo for assistance in gaining time on equipment, and so on.[153]   The third interviewee, a specialist in English literature, stated that the practice, which he termed "widely spread at Russian universities and academic institutes," had paradoxically been less of a problem in the 1970s than after the dawn of perestroika, when specialists, desperate for ever more scarce publication funding, allowed the numbers of coauthors to balloon into the hundreds in some cases.[154]   In summary, Perevedentsev's comment was correct: if a young specialist had a work that he or she wanted to have published, it needed the prestige and backing of established authorities and often got it by including them as coauthors.

Though widely acknowledged, the coauthorship system was clearly not what young Belov had expected when he reported to the institute. "I came here as to a temple of science, but it turned out to be a bazaar. That would be OK, if they'd honestly confess it, but they continue to cry: 'No, it's a temple!'"[155]

Belov, despite his protesting against a practice that seemed to be more or less accepted by other members of his generation as a means to a professional end, referred to one of the most significant images in the life experience of the young specialists—the heroic, noble vestige of science. In his insistence that "science must be done with clean hands" and his praise for scientific mentors who "scattered ideas to the winds and were glad if someone picked them up and developed them," Belov paid homage to the heroic myth of science as the key to human advancement. As mentioned earlier, the vision of such heroic science had been an important part of Soviet ideology from the beginning. The young specialists had been immersed in it since they began school in the Soviet system, with its heavy emphasis on math and science. The immersion left its mark, with young professionals repeatedly emphasizing "rational" and "objective" decision making, a traditional hallmark of the scientific method, in their public commentary, regardless of the subject.[156] This same emphasis also motivated the young specialists' demand for the statistics and data that they believed would help them solve the nation's economic problems, although those demands were relegated to the "hidden" commentary of archives. They believed so strongly in the ability of reason and science to solve problems and in their obligation to apply their expertise as specialists to those solutions that this aspect of Soviet ideology became one of the "principles" to which they adhered, as discussed further later.

As the emphasis on technological solutions to the USSR's economic problems intensified in the 1970s, the rationalism of the scientific influence increasingly came into conflict with the bureaucratic irrationality and arbitrariness of many decisions, such as those dispatching specialists to constructions sites and vegetable depots.[157]   While Belov's stance on coauthorship may have been unrepresentative of his generation, the worship of heroic, rational science was not. This emphasis on rationality stands as one of the key elements of the professional ethos of the Children of Victory, and it undermined their faith in the system. The conflict between the specialists' sense of rationality and the "chaos" of the Soviet workplace also became a key component of that professional ethos.

But didn't their parents worship at the altar of reason as well? Were they not also subjected to the immersion in heroic science? Again, Belov's case provides an answer.

Lab director Kozhin, representative of the parents' generation, emphasized the collective nature of modern science. He compared the development of complex scientific procedures (like the one that Belov invented) first to an assembly line, then to an orchestra, with many contributing to the final product.[158] In Kozhin's professional ethos, the combination of rationality and *collective* performance dominated. In a response to the Belov discussion, E. Kulaga, a peer of Kozhin in both age and position, condemned both Kozhin and Belov as "individualists." Kulaga, emphasizing the classic image of science as a collective effort, stated that Kozhin's proper role as laboratory director would have been to teach Belov the proper place of collective effort.[159] For Belov and increasingly for his generation, rationality combined with *individual* performance to shape the young specialists' professional ethos. That emphasis on individuality becomes more apparent when we examine the outlook of the Children of Victory toward living standards and wages.

Living conditions outside the major cities did not always favor the scientific specialist. An *Izvestiia* article from May 1982 cited the case of geologists working in Siberian gas and oil exploration. The specialists were still living in the old-style travel trailers that were originally used to open the settlements, while the petroleum and gas workers in the same areas "enjoy significantly better working conditions and their social needs are met more fully and promptly."[160]

In addition to geographical differences, specialists in the "nonproduction" sphere lacked the housing preferences so highly praised in the *Literaturnaia gazeta* survey. Recall A. Artsibashev's complaint that sometimes employees in the service sphere left for jobs in factories to gain the housing and other benefits not available to service workers.[161] Other, less "favored" specialties included the few forestry engineers who did actually accept jobs in the forests upon completion of the *vuz*.

The diploma-bearing specialists who work in the forests are placed in significantly worse situations than those specialists engaged in other economic branches. This includes both wages and living conditions. . . For years young specialists, assigned to forest areas without apartments, have lived wherever they had to, accepting "corners." . . . In addition to decent apartments, foresters must be supplied with modern transport and means of communication.[162]

Such young specialists, in effect, often "voted with their feet" and moved to jobs or areas with higher-quality housing. Despite the fact that Soviet legislation decreed that young specialists deserved higher-quality living quarters, the majority of the specialists interviewed for this study spent at least part of the early years of their careers in substandard housing arrangements. Thirty-eight of 53 lived either with their own or their spouse's parents or in a communal apartment. While the legislation and public discussion of it may have raised their expectations for better quarters, the facts of everyday life spoke for themselves.

Of course, housing is only part of one's living standard. Other forms of "material stimulation" (wages, access to scarce goods, free vacations, etc.) also shaped important parts of the ethos of the young specialist. The same *Literaturnaia gazeta* survey of scientific workers noted that "material stimulation" seemed even more important to young specialists than to older ones. Forty-one percent of the young professionals who responded to the survey listed material stimulation as "very important" to them, compared to only 31% of older specialists.[163] A *Pravda* survey on the subject of wage differentials produced more specific findings: "The [current] correlation of pay for the work of specialists and workers not only definitely undermines the prestige of engineering and technical work, but it is the reason for the reduction of interest toward receiving a higher education, especially a technical education."[164]

V. Belkin reached a similar conclusion in his analysis of the "costs" to society of training and employing engineers. "The correlation of workers' earnings and those of diploma-bearing specialists does not fully reflect the difference in the level of their professional knowledge."[165]

Professor A. Grigoriev, head of the Kalinin Polytechnical, institute whose views on specialization were discussed earlier, cited figures describing the wage differential between workers and industrial engineers (e.g., those doing applied work in factories and shops as opposed to theoretical research). In his words, "whereas [industrial] managers and engineers once made seventy percent more than workers, by the middle 1970's this figure had dropped to twenty percent. In the building industry, the change was even more dramatic, with the wage differential dropping from fifty percent to eight percent over the same time period."[166]

Scientific and engineering specialists were, of course, not the only ones concerned with their wages. In 1981, *Pravda* conducted a survey measuring the level of job satisfaction among school directors and assistant principals.[167] That survey discovered that most young school directors liked their jobs, especially the basic aspects of organizing teachers' work, helping students, and so on. Nevertheless, large numbers of young directors were leaving their jobs for other work. "Young school directors were least satisfied of all." The article summarizing the survey attributed this fact in part to the lack of knowledge and experience of young directors but also included a letter from a young director who specifically complained that his pay is the same as a starting teacher's salary. He considered this a "major problem," particularly when the only way that he could increase his own salary would be to increase the amount of administrative and outside work performed by his school.

Physicians working in clinics faced many of the same concerns regarding monetary compensation as did industrial engineers. N. Shestakova, chief physician at a Leningrad polyclinic, complained to *Literaturnaia gazeta* that "too many physicians work in research institutes and departmental polyclinics, where they have a much lighter workload than they would in general medical practice."[168]   In addition, "the pay that clinic physicians get is still inadequate. Their only major pay raise doesn't come until after thirty years of service."

At least some young specialists were sufficiently dissatisfied with their monetary compensation to propose alternative pay systems. R. Metelnitsky, a young architect, argued in a letter to *Literaturnaia gazeta* that architects should not be forced into salaried positions, that their pay should be awarded like that of writers and other creative workers, who were paid on the basis of their individual, creative work.[169]

Generally, however, the question of direct monetary compensation was not the paramount concern of most young specialists. All of the articles and letters discussed previously focused on a comparison of some sort. Specialists' wages were evaluated in the context of a comparison to workers, other specialists, and so on. The bulk of R. Metelnitsky's comments, for example, focused not upon the actual quantity of recompense but the categorization of the architects as salaried workers instead of creative ones and the limits imposed upon architects in selecting their coworkers on projects. This comparative discussion indicates the factors that young specialists *did* consider crucial, more crucial than money, in evaluating their income and status. Those factors were their reputation among their professional colleagues, their creative opportunities, and their professional dignity and autonomy. Once again, each of these factors emphasized individual performance.

Another architect, V. Melik-Karamov, echoed many of Metelnitsky's concerns about creativity in a 1974 letter to *Komsomolskaia pravda*. Melik-Karamov called for nationwide design competitions among architects to alleviate the "sameness" of modern Soviet architecture and to enhance the creative opportunities for architects.[170] Melik-Karamov described a crisis among young architects, in which their frustration with the lack of creative opportunity inspired them to leave the profession for work in theater, cinematography, graphics, and so on.

Both Metelnitksy and Melik-Karamov raised the issue of professional reputation and knowledge of one's contemporaries. Metelnitsky believed that the architect in charge of a project should be free to select which architects should work under him or her based on the chief's evaluation of their professional ability. Melik-Karamov argued that newly graduated architectural specialists should be assigned as a group to a housing and civil engineering design institute, where they could work for some of the same senior specialists who had supervised their graduation projects. This practice would enhance their effectiveness and creativity, given the senior specialists' knowledge of the new graduates' talents and abilities.[171]

This awareness of one's peers as a professional community was prominent among specialists of all disciplines, not just architects.

Literaturnaia gazeta surveyed scientific and technical specialists in 1970-1971 as to what factors motivated them to be productive, how their productivity should be evaluated, and what factors decreased their productivity. The survey indicated that "they most highly value the scholarly opinion of colleagues." Recognition by specialists in their own field was regarded as the "most important measure of scientific productivity." The only measure that they considered more important was that their work have some inherent creative satisfaction. These specialists considered their work to be truly successful if their peers often cited it.[172]

They made a distinction between reputation among colleagues and the more general notion of "fame." Fame in the sense of becoming a household name was not so important as earning the respect of one's peers.[173] According to the survey, only 9% of young specialists cited the desire for such broad notoriety as a motivator.[174]

The most succinct description of the importance of professional reputation to the young specialists was that rendered by Nikita Pokrovsky, a 1973 graduate of Moscow State University's philosophy department who specialized in English and American literature and philosophy and later became a professor in MGU's sociology department. When asked what professional aspirations he had achieved as a young specialist in the 1970's, Professor Pokrovsky replied: "The main professional objective that I was to achieve was professional progress in terms of getting better positions, higher positions, in the academic hierarchy. I would say I was a very fast runner. I made good progress . . . . However, what I really achieved was having a very good reputation among my colleagues. That is, an academic reputation."[175]

This distinction between "fame" and "academic reputation" is a vital portion of the young specialists' ethos and should not be confused with a more general notion of "prestige." The notion of prestige was much discussed in the Soviet press and in sociological works of the Brezhnev era and may be defined as respect for a position or occupation held by society at large. But, in this context, prestige much more closely resembled what the *Literaturnaia gazeta* survey cited earlier called "fame"—as in recognition of an individual by large segments of society. Two examples illustrate the distinction.

Aleksandr Kitaigorodskii, a professor of physical-mathematical science, wrote a scathing critique of the Soviet scientific community for *Literaturnaia Gazeta* in 1982. In describing the process by which some young specialists attain a candidate's degree, Kitaigorodskii discussed "prestige": "Having shown skill and dexterity, and having selected a suitable academic advisor, who is most interested in the quantity of printed work (to which he believes he has full rights as "coauthor") the young person, as a rule, has achieved his goal. He becomes a candidate of some science, by which he secures for himself, if not a high wage, then at least something that many value more than money—prestige."[176]

Certainly, attainment of the academic degree alone was not sufficient to gain the respect of one's peers, who, of course, also had the degree. Thus, this valued "prestige" was held only in the eyes of the general public. Another example illustrates the same notion from a dramatically different perspective.

One of the older members of the generation of young specialists, M. Klimov, graduated from a *vuz* with a degree in "technical cybernetics" in the early 1960s. In 1973, Klimov wrote to *Literaturnaia gazeta* to describe the fate of one of his classmates, identified only as Nikolai P. While the two were still students together, Nikolai, who seemed to Klimov a brilliant, successful student, had confessed to Klimov that his "heart was not really in all these scheming theories of graphs and multi variants."[177] When Klimov advised his friend to leave the discipline and pursue something more to his liking, Nikolai was insulted. Klimov believed that "for Nikolai to leave cybernetics would mean to admit some personal inferiority," and this he could not do. The two friends drifted apart until they met by accident in 1972 at a technical conference. Klimov described Nikolai's (by then a candidate of science) presentation of a "colorless" report, after which the two met to reminisce. Klimov concluded from Nikolai's "painful melancholy" that he remained unhappy in the cybernetics field, despite his advanced degree. Nikolai admitted, "I never fit into science. . . it is terrible to feel yourself a mediocrity, a person without a vocation." When Klimov asked his friend why he had never left the discipline, Nikolai admitted, "To where? I've tried a few times, but conversations with my wife and her mother led nowhere."

Clearly, Nikolai had chosen and attained the "prestige" of a candidate's degree. But he had not reached the level of professional success that the Children of Victory held dear. That success, defined by their links to, and their awareness of, their own professional community, was the critical motivation for the young specialists. It was also the basis of an awareness, of a fledgling notion of themselves as an important professional community, which shaped the evolution of the specialists' ethos as a unique entity within Soviet society.

SUMMARY

That young specialists had developed at least some sense of themselves as a unique group within Soviet society by the end of the Brezhnev era is evident in a letter from F. Vasiliev to *Sotsiologichekaia industriia* in 1981. Each department of the newspaper submitted samples of letters received to the CC for review. In addition to section-specific letters, 10 letters were included under the heading of "various proposals." Vasiliev's letter was the first included in that group.

I propose the introduction of a section "The Young Specialist in the National Economy." Here the young specialists' contributions to the fulfillment of Party and government decisions . . . would be recognized. In particular, [the section could] highlight the work of young engineers, whose work is inclined toward basic creativity and initiative. Here you could also reveal the facts about those *vuz* graduates who are not working in accordance with their specialty.[178]

The professional ethos of the Children of Victory was forged in the competitive fires of *vuz* entry examinations. This first personal victory gave the fledgling specialist a strong sense of self, which his or her initial professional experiences reinforced. Entering a workforce for which their educational experience had prepared them only in part, the young specialist often endured another "trial by fire" in developing professional competence and establishing a reputation among his or her professional peers. The emphasis on the respect of one's peers formed the basis upon which the young professionals defined their preference for a new type of collective—the closed professional association. Their affinity for affiliation with one another was further shaped by bureaucratic struggles between groups of young specialists and governmental and Party officials over issues of job assignment, menial labor, and additional duties. These struggles fostered among the specialists first a sense of negation, that is, a view of themselves in contrast to the system that seemed to oppose them. That negation grew into a sense of mutuality, or an awareness of the common traits that they as professionals shared. Incompletely, yet distinctly, the young specialists developed a sense of cohesion as professionals, manifested in advocacy for the opportunity to recognize their peers' accomplishments by membership in selective professional associations.

Simultaneously with the evolution of this sense of professional cohesion was the young specialists' recognition of themselves as distinct within Soviet society because of their age. As with their sense as professionals, this genealogical awareness was fostered at first by negation. The "stability of cadres" policy promoted by the Brezhnev regime endowed the young with a stability of environment unprecedented in the Soviet era, but, ironically, it simultaneously blocked opportunities for their advancement and inspired a fledgling awareness of themselves as a distinct group within Soviet society. This awareness did not develop so fully as their professional awareness and did not lead to the same kinds of concrete manifestations as the professional associations discussed earlier.

By the end of the Brezhnev era, the professional ethos of the young specialists had only just begun to give impetus to the development of potential horizontal connections within Soviet society. But some movement had begun, as this chapter has demonstrated.

Parallel to the growth of the young specialists' awareness of themselves as unique, this chapter has shown the evolution of aspects of the "public" and "private" transcripts concerning the young specialists in the Soviet press. Specialists' letters and complaints followed the traditional format of the Russian petition and exerted enough pressure on the regime to insert themselves at least partially into the public transcript. Ideas and issues that were classified as secret and discussed only among Party and state officials at the start of the era were openly discussed on the pages of *Pravda* itself by 1982.

NOTES

1. A. Rusov, "Mnogovariantnyi Posudnikov," *Literaturnaia gazeta*, 21 September 1977, 12.

2. Rusov was a doctor of chemistry. Obviously, his parents didn't agree with his decision to abandon laboratory work for work as a science correspondent for *Literaturnaia gazeta*.

3. "Dobrovol'no--ne prinuditel'no," *Uchitelskaia gazeta*, 17 April 1982, 2. The actual content of this article is discussed in detail later.

4. It is interesting to note that 27 of the 30 specialists interviewed in 1995 felt that they as individuals had no voice in the definition of society or the country in the Brezhnev era. At the same time, 19 of the 30 believed that public opinion did exist in various forms. Twenty-four of the 30 regularly read letters published in the press, and 28 of the 30 believed them to be genuine, not "staged" or fabricated. None of them, however, wrote letters of their own.

5. "Po normam morali i prava," *Pravda*, 27 January 1979, 3.

6. "Plenum verkhovnogo suda SSSR," *Pravda*, 4 September 1980, 6.

7. Donald R. Kelley, "Environmental Policy-Making in the USSR: The Role of Industrial and Environmental Interest Groups," *Soviet Studies* 28, no. 4, (October 1976) 570-589.

8. "Baikal: Novaia stranitsa biografii," *Literaturnaia gazeta*, 4 December 1974, 11.

9. Oleg Volkov, "Chem dal'she v les . . ." *Literaturnaia gazeta*, 4 December 1974, 11.

10. N.V. Timofeev, "Les nel'ziz zapirat' v kladovaia"'" *Literaturnaia gazeta*, 5 March 1975, 13.

11. F. Shtilmark, "Skol'ko kedrov na BAMe?" *Literaturnaia gazeta*, 5 September 1975, 10.

12. M. Podfordmikov and V. Travinskii, "Conflict on the River Bank," *Literaturnaia gazeta*, 23 January 1974, 11 and 30 January 1974, 11, as translated and presented in *Current Digest of the Soviet Press* 26, no. 5 (1974), 12-15.

13. D. Iurinov, "Ofitsialnyi otvet," *Literaturnaia gazeta*, 11 September 1974, 13.

14. Oleg Volkov, "Caucasian Preserve in Danger," *Komsomolskaia Pravda*, 10 January 1974, 2 as translated and presented in *Current Digest of the Soviet Press* 26, no. 26 (1974), 25.

15. The expression "objective necessity" was a standard Soviet euphemism for "unavoidable."

16. *Komsomolskaia Pravda*, 16 February 1974, 2 as translated and presented in *Current Digest of the Soviet Press* 26, no. 26 (1974), 25.

17. The final decision on the Caucasus State Preserve appeared under the heading "After *Komsomolskaia pravda* Spoke Out: Threat to Caucasian Preserve Removed." Ibid.

18. A recognized, officially sanctioned group, the All Russian Society for the Conservation of Nature, did exist and was occasionally mentioned in newspapers as contributing to the discussion (e.g., in the 16 February 1974 *Komsomolskaia pravda* article cited earlier), but this group was composed primarily of schoolchildren. For a brief summary of this group's activity and its effectiveness, see Kelley, 1976, 578-579.

19. Sadly, it is obvious to any visitor to the former USSR that pro environment forces were also largely impotent in terms of actually preventing widespread environmental destruction. However, the role of the "cause" in fostering civil society should not be underestimated.

20. Georgie Anne Geyer, *The Young Russians* (Homewood, IL: ETC, 1975), 33.

21. Gail Lapidus, "Society under Strain: The Soviet Union after Brezhnev," *The Washington Quarterly*, no. 6 (Spring 1983), 43.

22. Eugene Stolokov, interview by British journalist Tony Parker in *Russian Voices* (New York: Henry Holt, 1991), 374-379.

23. "Ostanovit' bul'dozer--v zashchitu pamiatnikov istoii i kul'tury," *Literaturnaia gazeta*, 26 May 1971, 10-11.

24. Vladimir Shlapentokh discussed such membership in *Public and Private Life of the Soviet People: Changing Values in Post-Stalin Russia* (New York: Oxford University Press, 1989), 109. His position is supported by the recollections of all the specialists interviewed in 1995, as discussed later.

25. Olga Nadimova, interview by British journalist Tony Parker, in *Russian Voices*, 289.

26. Boris Vidimskii, interview by author, tape recording, Moscow, Russia, April 1995.

27. All of the specialists interviewed in 1995 recollected their membership as "pro forma" but useful. They described various aspects of life with which their membership

helped, such as day care and vacations.

28.   Ranajit Guha and Gayatri Chakravorty Spivak also described this phenomenon in *Elementary Aspects of Peasant Insurgency in Colonial India* (Delhi: Oxford University Press, 1983), 28-29, 167-219. I chose Scott's "mutuality" in recognition of his much more concise and lucid description of the phenomenon. See James C. Scott, *Domination and the Arts of Resistance: Hidden Transcripts* (New Haven, CT: Yale University Press, 1990), 118-128.

29. "Molchit shkol'nyi zvonok," *Pravda*, 4 December 1981, 3. In the discussion that follows, note how this petition adheres to the classic elements of the petitioning process.

30. "Dobrovol'no--ne prenuditel'no," *Uchitel'skaia gazeta*, 17 April 1982, 2.

31. "Skol'ko piatnits na nedele?" *Uchitel'skaia gazeta*, 11 November 1982, 2.

32. Note the strong parallel here to Comrade Karpov's warning that "we must not abuse their optimism and patriotism," from the previous chapter--an excellent example of Karpov's entry in the "hidden transcript" making its public appearance.

33. Scott, *Domination and the Arts of Resistance*, xi-xii.

34.   That is not to say that they did not complain about wages or economic opportunity.   Economic considerations appeared often in the sources.   But never did economic considerations appear as the *sole* issue in a petition. On the other hand, questions of prestige as manifested in issues of dignity, autonomy, and responsibility often appeared without any simultaneous economic complaints.

35. "Ne srabotalis'," *Komsomolskaia Pravda*, 16 July 1977, 2.

36. "Poka ne grianuli morozy," *Uchitel'skaia gazeta*, 21 August 1979, 2.

37. TsKhSD F5O68 D387 L156.

38. Ibid.

39. "Nashli sebe zabotu," *Sotsiologicheskaia industriia*, 8 October 1972, 1.

40. Of the specialists interviewed 29 of 30 belonged to such *soiuzy*. Only the professional soldier did not.

41. *Pravda*, 25 June 1979, 2 as translated and presented in *Current Digest of the Soviet Press*, 31, no. 25 (1979), 19-20.

42. A. Kolesnichenko, "Professiia bukhgalter," *Pravda*, 3 August 1982, 3.

43. "Pri zvanii--prizvanie," *Komsomolskaia pravda*, 3 June 1981, 2.

44. RTsKhIDNI F638 O1 D23 L125.

45. Ibid., L15.

46. Ibid., L18. Each of these requests was made in 1969-1970.

47. Ibid., L24.

48. Ibid., L17.

49. Ibid., L26.

50. Ibid., L85.

51. Ibid., L86.

52. Ibid., L26.

53. The State Archive of the Russian Federation (GARF) holds the records of a large number of Scientific Technical Societies (NTO) in Fond R-5587. Many of those collections include such trip reports.

54. GARF F R-5587 O 28 D 84 L43-44.

55. RTsKhIDNI F638 O1 D23 L 29.

56. Ibid.

57. "Nauchnyi potentsial: Kak im rasporiadit'sia?" *Pravda*, 26 November 1981, 3.

58. "Kogda prikhodiat otkrytiia?" *Literaturnaia gazeta*, 2 June 1982, 13.

59. "Manage Economically," *Izvestiia*, 24 November 1981, 2, as translated and

presented in *Current Digest of the Soviet Press* 33, no. 47 (1981), 24-25.

60. "Glavnyi vrach," *Pravda*, 1 February 1981, 1.

61. "Ne vremennaia dolzhnost'," *Pravda*, 3 November 1981, 3.

62. Bogdan was just slightly older than the oldest of the Children of Victory. He opened this 1981 letter by saying that he had finished the medical institute "over twenty years ago." Nevertheless, it is reasonable to assess his views as similar to theirs and that they are the people to whom he refers as refusing to take on this post.

63. "Vy khotite stat' rukovoditelem?: pis'mo v redaktsiiu," *Literaturnaia gazeta*, 14 July 1970, 10.

64. E. Fainburg, "Vy khotite stat' rukovoditelem? Kommentarii sotsiologa," *Literaturnaia gazeta*, 14 July 1970, 10. Fainburg is listed in the article as director of the sociology lab at the Perm Polytechnical Institute and a corresponding member of the Soviet Academy of Sciences as a sociologist (his discipline is listed as "concrete social research," the Soviet term for sociology in the 1970s).

65. RTsKhIDNI F 638 O1 D23 L32.

66. *Smena*, no. 16, August 1975, 14.

67. V. Rutgaizer, "Diploma and Education," *Komsomolskaia pravda*, 9 February 1973, 2 as translated and presented in *Current Digest of the Soviet Press* 25, no. 26 (1973), 16.

68. *Istoricheskii arxiv*, 1994 no. 1 (1994), 176-177.

69. A number of Western observers described this phenomenon. See, for example, Mervyn Matthews. "Soviet Students--Some Sociological Perspectives," *Soviet Studies* 27 (January 1975), 97-98; Vladimir Shlapentokh, *The Politics of Sociology in the Soviet Union* (Boulder, CO: Westview Press, 1987), 79. William Taubman, *The View from Lenin Hills: an American Student's Report on Soviet Youth in Ferment* (New York: Coward-McCann, 1967), 27. A number of Soviet sociological works on this issue were cited in Chapter 1.

70. "Ne dalee sadovogo kol'tsa," *Literaturnaia gazeta*, 4 July 1973, 11.

71. *Smena*, no. 16, August 1975, 14.

72. Ibid.

73. Georgie Anne Geyer, *The Young* Russians (Homewood, IL: ETC.,1975), 90-91. The issue of pay, which in many cases was actually greater for workers than for young specialists, is addressed later.

74. The original text of Suslov's speech appeared in "Vysokoe prizvanie i otvetstvennost," *Pravda*, 15 October 1981, 2.

75. The rector's full name was not included. Reference was made only to his family name, Zhdanov.

76. TsKhSD F5 O69 D580 L6. The entire petition is contained on L6-12.

77. Ibid., L7. The training of technical specialists for administrative and leadership roles remained a major item of discussion throughout the Brezhnev era and is discussed in detail later.

78. Ibid., L8.

79. Ibid., L10-11.

80. "Mesto dlia inzhenera," *Pravda*, 7 June 1981, 3.

81. Again, this aspect of his position is supported by the Odessa informer and the Tumanov and Kurin interviews.

82. Aleksandr Kitaigorodskii, "Kogda prekhodiat otkrytiia?" *Literaturnaia gazeta*, 2 June 1982, 13.

83. V.I. Lenin, "The Tasks of the Youth Leagues" in *The Lenin Anthology*, Robert C. Tucker, ed., (New York: 1975), 664-674.

84. Kendall Bailes, *Technology and Society under Lenin and Stalin: Origins of the Soviet Technical Intelligentsia, 1917-1941* (Princeton, NJ: Princeton University Press, 1978), 317-318, 409-410.

85. Nicholas Lampert, *The Technical Intelligentsia and the Soviet State: A Study of Managers and Technicians, 1928-1935* (London: Macmillan, 1979), 151.

86. Harley Balzer, "Engineers: The Rise and Decline of a Social Myth," in *Science and the Soviet Social Order*, ed. Loren R. Graham (Cambridge: Harvard University Press, 1990), 141-167, esp. 160-161.

87. A. Rusov, "Mnogovariantnyi Posudnikov," *Literaturnaia gazeta*, 21 September 1977, 12.

88. G. Efimenko, Ukraine Republic minister of higher and specialized education, "According to the Five-Year Plan's Compass," *Pravda*, 7 March 1981, 3 as translated and presented in *Current Digest of the Soviet Press,* 33 (1981), no. 10, 18. In this article, the Minister proposed a change to the education system: a contractual arrangement between the Ministry of Higher and Specialized Secondary Education and the enterprises that employed personnel. A similar proposal was forwarded in "Ishchem partnerov," *Pravda*, 7 August 1981, 3, which argued that direct contracts be established between *vuzy* and enterprises.

89. V. Belkin, "Skol'ko stoit' inzhener?" *Literaturnaia gazeta*, 10 March 1971, 10.

90. Ibid.

91. Iu. Kantor, candidate of philosophy, "Kogo zhdut na kafedre?" *Literaturnaia gazeta*, 17 March 1976, 12. Kantor's letter appeared as one of two letters under the rubric "Zvaniia i znaniia" that examined the qualifications of instructors.

92. Letters in response to the rubric "Zvaniia i znaniia" appeared in *Literaturnaia gazeta*, 8 September 1976, 12.

93. This complaint, of course, is certainly not unique to the USSR!

94. A. Artsibashev, "Po tu storonu prilavka," *Komsomolskaia pravda*, 14 March 1975, 2.

95. This debate provides an excellent example of the interaction and relative "positions" of these three major Soviet newspapers, *Pravda, Komsomolskaia Pravda*, and *Literaturnaia gazeta*.

96. V. Primak, "Ne dalee Sadovogo Kol'tsa . . ." *Literaturnaia gazeta*, 4 July 1973, 11.

97. V. Lavrov, "Boiazn' vysoty," and L. Kondrat'eva, "Naiti sebia," *Literaturnaia gazeta*, 21 September 1977, 12.

98. TsKhSD F5 O64 D78 L34-5.

99. V. Perevedentsev, "Kollektivizm istinnyi i lozhnyi," *Literaturnaia gazeta*, 19 April 1972, 12.

100. M. Iaroshevskii, "Esli mozhesh' ne goret' . . . ," *Literaturnaia gazeta*, 21 September *1977, 12.*

101. V. Belkin, "Besplatnoe--dorozhe," *Literaturnaia gazeta*, 10 March 1971, 10-11.

102. G. Shagieva, "Ne nuzhny spetsialisty," *Komsomolskaia pravda*, 21 May 1981, 2.

103. Ibid.

104. The letter was undated but stamped as "received" by the CC section on 5 April 1976. TsKhSD F5 O69 D580 L1-2.

105. Ibid.

106. Thirty-one of 53 respondents said that they "chose" or "arranged" their own jobs independently of the assignment system. In addition, 1 noted that his choice and the job

assigned were the same.

107. "Paradoksy raspredeleniia," *Pravda*, 14 November 1981, 3.

108. TsKhSD F5 O63 D90 L16-17.

109. Ibid., L17.

110. "Ne srabotalis', ili pochemu ushla iz sel'skoi shkoly molodaia uchitel'nitsa," *Komsomolskaia pravda*, 16 July 1977, 2.

111. G. Efimenko, Ukraine Republic minister of higher and specialized education, "According to the Five-Year Plan's Compass," *Pravda*, 7 March 1981, 3, as translated and presented in *Current Digest of the Soviet Press*, 33, no. 10 (1981), 18.

112. "Ne srabotalis', ili pochemu ushla iz sel'skoi shkoly molodaia uchitel'nitsa," *Komsomolskaia Pravda*, 16 July 1977, 2.

113. Leonid Romanovich Veintraub, interview with the author, transcribed tape recording, Moscow, June 1999.

114. "Ofitsial'nyi otdel: V Mimisterstve prosveshcheniia SSSR," *Uchitel'skaia gazeta*, 15 January 1980, 2.

115. "They Never Arrived for Their Assigned Work," *Izvestiia*, 11 June 1980, 3, as translated and presented in *Current Digest of the Soviet Press* 32, no. 23 (1980), 16-17.

116. TsKhSD F5 O69 D580 L3. The specialties of the remaining 471 graduates were not specified.

117. Specific numbers of such shifts in requirements are not available, but the discussion in TSKhSD F5 O69 D580 L1-12 makes clear that such shifts occurred on a massive scale.

118. See, for example, F. Panachin, first deputy minister of education of the USSR, "Pedagogicheskie vuzy: problemy razvitiia," *Uchitel'skaia gazeta*, 9 February 1980, 2. For the proposal to withhold diplomas and E. Levchenko's response to A. Rusov's "Posudnikov" portrait in *Literaturnaia gazeta*, 23 November 1977, 13.

119. "Kak vam rabotaetsia?" *Literaturnaia gazeta*, 15 July 1970, 11.

120. "Kak vam rabotaetsia?: Kto pokorit vershinu," *Literaturnaia gazeta*, 4 August 1971, 10.

121. The term "condensations" here refers to the assimilation of data from different reference sources into one volume. Perhaps the best Western equivalents would be "desk references" or "almanacs."

122. "Kak vam rabotaetsia?" *Literaturnaia gazeta*, 4 August 1971, 10.

123. Doktorovich's letter appeared in *Literaturnaia gazeta*, 12 April 1972, 10. The reply from academician V. Glushkov was published in *Literaturnaia gazeta*, 24 May 1972, 12. It is impossible to say with any certainty whether Doktorovich's letter and the subsequent reply represented simply a well-timed coincidence, or if Doktorovich's letter was "staged" to allow the regime to publish a response that demonstrated its ability to successfully address specialists' concerns. In any event, the journal *Upravliiaiushchie sistemy i mashiny* did in fact begin its publication run in August 1972 with V. Glushkov as the editor in chief. The journal appeared bimonthly until 1990, when it shifted to a monthly format. It achieved success as an international reference work, listed in standard Western scientific sources.

124. The volume of information was presented as a "mountain," the "summit" of which must be scaled by specialists, in "Kak vam rabotaetsia?: Kto pokorit vershinu," *Literaturnaia gazeta*, 4 August 1971, 10.

125. "Kak vam rabotaetsia?" *Literaturnaia gazeta*, 11 August 1971, 11.

126. "Chto zabotit sotsiologa," *Pravda*, 28 December 1981, 2.

127. TsKhSD F 5 O 67D 180 L 47. Her comments were part of a *Literaturnaia*

gazeta "bulletin" on medical care submitted to the Central Committee. Originally classified as "secret," declassified 4 April 1995.

128. Boris Vidimskii, interview by author, tape recording, Moscow, April 1995.

129. This strong demand for hard data, combined with the specialists' expressed intention to use those data to compete with the West, is especially apparent in the commentary of propagandists in the archives of the journal *Agitator*, RTsKhIDNI F614 O1.

130. Georgie Anne Geyer, Research Notebook I, 1971, 18.

131. Geyer, 1975, 73.

132. Geyer, Research Notebook II, 1971, 40. This specialist, identified only as "Alec," insisted that he was "not a political man." Nevertheless, Geyer noted that every subject seemed to lead him to talk of nothing but politics. In this open political discussion, he was not representative of most young specialists.

133. Geyer, 1975, 39, 242-243.   Geyer believed that the increase in availability of literature and film was due to an ideological campaign to "fight something by knowing it." I have not been able to confirm any such conscious decision by Soviet ideologues, but the importation of Western technology and the increased scientific exposure that accompanied it are a well-documented phenomenon that had its roots in economic necessity.

134. Some Western analysts assert that this type of exposure shaped the values of the Gorbachev generation and inspired perestroika. See, for example, Judith Kullberg, "The Origins of the Gorbachev Revolution: Industrialization, Social Structure Change and Soviet Elite Value Transformation, 1917-1985," (PhD dissertation, rev. ed., 1995, Ohio State University),   which   termed   perestroika   "the   long-delayed   arrival   of Reformation/Enlightenment ideals in Russia" (80-81).

135. Both published and archival sources indicate that such labor was frequently assigned and almost always resented. It is important to note here that this was regularly assigned outside labor, not the normal "*sanitarny den'*" that every Soviet (and today, Russian) organization conducted monthly or the annual "*subbotnik*" labor associated with Lenin's birthday.

136. Aleksandr Rusov, "Mnogovariantnyi Posudnikov," *Literaturnaia gazeta*, 21 September 1977, 12.

137. "Grabli dlia . . . konstruktora," *Pravda*, 4 June 1978, 2.

138. That is, with Kocheshev's *former* supervisors. According to Lukin's commentary, Kocheshev no longer worked at the factory, having been discharged "according to his own request." Lukin does not specify whether Kocheshev's discharge came before or after his letter was published.

139. The parallel between this criticism and the 1970 criticism of sending students to harvest fields when farmers "are not inclined to such work" is striking. That criticism appeared earlier, and was taken from TsKhSD F5 O63 D90 L5-7. Originally classified "Secret," declassified May 1995. It was likely relegated to archival status because harvest work was such an integral part of the Soviet way of life that *Pravda* was unready to admit the widespread resentment of it in 1970 or even in 1978, given Velichko's comment that such labor was "understandable" when speaking of the harvest.

140. Again, it is important to note that central Party officials and regional or local officials often used citizens' grievances as tools to strengthen their positions relative one another or to bolster arguments or shift blame.

141. "Obzor pisem: Grabli ne dlia konstruktora," *Pravda*, 25 December 1978, 3.

142. "Privykli," *Pravda*, 11 November 1982, 3. The parallel to the 1968 portrayal by the KGB informer from Odessa of the factory as the place where "one is disqualified as a specialist" is striking. The fact that this perception was commonly held by specialists in 1968 but not openly admitted in *Pravda* until 1982 of itself attests to both the ability of the

system to stifle concerns and the inevitable pressure from below to see those concerns addressed.

143. "Tsena znanii," *Uchite''skaia gazeta*, 31 October 1981, 2. Again note the specialists' strong resentment toward the failure in performance of those who bore primary responsibility for the menial work.

144. "Kak moi ziat stal starshim inzhenerom," *Literaturnaia gazeta*, 23 November 1977, 13.

145. If this had appeared in *Pravda*, one might be tempted to argue that the regime sought to publicize rewards for long-suffering, virtuous service. The fact that it appeared in *Literaturnaia gazeta*, however, suggests that irony was, in fact, the intended message.

146. "Kak vam rabotaetsia?" *Literaturnaia gazeta*, 18 August 1971, 11.

147. "The Diploma's Prestige," *Komsomolskaia pravda*, 2 March 1973, 2; "How to Raise the Diploma's Prestige," *Komsomolskaia Pravda*, 16 March 1973, 2, both as translated and presented in *Current Digest of the Soviet Press* 25, no. 30, 31 (1973). The acute shortages of technicians, service personnel, and workers discussed here hark back to the story of the happy worker Sergei at the outset of this chapter and lend credence to the possibility that his letter, if genuine, was selected as a tool to help address this problem.

148. "Mnogovariantnyi Posudnikov," *Literaturnaia gazeta*, 21 September 1977, 12.

149. V. Perevedentsev, "Kollektivizm istinnyi i lozhnyi," *Literaturnaia gazeta*, 19 April 1972, 12.

150. A. Ianshchin, "Eto nedopustimo!" *Literaturnaia gazeta*, 26 January 1972, 11.

151. M. Boguslavskii, "Nuzhno razobrat'sia . . ." Ibid.

152. Vladimir Marukhlenko, interview by author, written transcript, Columbus, Ohio, August 1995.

153. Alexei Lebed, interview by author, written transcript, Columbus, Ohio, 1 September 1995.

154. Nikita Pokrovsky, interview by author, written transcript, Columbus, Ohio, 30 September 1995.

155. "Otkrytie sdelano, a kto zhe avtor," *Literaturnaia gazeta*, 26 January 1972, 11.

156. The best single-source Western summaries of the role of science in the ideology of the USSR are Loren R. Graham *Science, Philosophy and Human Behavior in the Soviet Union*, originally printed in 1972 and reissued (New York: Columbia University Press, 1989) and Loren R. Graham *Science and the Soviet Social Order*, (Cambridge: Harvard University Press, 1990).

157. The young dissident historian Boris Kagarlitsky discusses this conflict in *The Thinking Reed: Intellectuals and the Soviet State, 1917 to the Present*, trans. Brian Pearce (New York: Verso, 1988), 265-269.

158. "Otkrytie sdelano, a kto zhe avtor," *Literaturnaia gazeta*, 26 January 1972, 11.

159. E. Kulaga, "Konflikt bez podopleki," *Literaturnaia gazeta*, 1 March 1972, 12.

160. "Uiut taezhnogo poselka," *Izvestiia*, 15 May 1982, 3.

161. "Po tu storonu prilavka," *Komsomolskaia Pravda*, 14 March 1975, 2.

162. "Rezonans: Ne dalee Sadovogo kol'tsa. . ." *Literaturnaia gazeta*, 22 August 1973, 10.

163. "Kak vam rabotaetsia?" *Literaturnaia gazeta*, 18 August 1971, 11.

164. "O rubliax zarabotannyx i nezarabotannyx: chitatel' prodolzhaet razgovor,"

Pravda, 17 November 1980, 7.

165. V. Belkin, "Skol'ko stoit' inzhener?" *Literaturnaia gazeta*, 10 March 1971, 10. Western studies also noted the problem of decreased wage differentials between specialists and workers in Brezhnev's USSR. See, for example, Donna Bahry, "Rethinking the Social Roots of Perestroika," *Slavic Review* 52 no. 3 (Fall 1993), 532-535. Bahry noted that the ethic of "redistribution" of wealth was losing its appeal by the 1980s. Soviet sociological studies listed the wage ration of specialist to worker as having decreased from a high in the mid-1950s of 2.0:1 to a low of 1.08:1 by 1977. See N.A. Aitov, "The Dynamics of Social Mobility in the USSR," in *The Social Structure of the USSR: Recent Studies*, ed. Murray Yanowitch (Armonk, NY: M.E. Sharpe, 1986), 269.

166. "Mesto dlia inzhenera," *Pravda*, 7 June 1981, 3.

167. "Perepady rabochego samochuvstviia," *Pravda*, 17 March 1981, 3.

168. "How are you Feeling, Doctor?" *Literaturnaia gazeta*, 28 October 1981, 13, as translated and presented in *Current Digest of the Soviet Press* 33, no. 51 (1981), 4-5.

169. R. Metelnitsky, "Who Are We?" *Literaturnaia gazeta*, 11 October 1972, 11, as translated and presented in *Current Digest of the Soviet Press,* 25, no. 11 (1973), 22.

170. V. Melik-Karamov, "Begom ot prizvaniia: Molodoi zodchii ushel proektnogo instituta. Pochemu?" *Komosomolskaia Pravda*, 5 December 1974, 2.

171. Another architect, B. Svetlitskii, whose age is unknown, wrote an "open letter" to *Literaturnaia gazeta* in 1974 entitled "Legalize Initiative," in which he argued along lines similar to those of Metelnitsky that senior directors of projects must be given the legal freedom to make decisions to overcome unforeseen circumstances in design projects. Svetliskii's emphasis on a legislated solution to the problem is more typical of the "parents'" generation than that of the specialists, but his letter indicates the prominence of the issue in the early 1970s. "Uzakanit' initsiativu!" *Literaturnaia gazeta*, 6 February 1974, 10.

172. "Kak vam rabotaetsia?" *Literaturnaia gazeta*, 18 August 1971, 11.

173. Of course, it is possible that the regime manipulated survey data to "sponsor" this conclusion in order to discourage specialists from seeking just such fame.

174. Ibid.

175. Nikita Pokrovsky, interview by author, tape recording, Moscow, March 1995.

176. A. Kitaigorodskii, "Kogda prikhodiat otkrytiia?" *Literaturnaia gazeta*, 2 June 1982, 13.

177. "Razmyshleniia o neudachnike," *Literaturnaia gazeta*, 26 December 1973, 11.

178. RTsKhIDNI F 638 O1 D23 L62.

Conclusion

No longer "young," the specialists at the heart of this study play critical roles in the Russian Federation today. While their politically oriented contemporaries (Chubais, Feodorov, Gaidar, even President Putin) fill or have filled the highest posts of government, the vast majority of the Children of Victory carry lower international profiles. Nevertheless, these millions of specialists have shaped the uniquely Russian evolution of post-Soviet society. That Russian society today does not more closely resemble the "civil" society of the West is not surprising, given the ethos that these specialists developed in their youth. The major contribution of this study to understanding Russia today is its elucidation of that ethos.

Those born after 1940 who completed higher education during the Brezhnev era, were the principal benefactors of the Soviet military, industrial, and economic triumphs earned during the first 50 years of Soviet history. Some Western observers of this generation, both during the Brezhnev years and from the perspective of Gorbachev's era, concluded that the Children of Victory had come to reject the basic premises of the system which had made them the most highly educated and materially affluent generation in all of Russian history.

This study has shown that this assessment was not entirely correct. By examining how the young specialists of the Brezhnev era saw themselves, and exploring the means by which they expressed themselves, this study has shown that the Children of Victory accepted the basic premises of the Soviet system. They readily acknowledged the power of the Communist Party of the Soviet Union and expected the Soviet system to endure indefinitely. That is not to say, however, that they accepted all aspects of that system and its ideology. In contrast to their dissident contemporaries, the Children of Victory were largely apolitical; they avoided open challenges to the legitimacy or power of the Party.

Instead, young specialists worked within the parameters established by Party policy and attempted to confront and solve the problems facing Soviet society. They questioned shortcomings in the Soviet economy and tried to improve the standard of living enjoyed by Soviet society. These efforts inspired them to seek information and to question restrictions that the Soviet state placed upon access to various sources of data. According to the sources available, young specialists normally acted as individuals in these efforts and directed their inquiries to the Party as the repository of real power in the country. Such individual action was in keeping with both traditional Russian practices of petitioning and the generally accepted parameters of Brezhnev-era Soviet socialism.

The principal motivations behind specialists' efforts did not normally include material ambition or the desire for individual notoriety.   Young specialists sought to improve the Soviet system in ways that would enable Soviet citizens to pursue their own aspirations while being protected from arbitrary treatment, material poverty, and human indignity. Issues of material poverty, especially in the areas of housing conditions and shortages of basic foodstuffs, evoked particularly sharp responses from young specialists. They sought to create a system that treated citizens humanely, that is, one that satisfied basic human needs, and at the same time a system that recognized their value as talented individuals.   Young specialists developed this sense of "humanism" in reaction to the daily reality of "developed socialism."

The ideology of developed socialism demanded that all citizens place priority on achieving the goals of their *kollektiv*. Young specialists, in keeping with the extant social contract, paid lip service to *kollektiv* membership. They normally enrolled in professional unions automatically upon graduation from institutes of higher education and maintained such membership.   But young specialists in general did not internalize the notion of "building socialism." Many joined political organizations, such as the Komsomol and even the Party itself, as a matter of necessity rather than of conviction.

In contrast to their pro forma membership in officially accepted *kollektivy*, Soviet citizens, including young specialists, developed their internal sense of morality and humanism within a self-selecting community of friends, relatives, or others with common interests.   These informal associations, the famous "circles" (*kruzhki*) of Russian life, were tolerated by the regime as part of the Little Deal.   By the end of the Brezhnev era, some young specialists began to call for application of the same type of selectivity that they enjoyed in their informal associations to formal associations, such as professional unions. No such calls were successful.   However, calls for selectivity in professional associations were debated in the open press.   These public discussions of the potential for formally recognized Soviet groups to become self-selecting indicated that the notion of such selectivity was widespread.

This selectivity was just one example of the spread of genuine horizontal awareness within the vertically rigid orientation of Soviet society. The unique Russian and Soviet phenomenon of petitioning, the letters to Party and press, spread a sense of commonality among people with common interests or vocations (teachers, architects, and so forth in the cases studied here). While Soviet strictures prevented the coalescence of this awareness into physical organizations, this real awareness among such "virtual" groups spread increasingly as Soviet society became more educated and dynamic. These virtual groups of specialists evolved from the Russian tradition of individual petitioning. In combination with the increased literacy and education of Soviet society, these groups provided a basis for non-governmental, non-Party actors to have some limited influence on the decisions of the state.

While official Soviet organizations (professional unions, associations, etc.) never became self-selecting, recognized unofficial groups had become so on a very limited basis by the end of the Brezhnev era. Most notable among these were environmental groups and groups dedicated to the preservation of historical monuments. Young specialists formed important parts of such groups. While their influence was limited, such groups contributed to the potential expansion of the notion that citizens could build horizontal associations on the basis of values other than those of the official *kollektivy*.

This is not to say that young specialists rejected all aspects of socialist ideology. In keeping with their emphasis on "humanism," young specialists instead sought to strengthen those aspects of socialism in which they believed. The system of free medical care, however imperfect, represented a positive socialist value that young specialists sought to improve. The same was true for the educational, job assignment and food distribution systems as well. Archival documents, in the form of letters to the Party and press or in the form of questions posed to political activists, indicate that young specialists actively proposed solutions to problems within these systems. In so doing, they sought to narrow the gap between the words of Soviet ideology and the deeds of the Soviet state. They did this, not out of any political motive, but because of their own high expectations. Those expectations grew out of the stability, relative prosperity, and educational success that had been such critical formative elements of the specialists' lives. Their activity represented part of the increased, overall dynamism of Soviet society during the Brezhnev years.

As it had in the immediate postwar period, the regime responded to public opinion in general and to these suggestions specifically as well. As always, some aspects of the response were negative and some were positive, and in all cases the regime attempted to closely control the process. In many cases, the Soviet state censored citizens' petitions and stifled social initiatives in order to enhance society's short-term stability. This censorship led to the escalation of pressures and frustrations generated by the increasingly well educated society.

The regime did allow discussion of problems and issues in the public press. In this way, despite the censorship, issues raised by an individual specialist were brought to the attention of other specialists throughout the country. When issues resonated among specialists, as was often the case, subsequent discussions in the press created "virtual" groups of specialists. Members of such groups did not actually have contact with each other but developed a commonality of interests and an awareness of themselves as members of the group. In this way, issues raised in keeping with established parameters nevertheless created an initial sense of horizontal connection among young specialists.

The Soviet social contract of the Brezhnev era promised citizens a basic level of prosperity and the opportunity for social mobility in exchange for political quiescence. A comparison of the theoretical parameters of the contract to the realities of the young specialists' lives reveals an inherent conflict between the society proclaimed by the regime's ideology and their everyday lives—a gap between the regime's words and deeds. The tension generated by this gap shaped the ethos of the Children of Victory and undermined their faith in the Soviet system.

In their quest to build a humane, efficient system, they adapted official rhetoric and expression to serve their own purposes in an effort to overcome the "voiceless" status that they held in Soviet society.   Their confidence was reflected in their increasing willingness to criticize the Soviet social and economic systems for both philosophical and practical reasons, instead of merely criticizing corrupt or incompetent officials. Their confidence was also reflected in the value systems that they chose as their frame of reference. Linguistic markers in the public transcript portray the young specialists as having a different perspective from that of their immediate predecessors. They were more likely to act "for conscience" and "according to principle" than their parents, as well as to question fundamental practices of the regime for reasons of efficiency.   In the public transcript, they often found themselves more in harmony with members of their grandparents' generation (those born in the 1890s and 1900s) than with their parents. The hidden transcript of unpublished materials, however, indicates that the rift between young specialists and their parents may not have been so pronounced. This disparity may have represented an effort by the regime to publicly associate the young specialists more thoroughly with the "heroic" deeds of their grandparents' generation (the victories of the Revolution and Great Patriotic War) and, perhaps, overshadow the lack of such deeds by the Brezhnev regime.

Nevertheless, young specialists and other members of Soviet society continued to attempt to solve the nation's problems.   Educated, trained, and sophisticated elements of Soviet society naturally sought to confront problems of economic, social, and technological development.   Their energy and motivation inspired an impetus toward the solution of Soviet problems. Like a stream of water, this impetus grew along channels where it met less resistance. In those social spaces where such growth was blocked, the movement sought other channels or stopped. But, if stopped, the pressure exerted by the energy and motivation of certain social elements continued to build and seek new outlets. What is critical here is to keep in mind the interactive nature of the relationship between petitioning, censorship, and Soviet society.   The pressure generated from below inspired reactions from above.

Brezhnev's regime did adapt to the pressure of public opinion. But it did not do so quickly or efficiently enough to keep pace with the expectations of the USSR's increasingly educated and dynamic society. As a result, the stability with which the regime defined itself, in contrast with Stalin's terror or Khrushchev's "harebrained schemes" appeared as an obstacle to advancement and the cause of frustration for many, especially for many young specialists.

These frustrations make it possible to analyze the petitions, questions and activities of the young specialists from the perspective of domination-resistance paradigms usually associated with subordinate or subaltern groups in hierarchical societies.   Quite clearly, the well-educated, prosperous young specialists were not a subaltern group in the same sense as the peasants, serfs, or slaves traditionally at the center of subaltern studies. But the restrictions placed upon their avenues of expression by the regime make possible the application of domination-resistance paradigm to the search for source materials concerning their beliefs.

The second major contribution of this study is the location and exploration of just such sources. The letters to the Party and press did represent a "zone of interaction" between Soviet society and the regime. According to the classification rules applicable to most Russian Federation archives in 1999, documents of a "personal nature" will not be open to researchers for 30 years after their creation. Contrary to that rule, letters to the press and summaries of those letters are available. Equally valuable and available are records of the questions and requests that young specialists posed to the regime's activists, which also represent just such "points of interaction." Finally, KGB documents concerning young specialists have been declassified on a limited basis. The *fondy* used as source materials for this study represent merely the initial opportunity for the application of the domination-resistance paradigm to the society of the Brezhnev era.

The discovery of available archival materials is only part of the second contribution made by this study. As noted earlier, historian Gregory Freeze remarked on his choice of published documents over archival ones for his analysis of Russian history at the start of the twentieth century: "The documents that appeared in the contemporary press hold greater historical importance, for they not only expressed but also molded group consciousness and public opinion."[1] This study, through the comparison of published and unpublished letters and requests, demonstrates that Soviet censorship in the Brezhnev era was as active in shaping some public discussions as it was in prohibiting others. The revelation or, perhaps more accurately, the elaboration of this interaction between the Soviet state and society has only just begun. As the works of David Hoffmann and Sheila Fitzpatrick demonstrated, the interactive nature of state-society relationships in the USSR during the prewar Stalin era, and as Elena Zubkova's work showed for the immediate postwar era, this study has taken the first, tentative steps in demonstrating the continuity of such interaction in the "stagnant" years of the Brezhnev era as well.   The strength of the dynamism that underlay that interaction remained unclear until the coming of Mikhail Gorbachev and the dawn of glasnost' and perestroika.

NOTE

1. Gregory L. Freeze, *From Supplication to Revolution; A Documentary History of Imperial Russia*, (New York: Oxford University Press, 1988), 7.

Appendix

Graduates of Soviet Higher Education, 1965-1982

YEAR	NUMBER OF GRADUATES (TO NEAREST THOUSAND)	TOTAL SOVIET POPULATION
1965	403,000	229.3M
1966	432,000	232.2M
1967	480,000	234.8M
1968	511,000	237.2M
1969	565,000	239.5M
1970	630,000	241.7M
1971	672,000	243.9M
1972	684,000	246.3M
1973	692,000	248.6M
1974	693,000	250.9M
1975	713,000	253.3M
1976	734,000	255.6M
1977	752,000	257.9M
1978	772,000	260.1M
1979	790,000	262.4M
1980	817,000	264.5M
1981	831,000	267.0M
1982	841,000	270.0M

TOTAL 12,012,000

Source: "Vypusk spetsialistov vysshimi uchebnymi zavedeniiami po gruppam spetsial'notei," taken from various volumes of *Narodnoe khoziaistvo SSSR* published in Moscow by the Central Statistical Administration (Tsentral'noe statisticheskoe upravlenie SSSR), 1965-1982.

Bibliographic Essay

The increasing formal and social importance of the young professionals earned the scrutiny of observers of Russia, both domestic and foreign. It is therefore important to review how scholars have portrayed this generation, its influence, and its accomplishments.

While a vast body of scholarly literature regarding the Brezhnev-era society exists, that literature has traditionally been dominated by anthologies and articles produced by political scientists, sociologists, and economists. Historians (with the notable exception of Moshe Lewin) have been conspicuous only by their absence,[1] but the scholarly literature from these other disciplines has considered many of the same questions that this study has explored.

In general, the early-mid-1980s mark a watershed within the secondary literature. Both Soviet and Western works published before that time tended to focus on narrowly defined segments of Soviet society and to avoid generalizations.[2] Later Western literature, on the other hand, tended to emphasize the growing "crisis" in Soviet society and to link that crisis to the growth of "civil society." Soviet works likewise began to expand the scope of their focus in the mid-1980s.

Western studies published before the early 1980s tended to focus either on Soviet émigrés' portrayal of life in the USSR or on various single aspects of Brezhnev-era society. The émigré studies indirectly examined Soviet society as a whole. Single-aspect studies tended toward narrowly limited segments of society and quantitative analysis.

Émigré studies, such as the works resulting from the Soviet Interview Project (SIP), edited by James Millar (and in particular the chapters in those anthologies by Brian Silver and Donna Bahry), targeted the level of compliance exhibited by Soviet citizens of various backgrounds with the official norms of the regime as a function of educational and generational backgrounds. Yet they did so on the basis of interviews with a relatively small number of émigrés. The same reliance upon émigré interviews underscored the relevant works of Aryeh Unger, who studied the incongruity between the public and private behavior of Soviet citizens. Many scholars hesitated to generalize issues raised in these studies to all of Soviet society out of concern for the inherent limitations (possibilities for bias, etc.) of émigré studies. While such social science studies did indeed produce genuine insights and represented a valuable basis for comparison with the central findings of this study, they nevertheless constituted merely an initial inquiry.

Equally important, yet with similar limitations in scope, is the large number of Western studies, written prior to 1985, that addressed various single aspects of Brezhnev-era society. These works, such as those by Walter Connor (the conflict between the high expectations and restricted opportunities of Soviet citizens), Viktor Zaslavsky (the growth and impact of social inequality in the USSR), John Bushnell (economic dissatisfaction of Soviet middle class consumers), Mervyn Matthews (the difficult lot of Soviet students), and Ellen Mickiewicz (the evolution and effectiveness of the Brezhnev regime's propaganda and agitation networks) addressed social concerns as individual contemporary issues and examined these issues based primarily upon statistical data. Like the émigré literature, these works frequently noted tendencies or problems within Soviet society that later works would build upon, yet due to the limited scope of the studies (often imposed by limited access to Soviet sources), authors frequently refrained from reaching generalized conclusions about the state of Soviet society.[3]

In other cases, generalized conclusions about the nature of Soviet society were set forth, but the difficulty faced by Western scholars in gaining access to source materials undermined the popularity of such generalized conclusions. In addition, general conclusions sometimes seemed (or were deemed) to be due to the political or ideological positions of the authors involved, even when they focused upon early periods of the Soviet era for which sources were relatively plentiful.[4]

In a handful of cases, almost exclusively in the field of sociology, Western studies compiled before the late 1980s did attempt to place specific trends and tendencies within the general context of Soviet society. Basile Kerblay's 1983 study *Modern Soviet Society* evaluated many different aspects of Soviet society as functions of the interplay between historical and political factors and includes significant quantitative data on such social features as education levels, divorce rates, and family incomes (apparently gleaned from open Brezhnev-era Soviet sources), but his study did not attempt to analyze in detail the values or experiences of Soviet citizens in any qualitative sense.

Murray Yanowitch's 1977 work *Social and Economic Inequality in the Soviet Union: Six Studies* was based upon Soviet sociological data, but he went beyond the numbers to discuss the apparent inequality of social groups in terms of material rewards, opportunity, decision-making power, and gender considerations. Perhaps more than any other Western study prior to the mid-1980's this work sought to portray the quality of life in the USSR in a broad, society-wide context.[5]

Soviet sources written prior to the early 1980s dealt directly with issues of concern to the present study. This was especially true of sociological surveys. Yet those studies, like the Western sources previously mentioned, did so in relative isolation. Those written in the Brezhnev years were notorious for avoiding any sweeping conclusions or generalizations about the nature of Soviet society. For example, Iadov's 1977 study of engineers in Leningrad made no attempt to compare the interests and values of engineers to other social or professional groups but instead contrasted the role of the engineer at work (as a producer of social welfare) with the engineer's role after work (as a consumer of social welfare).[6]

By the mid-1980s, however, Soviet studies did begin to make more broadly oriented investigations. For example, Gordon and Nazimova's 1983 look at the social and professional structure of Soviet society emphasized its departure from the traditional focus on "certain economic branches or geographic zones" that had characterized earlier studies and declared that the time had come for the "cross-sectional analysis" of Soviet society using accumulated census data. Their study and many of those that followed it took the first tentative steps toward a more integrated study of Soviet society from the sociological point of view.[7]

Studies of Brezhnev-era Soviet society published in the West after 1985 frequently asserted that a "crisis of belief" existed in the Soviet Union by the 1970s and described that crisis as the source or inspiration for the growth of "civil society" in the USSR. That is, such studies stressed that more and more Soviet citizens, disillusioned with the policy and ideology of the regime, sought and found avenues of social expression and interaction that were largely independent of the party and government. Such tendencies had been identified in some of the literature published before 1985, as noted earlier, but the literature put out after that time began to group the tendencies described by the earlier literature into a general sense of malaise or crisis in Soviet society. Many of these works were more effective in describing the "crisis of belief" than the evolution of "civil society." Nevertheless, a detailed examination of some of this literature and the course of its development is necessary here, since it had a direct influence in inspiring the present study.

Scholars of different backgrounds analyzed the "crisis of belief" from their own various perspectives but came to similar conclusions. A young Soviet historian and activist concluded that, in the 1960s, "critical thinking" by intellectuals in Soviet society was still normally intended as the making of "corrections" within the framework of official Soviet dogma. But by the 1970s, the "ideology of 'true communism' had ceased to be operative."[8] An American political scientist noted that Soviet society of the late 1970s was "underfed, underhoused, and under-almost everything except under-ruled, under-policed and under-propagandized." In these conditions, the "myth" of building communism "no longer sustain[ed] more than a small minority, if that."[9] A Soviet émigré sociologist believed that Soviet people "manage to adjust to the state by developing a mythological level in their thinking, which accepts most official dogmas and at the same time in no way affects their material behavior."[10]

Each of these conclusions is consistent with the generally held retrospective view of Soviet society of the Brezhnev era that the citizens of the USSR were not faithful adherents to the official Soviet mythology that portrayed them as ardent builders of communism. Despite the diversity of their backgrounds, each of the scholars cited and the majority of the scholars who have analyzed Soviet society of the Brezhnev years focused on the Soviet state or on the Communist Party of the Soviet Union as the decisive factor in the shaping of Soviet history. Given their focus on the elite political elements of the USSR, their emphasis on "crisis" is not surprising. As Stephen F. Cohen noted in 1985, the political elite of the Brezhnev era was constantly undermined by three aspects of Soviet life: the past crimes of the regime, the inherent conflict between the society proclaimed by the regime's ideology versus the everyday lives of the people, and the notion of change, which formed an inherent part of Marxism-Leninism.[11]

More recent scholarship, however, has begun to take a wider view of Soviet society, going beyond sole reliance upon the actions of the elite. Accordingly, the views of life in the USSR produced by this scholarship have become increasingly sophisticated.

In 1991, Moshe Lewin described the increasing divergence between the elite and masses of post-Stalin Soviet society, such as those cited earlier as part of the evolution of a more "civil" society in the USSR, increasingly sophisticated and dynamic. Yet even his primary emphasis remained on the nature and policies of the Soviet political system, the "command-administrative" system established primarily in the 1930s. For Lewin, this top heavy state system played the decisive role by failing to adapt to the changing nature of the society that it ruled and "kept losing its capacity to solve problems, and hence to rule."[12] But by emphasizing the notion that Soviet society possessed "a changing nature," Lewin contributed to the process of shifting the historian's focus on Brezhnev's Russia from the elite as the critical actor, to an awareness of the impact made by nonelite elements of Soviet society.

Geoffrey Hosking attributed increased prominence to the influence of the nonelite. While he, like Lewin, noted that the Soviet political structure became increasingly stagnant, he highlighted the fact that ambitious and highly educated young people in the USSR found themselves barred from genuine advancement and from meaningful participation in the basic decision-making processes of their country.[13] As portrayed by Lewin and Hosking, the alienation of the society and the stagnation of the elite formed the "thesis" and "antithesis" of a dialectic tension that became a crucial factor in the evolution of Soviet history.

As the discussion in this study's chapters has shown, the "alienation of society" and "stagnation of the elite" were manifested most clearly in the "gap between words and deeds." That is, the everyday reality observed by the young specialists clearly and dramatically differed from the "developed socialist society" declared by the regime. More than any other factor, the tension created by this "gap" served to drive the evolution of Soviet civil society forward.

It is important to note here, however, that both this "gap" and the dialectical interaction of Soviet state and society had existed since the start of the Soviet era.   Social histories of the Stalin years and immediate postwar period, produced in the mid- to late 1990s, clearly illustrated both the divergence between the real world and the world of Soviet ideology as well as the interactive relationship between society and state.

In his 1994 study of peasant migration to Soviet cities of the late 1920s and 1930s, David Hoffmann demonstrated that peasant networks did as much to shape the evolution of the urban working class as did the regime's social engineering. In fact, Hoffmann argued, the desperate poverty and falling living standards among workers in the early 1930s undermined Soviet authority and reinforced traditional village networks. This, in turn, forced the state to alter its emphasis from revolutionary to traditional values and to seek extra systemic methods to improve productivity.[14]   Hoffmann concluded his study by noting that the Party leadership, deprived (via passive protest) of the large, politically supportive proletariat that was to build the socialist order, granted economic security in exchange for political quiescence. In addition to such non-Marxist incentives as Russian nationalism and the Stalin cult, the contradiction between Marxist ideology and non-Marxist appeals undermined the long-term stability of the Soviet system.[15]

In similar fashion, Sheila Fitzpatrick demonstrated both the gap between words and deeds and the genuine interaction of state and society in her social histories of the 1930s. In *Stalin's Peasants: Resistance & Survival in the Russian Village after Collectivization*, Fitzpatrick noted that the very first act of collectivization, the January 1930 seizure of livestock, discredited the regime and its proclaimed ideology from the start. As a result, peasants used both passive and active techniques of resistance to shape the state's rural policy in a process of give-and-take that changed both the regime and peasant society.[16] Subsequently, in her work on urban society in the 1930s, Fitzpatrick described the "normal" posture of the Soviet urban citizen as one of "passive conformity and outward obedience" toward the regime's words in the face of the daily confrontation with the reality of chronic shortages and housing problems— manifestations of the regime's deeds.[17]

Both of Fitzpatrick's works have special relevance to this study, in that she applied the analysis of Soviet peasants and workers as subordinate groups within Soviet society and noted how they applied techniques of resistance toward the domination of the regime. That resistance, in turn, shaped Soviet policy and forced the elite to modify its own public "transcript" in its interaction with its subjects. While Fitzpatrick applied this methodology much more effectively and rigorously in her history of the peasantry than in her work on the proletariat, she nevertheless set an important precedent for the current study.

The fourth major social history of the postwar era produced in the latter 1990s with particular relevance to this study was Elena Zubkova's analysis of the "complex of hopes and expectations" of the Soviet people from 1945 to 1957.[18] Zubkova used archival material to demonstrate the surprising level of influence that public opinion had upon the Soviet regime in the postwar period.

In each of these new social histories, the relationship between elements of Soviet society and the state as well as relationships within the social elements were portrayed as an interactive, "push-pull" process. While these works did not focus on the same time period as this study, they presented important applications of domination-resistance studies in the Soviet context and validation of the long-term existence of the "gap between words and deeds" that drove the evolution of Soviet society in the Brezhnev years as well.

S. Frederick Starr provided a warning that Western scholars must be cautious in tracing that evolution. In a wonderfully concise, yet insightful, article, Starr summarized the gradual change in Soviet society and provided two useful warnings to Western scholars attempting to classify that society as "civil." He reminded all that the Western notion of civil society as 'pluralistic,' with government distinct from society and but one of many institutions, might be too narrowly based on the Western tradition built by Locke, DeToqueville, and John Stuart Mill. Russian tradition, said Starr, may lead to unique traits. Starr's second warning noted that society must "gain influence" over government for civil society to exist.[19] In view of the social histories described earlier, Starr's comments proved prescient. Soviet society did gain influence over the state but did so in a uniquely Russian manner. As the source analysis of this study's chapters has shown, the young specialists at the heart of this study did gain some influence over the Brezhnev-era government in the same type of "push-pull" process as had the social elements highlighted by the previously mentioned studies. The inclusion of the nonelite elements of Soviet society as shapers of Soviet history was an important development in the historiography on the post-Stalin era, yet it represented only the initial expansion of the historian's view.[20]

Attempting to ascertain the genuine nature of the beliefs of Soviet citizens of the Brezhnev era remains a daunting task for historians, despite the widely expanded access to Soviet archival material in recent years. Trying to focus on a particular subgroup of Soviet citizens may prove even more difficult. Attempting to "get at" the essence of those beliefs has been termed "a real challenge" and a "scarcely touched subject," given the beliefs' "extremely private" nature.[21] Yet perhaps the difficulty lies not so much in the "private" nature of Soviet citizens' beliefs but rather in the methodology that historians have traditionally employed in attempting to understand them. Here, it seems, recent studies of subordination and subalternity within societies as well as notions of social domination and resistance may offer techniques that make traditional methodology more effective.

THE EVOLUTION OF SUBALTERN STUDIES[22]

In his analysis of the historiography of colonial India, Ranajit Guha declared that there were "vast areas in the life and the consciousness of the people" that were not integrated into the elite ideology and that, a "structural dichotomy" developed between the elite and nonelite elements of colonial Indian society that represented the "historic failure of the nation to come to its own."[23] Yet the two elements of this structural dichotomy were not mutually exclusive. In fact, they were in continuous interaction, and both were, therefore, represented within the historical records written by the elite. The critical reading of such records as discourses and the deciphering of elite and subaltern "codes" located within those discourses represented the essence of Guha's subaltern method.[24]   This study did not focus exclusively on elite-authored sources, as Guha was forced to do, since the young specialists were able to express their thoughts within the limited press forum, but the notion of press "discussions" as representing "continuous interaction" between the specialists and the regime represents a critical and relevant technique of subaltern studies drawn upon here. This continuous interaction represents the same "push-pull" process described in the works of Hoffmann, Fitzpatrick, and Zubkova mentioned earlier.

Guha's notion of "continuous interaction" between the governmental elite and remainder of society and the promise of subaltern studies as a technique for reaching voiceless social groups inspired the focus of the current work. But given that the young specialists were not completely "voiceless," more clearly relevant to this discussion is the more generalized discussion of domination and resistance conducted by James C. Scott, which places greater emphasis on the disguised expressions of belief inserted into historical sources by the subordinates themselves. When Scott and Guha's methods are combined with the specifically Soviet insights of émigré sociologist Vladimir Shlapentokh, they seem to hold great promise indeed.

It is important to note here that it is no secret that many practitioners of subaltern studies techniques zealously advocate for the exclusive use of those techniques to "empower" or "find the voice of" subaltern groups (almost always poor, Third World, ethnic, or religious minorities). Yet the discussion in the December 1994 American Historical Review among Prakash, Florencia Mallon, and Frederick Cooper clearly indicates that subaltern studies has evolved beyond this, the original, positivist political agenda of its founders. In a sense, the dialectical "thesis" of traditional elite-centered historiography has combined with the subaltern "antithesis" to create a new "synthesis": the application of subaltern studies techniques to persons who are neither poor nor ethnic or religious minorities.

In his 1990 study Domination and the Arts of Resistance, Scott argued that groups that occupy a subordinate status within any society must measure and restrain their responses in the presence of members of the dominant group. Such self-restraint inspires a sense of frustration. This frustration, in turn, leads subordinates "to create and defend a social space in which offstage dissent to the official transcript of power relations may be voiced" behind the scenes.[25]   In Scott's terminology, this "offstage dissent" represents a "hidden transcript" that can provide insight into the beliefs, feelings, and functions of the subordinate group.

In analyzing Soviet society, Vladimir Shlapentokh concluded that "due to the pressure to conform to official interpretations of reality, facts and feelings in contradiction with the official view tend to be suppressed . . . they accumulate, increasing pressure . . . awaiting an opportunity for a release."[26] Clearly, Shlapentokh's "suppressed facts and feelings" would seem to indicate the presence of "hidden transcripts" within Soviet society.[27]

Deciding exactly where to look for those transcripts required a comparison of Scott's broad definition of subordination and Guha's specific techniques for finding the voice of the subaltern.   As noted earlier, Guha considered that the two elements of his "structural dichotomy," the voices of the elite and subaltern, were in continuous interaction. Scott likewise portrayed the interaction of the hidden transcripts of the subordinate and the elite as occurring in a "zone of constant struggle" in the public domain.[28]   Prakash also emphasized that subalterns and subalternity exert pressure against the very structures that subordinate them.[29] Frederick Cooper, writing in the same forum as Prakash, went a step further and insisted that subordinate groups are much more heavily and openly "engaged" in interaction with elite elements than even Scott's "hidden transcripts" would indicate.[30] Therefore, this study sought out and explored points of interaction between the representatives of the political elite and the young, well-educated, often frustrated, alienated, or otherwise subordinated citizens at the heart of the evolution of late Soviet society.

My first search for archival materials for use in this study in 1995 was extraordinarily frustrating. Most of the documents used here were declassified shortly after I departed the Russian Federation in May 1995. By the summer of 1999 significant numbers of *fondy* containing valuable letters had been opened to researchers, albeit in a haphazard fashion. The intricacies of Russian politics and the funding problems faced by Russia's archives account for the uneven pace of declassification. Nevertheless, as declassification continues, additional archival documents will enrich and broaden the portrait of the young specialists and their influence on the evolution of Soviet and Russian society.

NOTES

1. Stephen F. Cohen offers some fascinating explanations for the lack of extensive historical research on post-New Economic Policy Soviet-era topics in *Rethinking the Soviet Experience: Politics and History since 1917* (New York: Oxford University Press, 1985). Of course, with the passage of time, the Brezhnev era is now becoming a more conventional subject for historians.

2. Anecdotal works, such as those of William Taubman, *The View from Lenin Hills* (New York: Coward-McCann, 1967), Georgie Anne Geyer, *The Young Russians* (Homewood, IL: ETC, 1975) and Hedrick Smith's *The Russians* (New York: Ballantine, 1976) represent important exceptions to this tendency. These accounts frequently noted the widespread disillusionment and sense of "purposelessness" among Soviet citizens, in contrast to the more "scholarly" studies of that time.

3. For example, Ellen Mickiewicz noted that the increasing general education level in the USSR was leading to a sense of lost mobility and frustration. Her conclusion, focused completely on the political elite, was that some CPSU elements would attempt to inject greater "pragmatism" into administrative decision making. See Mickiewicz, "The Modernization of Party Propaganda in the USSR," *Slavic Review* 30 (June 1971), 257-276.

4. For example, reviewers of E.H. Carr's *The Russian Revolution, 1917-1929: From Lenin to Stalin* (New York: Free Press, 1979), questioned Carr's personal philosophy even more than they did his conclusions. See *Book Review Digest* (1980), 193-194, and this when Carr was considered one of, the foremost specialists of that time on revolutionary Russia, if not the foremost specialist.

5. Yanowitch went so far as to discuss the development of Soviet management principles in a historical context, describing them as having been "enshrined" in the pre-World War II drive to industrialize. Murray Yanowitch, *Social and Economic Inequality*

in the Soviet Union: Six Studies (White Plains, NY: M.E. Sharpe, 1977), 141. Kendall Bailes and Nicholas Lampert subsequently validated Yanowitch's assertion. Bailes, *Technology and Society under Lenin and Stalin* (Princeton, NJ: Princeton University Press, 1978); Lampert, *The Technical Intelligentsia and the Soviet State* (New York: Macmillan, 1979).

6. V. Iadov, ed. *Sotsial'no-psikhologicheskii portet inzhenera*, (Moscow: Mysl', 1977).

7. L.A. Gordon and A.K. Nazimova, "Sotsiol'no-professiol'naia struktura sovremennogo sovetskogo obshchestva" in Yanowitch 1986, 3-61. Titma, Shkaratan, Osviannikov, and Aitov likewise conducted studies during this time period that expanded the traditional scope, which had been limited to geographic areas or even to certain institutes, universities, or enterprises.

8. Boris Kagarlitsky, *The Thinking Reed: Intellectuals and the Soviet State, 1917 to the Present*, trans. Brian Pearce (London: Verso, 1988), 181.

9. Robert C. Tucker, *Political Culture and Leadership in Soviet Russia: From Lenin to Gorbachev* (New York: W.W. Norton, 1987), 131-132.

10. Vladimir Shlapentokh, *Public and Private Life of the Soviet People: Changing Values in Post-Stalin Russia* (New York: Oxford University Press, 1989), 229.

11. Cohen, *Rethinking the Soviet Experience*, 151.

12. Moshe Lewin, "Russia/USSR in Historical Motion: An Essay in Interpretation," *Russian Review* 50 (1991), 249-266.

13. Geoffrey Hosking, *The Awakening of the Soviet Union*, enlarged ed. (Cambridge: Harvard University Press, 1991), 69. Hosking's chapter "A Civil Society in Embryo" gives an excellent narrative on the development of informal groups and horizontal connections from the mid-1960s forward.

14. David L. Hoffmann. *Peasant Metropolis: Social Identities in Moscow, 1929-1941.* (Ithaca, NY: Cornell University Press, 1994), esp. 156-177.

15. Ibid., 219.

16. Sheila Fitzpatrick, *Stalin's Peasants: Resistance & Survival in the Russian Village after Collectivization* (New York: Oxford University Press, 1994).

17. Sheila Fitzpatrick *Everyday Stalinism, Ordinary Life in Extraordinary Times: Soviet Russia in the 1930s* (New York: Oxford University Press, 1999).

18. Elena Iurevna Zubkova, *Russia after the War: Hopes, Illusions and Disappointments, 1945-1957*, trans. and ed. Hugh Ragsdale (Armonk, NY: M.E. Sharpe, 1998).

19. S. Frederick Starr, "Soviet Union: A Civil Society," *Foreign Policy* 70 (Spring 1988), 26-41.

20. It is critical to note that this study offers Lewin and Hosking only as *examples* of scholars who considered the nonelite as having an active role in the shaping of Soviet history. They were neither the first nor the only ones to take such a view. Many social historians in the late 1960s and 1970s looked at other periods of Russian history "from below." Few, if any, scholars have applied such a perspective to the non dissident society of the Brezhnev years. Lewin was chosen in recognition of his long-standing emphasis that "society was always an active shaper of long-term political and social trends in the Soviet Union, most clearly annunciated in *The Making of the Soviet System* (New York: Pantheon, 1985), 7. Hosking's was one of the first books by a Western author to discuss the "civil" nature of Soviet society as a factor in the revolutionary events of the late 1980s. It should be noted that dissident émigré Evgeni Gnedin declared that the Soviet state and Soviet society were "evolving in different directions," with society becoming increasingly pluralistic in 1982. Evgeni Gnedin, *Vykhod iz labirinta* (New York: Chalidze Press 1982), 115-117.

21. Such were the comments of the late Professor Allan K. Wildman in response to an exploratory analysis of the historiography on Soviet culture in the Brezhnev era that the author submitted in the fall of 1993.

22. The best concise history of the evolution of subaltern studies as a an analytical approach within the historical discipline to date may be found in Gyan Prakash, "Subaltern Studies as Postcolonial Criticism," *American Historical Review* (December 1994), 1475-1490, esp. 1477-1480.

23. Ranajit Guha, "On Some Aspects of the Historiography of Colonial India," in Ranajit Guha and Gayatri Chakravorty Spivak, *Selected Subaltern Studies* (New York: Oxford University Press, 1988), 36-43, esp. 40-43.

24. Guha discusses the specifics of historiographic sources, codes, and interpretations in "The Prose of Counterinsurgency," in Guha and Spivak, 1988, 45-84, esp. 47-59. Guha applied his methodology to the study of peasant rebels in colonial India and was successful in finding a voice of these subalterns within the elite-authored historiography of the colonial period in his book *Elementary Aspects of Peasant Insurgency in Colonial India* (Delhi: Oxford University Press, 1983). Some of the specific aspects that he described are discussed later when considering Soviet sources.

25. James C. Scott, *Domination and the Arts of Resistance: Hidden Transcripts* (New Haven, CT: Yale University Press, 1990), x-xi. Scott discusses the impulses generated by such frustration in more detail on pages 26-35.

26. Vladimir Shlapentokh, *Soviet Public Opinion and Ideology: Mythology and Pragmatism in Interaction* (NewYork: Praeger, 1986), 128. In the introduction to this book, Shlapentokh even went so far as to recommend methods for deciphering the "hermeneutics" involved in assessing the official ideology of the USSR, xv-xx.

27. The notion that Soviet citizens, especially those of the 1960s and 1970s, held personal beliefs that stood in contrast to their public actions has been frequently acknowledged, though rarely explored. A few examples of the many sources that acknowledge this dual nature of Soviet society include Kagarlitsky, 181-215; Tucker, 1987, 184; Nicholas Lampert, *Whistleblowing in the Soviet Union: A Study of Complaints and Abuses under State Socialism*, (NewYork: Schrocken Books, 1985), 59-60, 85; Shlapentokh 1989, 97-98.

28. Scott, 14-15.

29. Prakash, 1482.

30. Frederick Cooper, "Conflict and Connection: Rethinking Colonial African Histor," in *American Historical Review* (December 1994), 1516-1545, esp. 1534-1535.

Bibliography

ARCHIVES

GARF=Gosudarstvennyi arkhiv Rissiiskoi federatsii (State Archive of the Russian Federation)
RTsKhIDNI=Russian tsentr khraneniia i izucheniia dokumentov novoi istorii (Russian Center for the Preservation and Study of Documents on Contemporary History)
TsKhSD=Tsentr khraneniia sovremennoi dokumentatsii (Center for the Preservation of Contemporary Documentation)

NEWSPAPERS AND JOURNALS

Agitator. Journal for Activists of the Communist Party, produced under authority of the Central Committee
Izvestiia. Daily of the Soviet Government
Kommunist. Journal of the Communist Party of the Soviet Union
Komsomolskaia pravda. Weekly of the Young Communist League
Literaturnaia gazeta. Weekly of the Soviet Writer's Union
Pravda. Daily of the Communist Party of the Soviet Union
Sotsialisticheskaia industriia. Weekly produced under authority of the Central Committee

MONOGRAPHS AND ARTICLES

Aitov, N.A. *NTR: Sotsial'noe planirovanie*. Moscow: Profizdat, 1978.

Alekseev, V.K., B.Z. Doktorov, and B.M. Firsov. "Izuchenie obshchestvennogo mneniia: opyt i problemy." *Sotsiologicheskie issledovaniia,* no 4 (1979), 23 --32.

Alexander, John T. *Catherine the Great: Life and Legend.* New York: Oxford University Press, 1989.

Alexeyeva, Ludmilla, and Paul Goldberg. *The Thaw Generation: Coming of Age in the Post-Stalin Era.* Pittsburgh: University of Pittsburgh Press, 1993.

Bailes, Kendall. *Technology and Society Under Lenin and Stalin* New York: Princeton University Press, 1978.

Balmuth, Daniel. *Censorship in Russia, 1865-1905.* Washington, DC: University Press of America, 1979.

Blinov, N.M. "The Sociology of Youth: Achievements and Problems." *Soviet Sociology* 21 (1983), 3-19.

Bogdanov, V.,and B. Viazemskii. *Spravochnik zhurnalista.* Leningrad: 1965.

Bokarev, N. *Sotsiologicheskkiie issledovaniia effektivnosti lektsionnoi propagandy.* Moscow: Znanie, 1980.

Bushnell, John. "The 'New Soviet Man' Turns Pessimist." *Survey* 24, no. 2 (1979),1-18.

Byrnes, R.F., Ed. *After Brezhnev: Sources of Soviet Conduct in the 1980's.* Bloomington: Indiana University Press, 1983.

Carnaghan, Ellen. "A Revolution in Mind: Russian Political Attitudes and the Origins of Democratization Under Gorbachev." Ph.D. Dissertation, New York University, 1992.

Chernovolenko, V.F., V.L. Ossovskii, and V.I. Paniotto. *Prestizh professii: problemy sotsial'noi professial'noi orientatsii molodezhi.* Kiev: Naukova Dumka, 1979.

Chichanovskii, A.A. *Instantsiia istiny: sredstva massovoi informatsii i zhizn': vozhmozhnosti, poisk, otvetsvennost.* Moscow: Izdatel'stvo politicheskoi literatury, 1989.

Choldin, Marianna. *A Fence around the Empire: Russian Censorship of Western Ideas under the Tsars.* Durham, NC: Duke University Press, 1985.

Choldin, Marianna, and Maurice Friedberg, eds. *The Red Pencil: Artists, Scholars and Censors in the USSR.* Boston: Unwin Hyman, 1989.

Cohen, Stephen F., ed. *An End to Silence: Uncensored Opinion in the Soviet Union.* New York: W.W. Norton, 1982.

Cohen, Stephen F. *Rethinking the Soviet Experience: Politics and History since 1917.* NewYork: Oxford University Press, 1985.

Cohen, Stephen F., and Katrina Vanden Heuvel, eds. *Voices of Glasnost': Interviews with Gorbachev's Reformers.* New York: W.W. Norton, 1989.

Connor, Walter. "Dissent in a Complex Society." *Problems of Communism* 22 (1973), 40-52.

Connor, Walter D. *Socialism, Politics and Equality. Hierarchy and Change in Eastern Europe and the USSR.* New York: Columbia University Press, 1979.

Cook, Linda. "Brezhnev's Social Contract and the Gorbachev Reforms." *Soviet Studies* 44, no. 1 (1992), 37-56.

Cooper, Frederick. "Conflict and Connection: Rethinking Colonial African History." *American Historical Review* (December 1994), 1516-1545.

Darst, Robert G. "Environmentalism in the USSR: The Opposition to the River Diversion Projects." *Soviet Economy* 4, no. 3 (July-September 1988), 232-252.

Dewey, Horace W., and Ann Marie Kleimola. "The Petition as an Old Russian Literary Genre" *Slavic and East European Journal* 14, no. 3 (1970), 284-301.

Dewhirst, Martin, and Robert Farrell, eds. *The Soviet Censorship.* Metuchen, NJ: Scarecrow Press, 1973.

Dunham, Vera S. *In Stalin's Time: Middle Class Values in Soviet Fiction.* New York: Columbia University Press, 1990.

Dzirkals, L., T. Gustafson, and R. Johnson. *The Media and Intra-Elite Communication in the USSR.* Santa Monica, CA: RAND, 1982.

Ermolaev, Herman. *Censorship in Soviet Literature, 1917-1991.* Lanham, MD: Rowman and Littlefield, 1997.

Fields, Daniel. *Rebels in the Name of the Tsar.* Boston: Houghton Mifflin, 1976.

Figes, Orlando. *A People's Tragedy: A History of the Russian Revolution.* New York: Viking, 1996.

Finifter, A. and E. Mickiewicz. "Redefining the Political System of the USSR: Mass Support for Political Change." *American Political Science Review* 86 (1992), 857-874.

Fitzpatrick, Sheila. *Stalin's Peasants: Resistance & Survival in the Russian Village after Collectivization.* New York: Oxford University Press, 1994.

Fitzpatrick, Sheila. *Everyday Stalinism, Ordinary Life in Extraordinary Times: Soviet Russia in the 1930s.* New York: Oxford University Press, 1999.

Fomicheva, I. *Literaturnaia gaezta i ee auditoria.* Moscow: Izdatel'stvo MGU, 1978.

Freeze, Gregory L. *From Supplication to Revolution: A Documentary Social History of Imperial Russia.* New York: Oxford University Press, 1988.

Georgiev, D. *Rezhissura gazety.* Moscow: Mysl', 1979.

Geyer, Georgie Anne. *The Young Russians.* Homewood, IL: ETC, 1975.

Gnedin, Evgeni. *Vykhod iz labirinta.* New York: Chalidze Press, 1982.

Gordon, L.A., and V.V. Komarovskii. "Dinamika sotsial'no-professional'nogo sostava pokolenii." *Sotsiologicheskie issledovaniia,* 100-112.

Goriaeva, T.M., ed. *Istoriia sovetskoi politicheskoi tsnzury: Dokumenty i kommentarii.* Moscow: ROSSPEN, 1997.

Gorsheneva, N.A. *O rabote s pis'mami trudiashchikhsia.* Moscow: Znanie, 1979.

Gorshkov, M.K., A. Iu. Chepurenko, and F.E. Sheregi, eds. *Osennii krizis 1998 goda: rossiiskoie obshchestvo do i posle.* Moscow: Rossiiskaia politicheskaia entsiklopediia, 1998.

Grushin, B. *Mneniia o mire i mir mnenii.* Moscw: Politizdat, 1967.

Grushin, B.A., and L.A. Onikov, eds. *Massovaia informatsiia v sovetskom promyshlennom gorode.* Moscow: Politizdat, 1979.

Guha, Ranajit, and Gayatri Chakravorty Spivak. *Elementary Aspects of Peasant Insurgency in Colonial India.* Delhi: Oxford University Press, 1983.

Herlemann, Horst, ed. *Quality of Life in the Soviet Union.* Boulder, CO: Westview Press, 1987.

Hoffmann, David L. *Peasant Metropolis: Social Identities in Moscow, 1929-1941.* Ithaca, NY: Cornell University Press, 1994.

Hollander, Gayle Durham. *Soviet Political Indoctrination: Developments in Mass Media and Propaganda since Stalin.* New York: Praeger, 1972.

Hopkins, Mark W. *Mass Media in the Soviet Union.* New York: Pegasus, 1970.

Hosking, Geoffrey. *The Awakening of the Soviet Union.* Enlarged Edition. Cambridge: Harvard University Press, 1991.

Hough, Jerry F. "Political Participation in the USSR." *Soviet Studies* 28, no. 1 (1976), 3-20.

Iadov, V., Ed. *Sotsial'no-psikhologicheskii portet inzhenera.* Moscow: Mysl', 1977.

Iakovlev, B.P. "Vazhnaia forma sviazi s massami." *Partinaia zhizn'* 17 (1979), 22-37.

Ianitskii, O.N.   "Chelovecheskii   factor   sotsialisticheskoi   urbanizatsii: stanovlenie novykh orientirov." *Sotsiologicheskie issledovaniia* 2 (1986).

Jacobson, Helen Saltz, ed. and trans. *Diary of a Russian Censor: Aleksandr Nikitenko.* Amherst: University of Massachusetts Press, 1975.

Kagarlitsky, Boris. *The Thinking Reed: Intellectuals and the Soviet State, 1917 to the Present.* Trans. Brian Pearce. London: Verso, 1988.

Kagarlitsky, Boris. *The Disintegration of the Monolith.* Trans. Renfrey Clarke. New York: Verso Books, 1992.

Kazakevich, N.N., and A.V. Kalitsevskaia.   *O rabote s pismami trudiashchikhsia.   Sbornik dokumental'nykh materialov.*   Moscow: Iuridicheskaia literatura, 1980.

Keep, John L.H. *Last of the Empires: A History of the Soviet Union, 1945-1991.* Oxford: Oxford University Press, 1995.

Kelley, Donald R. "Environmental Policy-Making in the USSR: The Role of Industrial and Environmental Interest Groups." *Soviet Studies* 28, no. 4, October (1976), 570-589.

Kerblay, Basile. "Social Inequality in the USSR." *Problems of Communism* 31 (1982).

Kerblay, Basile. *Modern Soviet Society.* Translator Rupert Sawyer. New York: Pantheon, 1983.

Kharchev, A.G. *Brak i semia v SSSR.* Moscow: Mysl', 1979.

Kharkhordin, Oleg. *The Collective and the Individual in Russia: A Study of Practices*. Berkeley: University of California Press, 1999.

Khoros, V.G., ed .*Grazhdoanskoe obshchestvo. Mirovoi opyt i problemy Rossii.* Moscow: Editorial, URSS, 1998.

Kivelson, Valerie A. "The Devil Stole His Mind: The Tsar and the 1648 Moscow Uprising." *American Historical Review* 98, no. 3 (June 1993), 733-756.

Kivelson, Valerie A. *Autocracy in the Provinces*. Stanford, CA: Stanford University Press, 1996.

Kolkov, Iu. "Ostrova blazhennykh." *Strana i mir* 1-2 (1985), 104-114.

Kullberg, Judith. "The Origins of the Gorbachev Revolution: Industrialization, Social Structure Change and Soviet Elite Value Transformation, 1917-1985." Ph.D. Diss. Ohio State University, Columbus, 1995.

Lampert, Nicholas. *The Technical Intelligentsia and the Soviet State*. London: Macmillan, 1979.

Lampert, Nicholas. *Whistleblowing in the Soviet Union: A Study of Complaints and Abuses under State Socialism*. New York: Schocken Books, 1985.

Lapidus, Gail. "Society under Strain: The Soviet Union after Brezhnev." *The Washington Quarterly*, no. 6, (Spring 1983), 29-47.

Levin, A.I. *Nauchno-tekhnicheskii progress i lichnoe potreblenie*. Moscow: Mysl', 1979.

Lewin, Moshe. *The Making of the Soviet System,*New York: Pantheon, 1985.

Lewin, Moshe. *The Gorbachev Phenomenon: A Historical Interpretation*. Berkeley: University of California Press, 1991.

Lewin, Moshe. "Russia/USSR in Historical Motion: An Essay in Interpretation." *Russian Review* 50 (1991), 249-266.

Lim, A. "Intellektualy i novyi obshchestvennyi dogovor." *Problemy vostochnoi evropy* 2 (1981).

Lincoln, W. Bruce. *Nicholas I: Emperor and Autocrat of All the Russias*. DeKalb: Northern Illinois Press, 1989.

Lopata, P., and V. Petukhov. *Sozidatel'naia sila sotsialisticheskogo samoupravleniia naroda*. Moscow: Znanie, 1986.

Losenkov, V. *Sotsial'naia informatsia v zhizhni gorodskogo naseleniia*. Leningrad: Nauka, 1983.

Massie, Robert K. *Peter the Great: His Life and World*. New York: Ballantine Books, 1980.

Matthews, Mervyn. *Class and Society in Soviet Russia*. New York: Walker, 1972.

Matthews, Mervyn. "Soviet Students—Some Sociological Perspectives." *Soviet Studies* 27 (1975), 86-108.

McAuley, Alastair. *Economic Welfare in the Soviet Union: Poverty, Living Standards and Inequality*. Madison: University of Wisconsin Press, 1979.

Medvedev, Roy. *On Socialist Democracy.* Trans. Ellen de Kadt. New York: Alfred A. Knopf, 1975.

Medvedev, Vadim. *The Administration of Socialist Production: Problems of Theory and Practice.* Moscow: Politizdat, 1983.

Mendeleev, A.G. *Chto za gazetnym slovom?* Moscow: Mysl', 1979.

Mickiewicz, Ellen. "The Modernization of Party Propaganda in the USSR." *Slavic Review* 30 (June 1971), 257-276.

Mickiewicz, Ellen Propper. *Media and the Russian Public.* New York: Praeger, 1981.

Millar, James R. "The Little Deal: Brezhnev's Contribution to Acquisitive Socialism." *Slavic Review* 44, no. 4 (Winter 1985), 694-706.

Millar, James R., ed. *Politics, Work and Daily Life in the USSR: A Survey of Former Soviet Citizens.* New York: Cambridge University Press, 1987.

Millar, James R., ed. *Cracks in the Monolith: Party Power in the Brezhnev Era.* Armonk NY: M.E. Sharpe, 1992.

Miller, Arthur M., William M. Reisinger, and Vicki L. Hedli. eds. *Public Opinion and Regime Change: The New Politics of Post-Soviet Studies.* Boulder, CO: Westview Press, 1993.

Monas, Sidney. *The Third Section: Police and Society under Nicholas I.* Cambridge: Harvard University Press,

Morozov, Boris. *Sotsiologicheskie issledovaniia kaka sredstvo povysheniia effektivnosti partinogo rukovodstva pressoi.* Moscow: AON, 1981.

Panachin, F.G. *Shkola i obshchestvennyi progress.* Moscow: Prosveshchenie, 1983.

Papmehl, K.A. *Freedom of Expression in Eighteenth Century Russia.* The Hague: Martinus Nijhoff, 1971.

Parker, Tony. *Russian Voices.* New York: Henry Holt, 1991.

Pimenova, V. *Svobodnoe vremia v sotsiolisticheskom obshchestve.* Moscow: Mysl', 1974.

Prakash, Gyan. "Subaltern Studies as Postcolonial Criticism." *American Historical Review* (December 1994), 1475-1490.

Raeff, Marc. *Understanding Imperial Russia.* New York: Columbia University Press, 1984.

Remnev, V.I. *Predlozheniia, zaiavleniia i zhaloby grazhdan.* Moscow: Iuridichesakia literatura, 1972.

Remnick, David. *Lenin's Tomb: The Last Days of the Soviet Empire.* New York: Vintage Books, 1994.

Rhodes, Mark S. "Letters to the Editor in the USSR: A Study of Letters, Authors and Potential Uses." Ph.D. Diss., Michigan State University, East Lansing, 1977.

Richmond, Steven. " 'The Eye of the State': An Interview with Soviet Chief Censor Vladimir Solodin." *The Russian Review* 56 (October 1997), 581-590.

Ries, Nancy. *Russian Talk: Culture and Conversation during Perestroika,* Ithaca, NY: Cornell University Press, 1997.

Rowland, Daniel. "The Problem of Advice in Muscovite Tales about the Time of Troubles." *Russian History* 6, Part 2 (1979), 259-283.

Rutkevich, M.N.   *Intelligentsia v razvitom sotsialisticheskom obshchestve.* Moscow: Politizdat, 1977.

Rutkevich, M.N., and F.R. Filippov. *Vysshaia shkola kak factor izmeneniia sosial'noi stuktury razvitogo sotrialisticheskogo obshchestva.* Moscow: Nauka, 1978.

Sablinsky, Walter. *The Road to Bloody Sunday: Father Gapon and the St. Petersburg Massacre of 1905.* Princeton, NJ: Princeton University Press, 1976.

Saturin, V. *Molodezh: Doveriie i otvetsvennost'.* Kiev: Nauka Dumka, 1984.

Sbytov, V.   *Upravleniie Sotsial'nymi i ideologicheskimi przessami v period razvitogo sotsialisma.* Moscow: Nauka, 1983.

Schulz, Donald E., and Jan S. Adams, eds. *Political Participation in Communist Systems.* New York: Pergamon, 1981.

Scott, James C. *Domination and the Arts of Resistance: Hidden Transcripts.* New Haven, CT: Yale University Press, 1990.

Sedaitis, Judith B., and Jim Butterfield. eds. *Perestroika from Below: Social Movements in the Soviet Union.* Boulder, CO: Westview Press, 1991.

Seniavskii, Aleksandr S. *Sotsia'lnaia osnova SSSR.* Moscow: Mysl', 1987.

Shlapentokh, Vladimir. *Soviet Public Opinion and Ideology: Mythology and Pragmatism in Interaction.* New York: Praeger, 1986.

Shlapentokh, Vladimir. *The Politics of Sociology in the Soviet Union.* Boulder, CO: Westview Press, 1987.

Shlapentokh, Vladimir. *Public and Private Life of the Soviet People: Changing Values in Post-Stalin Russia,* New York: Oxford University Press, 1989.

Shlapentokh, Vladimir. *Soviet Intellectuals and Political Power: The Post-Stalin Era.* Princeton, NJ: Princeton University Press, 1990.

Shubkin, V. N. *Sotsiologicheskie opyty.* Moscow: Mysl', 1970.

Shubkin, V. N.   *Nachalo puti.   Problemy molodezhi v zerkale sotsiologii i literatury.* Moscow: Molodaia gvardia, 1979.

Shubkin, V.N. *Trudiashchaiasia molodezh'.* Moscow: Nauka, 1984.

Smith, Hedrick. *The Russians.* New York: Ballantine Books, 1976.

Smith, Hedrick. *The New Russians.* New York: Avon Books, 1991.

Starr, S. Frederick. "Soviet Union: A Civil Society," *Foreign Policy* 70 (Spring 1988), 26-41.

Starr, S. Frederick.   "Prospects for Stable Democracy in Russia." Mershon Center Occasional Paper.   Columbus: Ohio State University Press, 1991.

Taubman, William. *The View from Lenin Hills: An American Student's Report on Soviet Youth in Ferment.* New York: Coward-McCann, 1967.

Titma, M. Kh.   *Vybor profesii kak sotsial'naia problema.* Moscow: Mysl', 1975.

Tucker, Robert C. *Political Culture and Leadership in Soviet Russia: From Lenin to Gorbachev.* New York: W.W. Norton, 1987.

Unger, Aryeh L. "Political Participation in the USSR: Young Communist League and Communist Party of the Soviet Union." *Soviet Studies* 33 (1981), 107-124.

Van Het Reve, Karel, ed. *Dear Comrade: Pavel Litvinov and the Voices of Soviet Citizens in Dissent.* New York: Pitman, 1979.

Vasilieva, E.K. *Sotsial'no-professional'nyi uroven' gorodskoi molodezhi.* Leningrad: University of Leningrad, 1973.

Vasilieva, Evelina K. *The Young People of Leningrad: School and Work Options and Attitudes.* Trans. A. Schulz and A. Smith. White Plains, New York: International Arts and Sciences Press, 1975.

Vel'sh, A. "Motivetsionnye orientatsii inzhenerov prmyshlennogo predpriatiia." *Sotsiologicheskie issledovaiia* 3 (1975), 100-111.

Verkhovskaia, A.I. *Pis'mo v redaktsii chitatel'.* Moscow: Izdatel'stvo MGU, 1972.

Vitaliev, Vitali. *Special Correspondent: Investigating in the Soviet Union.* London: Hutchinson, 1990.

Vozmitel', A. "Ustnaia propaganda v prozesse formirovaniia obshchestvennogo mneniia." In N. Bokarev, ed. *Sotsiologicheskiie problemy sovershentsvovania ideologicheskoi raboty.* Moscow: Institut Sotsiologicheskikh Issledovanii, 1978.

Vychub, G.S. *Pis'ma trudiashchikhsia v sisteme massovoi raboty gazety.* Moscow: Izdatel'stvo MGU, 1980.

White, Stephen. "Political Communications in the USSR: Letters to the Party, State and Press." *Political Studies* 31 (1983), 43-60.

Yanowitch, Murray. *Social and Economic Inequality in the Soviet Union: Six Studies.* White Plains, NY: M.E. Sharpe, 1977.

Yanowitch, Murray, ed. *The Social Structure of the USSR: Recent Soviet Studies.* Armonk, NY: M.E. Sharpe, 1986.

Yanowitch, Murray, and Wesley A. Fisher, eds. *Social Stratification and Mobility in the USSR.* White Plains NY: International Arts and Sciences Press, 1973.

Zaslavskaia, Tatiana. "Paper to a Moscow Seminar." *Russia* 9 (1984), 27-42. Also published as "The Novosibirsk Report." *Survey* 28, no 1 (Spring 1984), 83-108.

Zaslavskaia, Tatiana. *The Second Socialist Revolution: An Alternative Soviet Strategy.* Bloomington: Indiana University Press, 1990.

Zaslavsky, Victor. *The Neo-Stalinist State: Class, Ethnicity and Consensus in Soviet Society.* Armonk, NY: M.E. Sharpe, 1982.

Zubkova, Elena Iurevna. *Russia after the War: Hopes, Illusions and Disappointments, 1945-1957.* Trans. and ed. by Hugh Ragsdale. Armonk, NY: M.E. Sharpe, 1998.

Index

About the Author

DAVID L. RUFFLEY is Assistant Professor of History and Deputy Director of International Program Plans and Development at the United States Air Force Academy.